Ian Gregg is a former MD of Greggs the Bakers and the son of its founder. Actively involved in the company until 2007, first on the shop floor and finally as Chairman, he was responsible for developing the business from a single shop in 1964 on Tyneside into a public company with several regional bakeries and hundreds of shops. He established the Greggs Charitable Trust, focussing on relieving social deprivation, and has been actively involved in environmental conservation for many years. He lives in Cumbria.

BREAD

The Story of Greggs

Ian Gregg

CORGI BOOKS

TRANSWORLD PUBLISHERS
61–63 Uxbridge Road, London W5 5SA
A Random House Group Company
www.transworldbooks.co.uk

**BREAD: THE STORY OF GREGGS
A CORGI BOOK: 9780552169493**

First publication in Great Britain
in 2013 by Corgi, an imprint of Transworld Publishers
Corgi edition published 2013

This book is a work of non-fiction.

A CIP catalogue record for this book
is available from the British Library.

Addresses for Random House Group Ltd companies outside the UK
can be found at: www.randomhouse.co.uk
The Random House Group Ltd Reg. No. 954009

The Random House Group Limited supports The Forest Stewardship
Council® (FSC®), the leading international forest-certification
organisation. Our books carrying the FSC label are printed on
FSC®-certified paper. FSC is the only forest-certification scheme
supported by the leading environmental organisations, including
Greenpeace. Our paper-procurement policy can be found at
www.randomhouse.co.uk/environment

Typeset in 10.25/13.25pt Century Schoolbook
by Falcon Oast Graphic Art Ltd.
Printed and bound by CPI Group (UK) Ltd, Croydon, CR0 4YY.

2 4 6 8 10 9 7 5 3 1

This book is for all the great people who work and
have worked for Greggs, and all the customers
who keep coming every day.

The Greggs Foundation was established in 1987 by Ian Gregg. Now in its 27th year, it has grown from a small grant-making trust to an independent charity currently donating £1.5 million per year. In the north-east, its major grant programme gives grants of up to £45,000 over three years to help sustain the work of organizations that make a difference to the lives of people in need at the heart of Greggs local communities. Also in the north-east, the hardship fund provides grants of £50–150 for individuals who suffer from poverty and financial exclusion via recognized social organizations, enabling the purchase of mattresses, cots, clothing, white goods and furnishing. The Greggs Foundation regional grants programme makes small grants nation-wide of up to £2,000 via seven regional charity committees comprised of volunteer staff from Greggs to help community organizations provide new experiences for the most disadvantaged people. Finally, the Greggs Breakfast Club programme provides funding to give a free, nutritious breakfast each school day to over 10,000 primary school children across the country. In 2012, the Greggs Foundation provided £250,000 to fund 220 Clubs and is now working in partnership with over 30 businesses and social housing organizations to open even more Clubs.

Ian Gregg will donate all of his royalties and Greggs plc will donate all its profits from the sale of this book to the Greggs Foundation to help fund more Breakfast Clubs for children.

CONTENTS

LIST OF RECIPES

The recipes included in the book are not the recipes used by Greggs today. They are small-scale, traditional or regional recipes similar to the ones from which Greggs recipes evolved.

INTRODUCTION

Bread

Bread has been an important part of our diet for thousands of years, but since 1945 consumption has decreased nationally by two thirds

Greggs serves more than a million customers each day, employs at least 20,000 people, and operates more than 1,600 shops in the UK, from Aberdeen in the north to Bournemouth in the south, and from Lowestoft in the east to Haverfordwest in the west. The shops are served by strategically located bakery and distribution centres, which produce more than twenty-five million products each week, including approximately 2.5 million sausage rolls, two million doughnuts and at least three million bread rolls. Two million sandwiches are made fresh each day in the shops and are consumed by six million customers every week. Profits exceeded £53 million in 2011 and the staff share 10 per cent of the annual profits under the Greggs' profit-sharing scheme.

It all began in the 1930s when my father, John Robson Gregg, started selling eggs and yeast from a bike around Newcastle upon Tyne. This book records the expansion of his business to what Greggs is today, some of the tragedies and triumphs along the way and the contribution of some of the main players, which unfolded not as part of any planned strategy (at least, not in the early years), but as the result of serendipity – or managing serendipity.

The backdrop was the most extraordinary period in world history: the 1939–45 war and defeat of Hitler, followed by post-war recovery (during which periods my mother and father managed one way or another to keep Greggs going); the sweeping away of the traditional foundations of society that began in the 1960s as people sampled more freedom in their behaviour; the union domination and industrial unrest of the 1970s; the decline of the traditional heavy industries of coal, steel and ship-building on which the north-east was so dependent; and the controversial Thatcher years, which solved some of the most pressing problems, but also ushered in a period of greed and self-interest. It continues unabated today, after three terms of New Labour, the banking crash of 2008 and the prolonged recession that followed it.

Businesses have grown larger and more complex and the position of individuals has become less important. Banks, petrol companies, hedge funds and now new IT companies, like Google and Facebook, measure profits in billions. The men who run them are paid millions – as are footballers, pop stars and celebrities – creating a culture of smash-and-grab consumerism and brand worship that will destroy the planet during this century, unless we swiftly and significantly reduce our consumption to what the planet can sustain. We all know this but few do anything about it.

All this is in stark contrast to what Greggs is about: simple, old-fashioned values that reflect roots and family traditions; the production of great-tasting, good-value products and treating people fairly. In the process of writing this book I have become increasingly aware that old-fashioned values have a contribution to make to the current debate on corporate greed, and the changes required to create a more sustainable form of capitalism. This has become as important to me as my original objective in writing a history of Greggs.

For much of this period I had my head stuck too far into a dough bowl to take more than a passing interest in current events and the world stage, and when I did manage to extract it in the mid-1980s, I stuck it into protecting the environment, particularly rivers and wildlife in the UK. One way or another, Greggs has navigated its way through the decades and seems to go from strength to strength. In the 1970s the Gosforth business found its way into the hearts, as well as the stomachs, of the north-east. In the 1990s in Glasgow, Greggs replaced the long-established City Bakeries in the jokes of the Christmas pantomime and stand-up comedians, marking it as the number-one bakery in Scotland.

Today Greggs seems to have penetrated the national psyche. Hardly a day goes by without a comment in the press or a joke on TV or radio. Greggs' Facebook site boasts over 650,000 fans. Regular initiatives urge Greggs to open new shops in particular areas, including schoolboy 'Hungry Harry's' successful Facebook campaign for a shop in Lydney in Gloucestershire, which was supported by the local MP. When the BBC moved to Salford in 2011, we were told a major concern of its staff was that there was no Greggs nearby. John Stevenson, MP for Carlisle, led another successful Facebook campaign to bring back to Cumbria the Greggs coffee-cream puff – a large, light choux-pastry case filled with fresh cream and topped with soft coffee fondant – a local favourite known further south as 'Elephant's Feet'. Greggs' Superstar doughnut range attracted national press attention, even from the broadsheets; the former BBC Radio 1 *Breakfast Show* host Chris Moyles frequently told a Greggs anecdote, and his guest Jimmy Carr even complained that the iced buns had sold out. When British troops serving abroad were asked what they missed most from the UK they answered, 'Greggs'; in September 2012 Greggs launched a trial with the NAAFI, the armed forces caterer, to supply frozen savouries to the British military base in Gütersloh, Germany; it even exported a Greggs-branded display counter to make the customers feel more at home.

I was recently asked by a financial journalist for a few lines to round off an article about Greggs. She wanted to know whether I thought my parents would have been surprised at what Greggs has become today. 'I assume they would be very surprised,' I said, 'but no more so than me!'

Perhaps customers identify with a business that still retains old-fashioned values, that seems local rather than global and doesn't put shareholders before customers and staff. Maybe it's simply because the sandwiches, sausage rolls and doughnuts taste great, are good value and are a treat most people can afford. One thing is certain, Greggs' success is largely due to the wonderful people who have worked for Greggs over the past seventy years. Regrettably, space available and a failing memory permit only some of these people to go on record in this book. To those not mentioned please accept my apologies – and my very sincere thanks.

EARLY DAYS
Hot cross bun

*Greggs Bakers still hand-pipe dough crosses onto every one
of the 4 million hot cross buns sold each year*

My great-grandfather, William Gregg, was born at Scremerston, a coal-mining area near Berwick. He was a miner until 1891, when he and his son, George Gregg, born in Bedlington in 1873, went into business together in Newcastle upon Tyne, as egg and yeast merchants. William is also listed as a shopkeeper and grocer at Wigham Street, Newcastle. My father, John Robson Gregg, was born at Canada Street, Newcastle, in 1909 and straight from school, aged fourteen, he joined the family egg and yeast business.

My mother, Elsie Davis, was born in 1908 in South Shields, and married Dad in 1937. I arrived two years later, in 1939. That's all I know of our family history, and most of it has been established as a result of recent enquiry. As a family, we rarely talked about our history and relations. However, it is immediately evident that the Gregg family had a close association with yeast and shopkeeping, and with the mining communities of Northumberland, which have played such a key part in the Greggs story.

My father began his working life during the hard times of the 1920s and 1930s, pedalling a bike around the streets of Newcastle, selling the yeast and eggs that he carried in a large wicker basket attached to the handlebars. It was one of the old, heavy, iron-framed 'sit up and beg' models and it must have been gruelling work pedalling up the steep streets leading away from the Tyne; I like to imagine him at the end of the day, with his basket empty and a few coins jingling in his pocket as he freewheeled back down the hill, like the boy in the old Hovis television commercial. At some point in the 1930s, he graduated to a van (or travelling shop), and following the death of his father, he took over the business, adding bread and confectionery as side-lines, and beginning to travel further outside the city in the search for customers.

I was only a baby when war was declared and my father enlisted. While he was away, my mother stepped in. With two small children, me and my brother Colin, to look after, it must have been exhausting for her, but she managed to keep the van round going and started another. The pressure increased in 1945 when, after my father had been home for a brief leave, she found she was pregnant again. The war in Europe ended with the German surrender on 8 May 1945, and my mother waited with mounting impatience for my father to return home. Weeks and then months dragged by and he was still in uniform, apparently no nearer to being demobbed. In desperation, she wrote to the minister of war, explaining that she was now seven and a half months pregnant and having to run the family business alone. Unless her husband was demobbed soon, she would no longer be able to cope and the business would have to close, throwing the family into destitution. It did the trick: within seven days my father had returned to take over running the business while my mother prepared for the birth of my sister, Gay.

In 1946 my parents must have appeared a striking and fortunate couple. Mum was blonde, slim, blue-eyed and beautiful. She had looked after her family well during the war, moving out of Newcastle into the country for a time. She had managed to keep the business going, and had increased the number of travelling shops from one to two. Dad was good-looking too: he was slim, of average height, with sharp features, brown eyes and jet black hair combed flat and slicked down with Brylcreem – there was never a hair out of place.

He expanded the business steadily, adding two additional rounds. The vehicles they used were blue Bedford vans, with 'J R Gregg, Baker and Confectioner' on both sides, a picture of a swiss roll on one and another of a jam sandwich cake on the other.

I was only six when my father came home from the war. I know almost nothing about his life before then, and relatively little even of what he did after that. He was never the most communicative of men, and before 1951 there are no written records or minutes of what took place in the business. All that remains are my recollections, with those of Colin and Gay. We lived at Brunton Park in the northern outskirts of Newcastle, a new middle-class suburb sandwiched between the city and the traditional mining areas, which began at Seaton Burn and Wideopen and stretched north over large swathes of Northumberland.

It was to these mining districts that my father drove his Bedford van, loaded with bread, cakes and pies bought from Laws Bakery in the west end of Newcastle. As a young child I used to go with him, through the cobbled yard with a great heap of coke at one side and past the vans waiting to be loaded, into what seemed an impossibly huge and rambling building, housing massive dough bowls, coke-fed ovens and pale-faced bakers, but it was the heavy, clinging smell of ferment-ing dough and the clouds of flour covering everything that evoke the strongest memories. From this sprawl-ing, scruffy building with its ancient machines, floury dust and ghost-like people came delicious crusty breads, sweet-smelling pies and heavenly pastries, which Dad packed into neat rows on the large wooden bread trays and carried on his head (protected sometimes by a flat cap and at others only by Brylcreem) to the metal angle racks on the inside of his Bedford van.

There was just time for a mug of tea, sweet and strong, and another Player's Navy Cut cigarette (which did for him in the end) and we were off, slowly and care-fully, always conscious of the precious and fragile load, changing gear only when absolutely necessary, using the brakes sparingly and coasting as much as possible to preserve the cargo, reduce petrol consumption and prolong the vehicle's life.

We drove north through the fringes of Newcastle,

passing the well-to-do areas of Jesmond and Gosforth, and then our own home in the new suburbia, to Seaton Burn, three miles north of the city and ten miles south of Ashington. The local colliery was known as Brenkley. The first shaft had been sunk in 1844 and, more than a century later, it was still employing at least six hundred people. The entire workforce came out in the 1984 miners' strike, and the colliery closed in 1985.

It was a solid, old-fashioned mining community, with rows and rows of back-to-back, brick-built terraced houses, with outside loos and no gardens. Most of them have now been cleared, as have the so-called 'slums' of Scotswood Road (made famous in the song 'Blaydon Races') and the west end of Newcastle, but whatever their physical inadequacies, they made for a close and cohesive community. Many of the men had allotments where they grew much of their food, kept their pigeons and watched over their leeks. There were few shops but a succession of vans brought fruit and vegetables, meat and general provisions, and there was the pub or club for the weekend.

No one would suggest that the lifestyle of those mining communities compares favourably with today. Housing standards, education, health, life expectancy, leisure opportunities and much more have made huge strides forward, but in the process of that change and progress, we seem to have lost some of the best aspects of those old communities: the physical proximity of families, identification with the community and a willingness to try to make the status quo work, rather than always questioning and looking for new pastures. Somehow we have lost the ability to be content.

At Seaton Burn, between the rows of back-to-back

brick cottages, Dad blew the horn of the van and out streamed the women, wearing pinnies and headscarves, tied on top, turban-style, sometimes concealing curlers. Some carried plates or boxes for their purchases while others took them back to the house cradled in their pinnies.

Some purchases were entered in the 'tick' (credit) book but most were paid for in cash, which went into the shiny leather satchel-purse Dad slung across his shoulder with separate sections for coppers, threepenny bits, small silver and large. He put any notes into a homemade cardboard wallet with different elastic con-figurations on the interior of each side. He closed the wallet, then reopened it from the other side and – presto! – the note was securely fastened under the elastic, ten shilling notes on one side, pound notes on the other. I never figured out how this worked.

The women who were our customers were the back-bone of the mining communities, working as hard as their husbands and for longer hours to keep one gener-ation fit for work and raise the next. It was an endless round of washing, for which water had to be carried and boiled, and the clothes, thick with coal dust, pummelled with a wooden baton in the washtub, then wrung through the mangle. The house and contents had to be cleaned, there was daily polishing of pit boots and safety helmets, carrying the coal, clearing the ashes, setting the fire, cooking, making ends meet and generally keeping the family going. All this required thrift and imagination, particularly when many husbands practised 'keepies back' with their wage packet, retaining a proportion for their own purposes, usually cigarettes, a few pints and a bet on the dogs or horses.

The exhausting process offered no escape and few thanks for the women, but the physical aspects were only part of the strength they needed. They also had to be emotionally strong to manage the tensions that arose within the close-knit family and community. The men did not deal in or with emotions. And there was always the dread that the next knock on the door would be news of an accident at the pit, whether death or injury, depriving the family of its wage-earner, its home and its dignity. 'Stoic' was a term that might have been devised with these women in mind.

The visit to Dad's van might be their only escape that day from the daily grind. To him they were more like friends than customers. The conversation was friendly, spontaneous and full of Geordie lilt, everyone happy to wait while others were served, and to wait again afterwards to continue the chat. It was 'Jack this' and 'Jack that' (as Dad was known), 'How's Elsie?' and 'Lovely to see the bairn'. I was subjected to a stream of generosity and compliments in relation to my size, handsomeness, the colour of my eyes and hair, and how like my parents I was – not to mention a bombardment of cakes, sweets and goodies. It was all very sociable and pleasant.

I was even invited on the miners' annual fishing trip by coach to the river Till (a tributary of the Tweed) where the women's husbands introduced me to the skilled techniques of taking trout with a worm cast upstream and allowed to drift with the current, while Dad sat quietly by a pool waiting for a trout to find his static worm and smoked another Player's. The trip was a revelation to me. My normal fishing trips were to the tiny rivers Pont and Blyth, some eight or nine miles from Newcastle, sometimes in the car with Dad but usually on my bike, rod strapped to the crossbar and the picnic Mum had made in the bag behind the saddle.

The river Till at Chatton seemed huge, compared to my usual Northumbrian streams, but it was not the most memorable thing: even more awesome was the tackle that some of the miners used. Many had short, clumsy, stubby rods like Dad's and mine, but others were the proud owners of long, light, delicate poles, twice the length, maybe twelve or thirteen feet, beauti-fully bound with silk; they had brass fittings and were made of whole cane, with a split cane or greenheart section at the end. The brandling worms they fished with had been kept in large cans in moss sprinkled with red brick dust, for colour, and milk, for flavour, the tin turned daily to maximize toughness and vigour. These worms could be dropped gently in any likely riffle or eddy, frequently attracting a red and black spotted trout, which always went into the basketwork creel. Catch and release had not been heard of in those days.

I was always sad when the last customers in that street had been served and the women returned to their homes. Even when it rained, they still came out and sheltered under the little awning that Dad could pull out from above the back of the van. The casual and good-humoured exchanges between him and his customers, and between the customers themselves, were more relaxed and friendly than what took place on the housing estate where we lived.

At a very early stage, it surprised me that Dad concentrated on the so-called 'working-class' communities at Backworth, Seghill, Fawdon, Seaton Burn, Wideopen, Dudley, Burradon, West Moor, Forest Hall and Killingworth, rather than going to the more well-to-do areas, like Jesmond, Gosforth, Ponteland or Darras Hall. Those people were wealthier, owned their houses, and some had a car. Surely they would spend more than the families he served.

When I suggested this, Dad explained that it was a waste of time calling on the better-off. They would not come out at the sound of the horn. He might have to walk up the often long drive, wait for a reply, take an order, return to the van, wrap the order, return to the customer, then wait for her to find her purse. He could serve a street in Seaton Burn in the time it would take to serve one customer in Gosforth. On top of that, most customers in Seaton Burn bought bread, cakes, pies and biscuits while in Gosforth the customer might want just one tea cake – and might return it the following week for lack of fruit. He couldn't argue: the customer was always right! Dad did feel obliged, though, to call on some friends and neighbours, which he did on a Monday: it was difficult on Mondays to access the narrow terraced houses in the mining communities because it was washing day and the streets were lined with hanging clothes. So, I learned Lesson Number One of retailing: the lower socio-economic groups spend most on bread, pies and confectionery; the middle and upper classes spend more on fruit, vegetables and meat. You must be where your customers are – location, location, location.

Lesson 1: You must be where your customers are – location, location, location.

Against this backdrop, it was surprising that my parents chose Gosforth, a very middle-class area, in which to open their first retail outlet and bakery, purchasing Mason's at 69/71 High Street for £7,750 in 1951. Their main motive in making the purchase was the bakery behind the shop. My father had become increasingly dissatisfied with the range and quality of the goods he could buy from other bakeries and wanted to supply his vans with his very own top-quality confectionery.

There were other factors at work as well. Gosforth was an appropriate place for a couple moving up life's ladder and wishing to provide the best upbringing and education for their children. It was also a sound invest-ment: the value of the building increased significantly over the next few years. However, with that exception, in the early years of Greggs' expansion in the north of England, we consistently applied the basic marketing lesson learned from the vans to our choice of shop locations, finding busy sites in working-class neighbour-hoods rather than middle-class areas.

My father also acquired the lease of a pork shop at 13 Eccleshaw Way, Longbenton. It was a very poor trading location but his main purpose in buying it was to provide meat for the pies and sausage rolls and cooked meats, black pudding, pease pudding and saveloys to sell on the vans.

My mother ran the shop and the catering, and my father did everything else, out on the vans, paying the bills, calculating and making up the wages, counting the money and taking it to the bank, everything, in fact, but the baking. He did not understand the processes involved and, anyway, was too busy working a twelve-hour day for six days a week. He took on a bakery manager and made him a partner in the business.

The partnership ended in 1953, when the manager resigned his directorship and transferred his share to my father, but he continued to be employed as bakery manager at twelve pounds per week. He also remained my father's regular companion on his trips to the greyhound racing track. It was one of Dad's few recreations, which usually involved a visit to Brough Park in Newcastle, but occasionally took the form of a clandestine visit to a 'flapping track', one of the many unregulated greyhound racing venues in the UK. Those jaunts sometimes involved one of the travelling shops (empty!), presumably to transport a greyhound, and a night away from home. We had no idea whether such activities resulted in profit or loss, but they provoked regular rows between my parents.

My dad was a lonely figure, whom none of us – not even, I suspect, my mother – really got to know. He was proud of what the business was achieving but exhausted by keeping it going. All he seemed to want after a hard day's work was his supper and to sleep. A couple of visits to his local, the Three Mile Inn, at weekends and the occasional fishing trip or visit to the dog track appeared to be the limit of his ambitions. Yet he was an able man who established a business from small beginnings, and when he became involved in anything, he did well at it. He was a former 'master' of his Masonic lodge and, in a brief period of involvement with the local church, was made a churchwarden, but with these two exceptions, he showed no interest in moving out of his routine to explore new horizons.

His lack of leisure ambition drove Mum to distraction. After a week working in the shop and on her catering business, she wanted to get away, to the coast, the Lake District, anywhere at all, rather than staying at home and having to cook the Sunday roast, which Dad always required on his return from the pub at lunchtime. As a result, Sunday lunches were not relaxing affairs and usually ended in rows caused either by Mum's frustration, Dad's beery boldness or simply the opportunity to release the unspoken tensions that had built up during the week.

Mum used every one of the rare opportunities she had to get away and enjoy herself, often with one or all of us. She took Colin and me out when we were at boarding school and, years later, at university, and accompanied Gay on her many successful horse-riding engagements. Her other great pleasure was the house they bought at 3 Linden Road, Gosforth, a large end-of-terrace Victorian home. She had always felt cramped and frustrated by the semi-detached house at Brunton Park, and Linden Road gave her all the scope and opportunity she wanted – without the money to match. She sought out amazing painters, joiners and plumbers, who worked miracles for very little, although they were never available the next time she wanted them because she had sung their praises to so many people that they were fully booked for years ahead. She also searched the sale rooms for bargains to furnish the spacious rooms.

My parents formed Greggs of Gosforth as a limited company on 30 December 1951, when they held its first board meeting. A legal requirement for all limited companies, a board is made up of formally appointed directors, who, in Greggs' early years, were just my father and mother. Directors are responsible for seeing that the company is properly managed; if it is not, they can be personally liable. However, in a small family company, most decisions tend to be taken informally and often 'on the hoof'; the next formal meeting of the board of directors did not take place until two years later, when a modest profit of £69 15s 6d (£69.77) was carried forward, with no dividend declared.

There are occasional further minutes of directors' meetings and other papers relating to the 1950s, which show that the business broke even or made a small profit each year. Given how hard my parents worked, this seems an inadequate return, but they were able to maintain a reasonable standard of living, including an annual holiday to Beadnell. The village is set in a sheltered, sweeping bay, with one of those beautiful, sandy Northumbrian beaches where we would play all day, making sandcastles, shrimping in the rock pools and watching the seals, sea birds and sometimes dolphins just off shore. It was here that my dad taught me to fish from the sea-wall around the harbour, sparking in me a lifelong love of angling.

To my parents, the most important aspect of their rising standard of living was not the holidays we could take or the house in a middle-class neighbourhood, but that it enabled them to provide their three children with what they considered to be the best possible education. Colin and I went to Durham School and then to university, and Gay to La Sagesse School for Girls, in a Victorian Gothic building overlooking Jesmond Dene, to the north-east of Newcastle.

There was never any intention that Colin, Gay or I would join the business, quite the opposite. Our parents worked all hours to pay for an education that would allow us to pursue professional careers. We were never encouraged to take an interest in what was happening at the bakery, required to help only at really busy times, making mince pies at Christmas and hot cross buns at Easter. In those days, such seasonal products were sold in huge numbers for just a few days, not for several weeks or throughout the year as now happens.

The sale of hot cross buns was confined to Maundy Thursday, Good Friday (vans only, the shop being shut) and Easter Saturday. From the Wednesday night through to Friday, the bakery was dominated by huge bowls of sweet, fermenting dough, and the air was rich with the scent of spices, peel, sultanas and yeast. Large lumps of the dough were scooped from the bowls, rested, and then put into dividers, which cut them into small pieces. The most skilled bakers laboriously hand-moulded the buns into perfect little globes, placing them on steel baking sheets – twenty-four to a sheet – in immaculate rows. Fifteen sheets at a time went into the steaming provers, then each bun was sprayed or brushed with spicy glaze and crossed with soft liquid dough, piped from bags in long sweeps across the whole sheet each way. Then they went into the oven, balanced on a 'peel', a long wooden pole with a flat end, which could reach into the recesses for loading and unloading. The soft dough crosses were a major contributor to the mess and mayhem. We did try to replace them with a stamped impression or a rice paper cross but they were no match in colour or texture for the dough cross. In fact, Greggs still hand-pipes the crosses today.

For those four days it seemed as though hot cross buns had taken over the world. The smell filled our

■ HOT CROSS BUNS ■

For the buns

1lb 2oz/500g strong white bread flour

1 tsp salt

2 tsp mixed spice

1 tsp ground cinnamon

2oz/55g cold butter, cut into small pieces (sugar cube size)

1 tsp dried yeast

2oz/55g soft brown sugar

10fl oz/300ml lukewarm milk

3oz/100g mixed dried fruits

1oz/25g candied mixed peel

For the crosses

2½oz/75g plain flour

For the glaze

1½ tbsp apricot jam, warmed

1 Mix together the flour with the salt and spices. Add the butter pieces and rub into the flour until it resembles coarse sand. Dissolve the yeast and sugar in the warm milk, add to the flour mixture and mix with your hands until a soft sticky dough is formed.

2 Tip the dough onto a lightly floured surface and knead for about 10 minutes or until the dough is smooth. Place in a large, lightly oiled bowl, cover with a clean teatowel and leave to rise in a warm place until it has doubled in size (about 1½ hours).

3 Tip the dough onto a lightly floured surface and knock the air from it. Sprinkle the dried fruits and mixed peel onto the dough and knead again for 2 minutes. Rest for 10 minutes and then divide into twelve. Roll each piece into a bun shape and place on lightly floured baking parchment. Cover with a teatowel and leave to rise again for approximately 45 minutes or until well risen.

4 Preheat the oven to 220°C/425°F/Gas 7.

5 To make the crosses, add a little cold water (½ tbsp) to the flour and stir to make a paste. Spoon the paste into a piping bag and pipe crosses onto the risen buns.

6 Bake for 15–20 minutes or until the buns are golden brown. Remove from the oven and brush the buns with warm jam. Leave to cool.

nostrils; floor, tables and machines were coated with the sticky cross mixture; spice and fruit clung to everyone's clothes, shoes, hands and hair. When it was all over and the remnants had been washed away, the spicy smell still lingered, and the last thing we wanted for breakfast over Easter was a hot cross bun.

We also helped out in emergencies. When Colin was only ten, he was put in charge of a van round on a day when both our parents had flu! As the less ill of the two, my mother drove, wrapped in blankets, while Colin, kept off school for the day, served as best he could from the back. That event might have been forgotten, had it not been for an unfortunate accident. As Mum set off from one stop, she made a 'kangaroo' hill start and heard a bang behind her. When she looked in the rear-view mirror, she saw the back doors wide open and her entire load of bread, savouries and cakes disappearing through them.

To me, in the 1950s, the business was something that went on in the background without any real involvement from me, and my memories of that time are largely of being away at school and then at university. My education centred on the classics and I never did any science whatsoever. My direction was set very early, at Askham House Preparatory School in Gosforth. From the age of eight or nine, Latin, Greek and ancient history became my main educational intake, leavened until I was fifteen with some English, history, maths and geography, but not even the most basic grounding in biology, chemistry or physics. Such omissions seem serious enough for any child, let alone one who spent weekends, holidays and any available spare moments with net and jam jar, combing the burns and countryside around Newcastle in pursuit of stickle-backs, butterflies and anything that flew, swam or moved. I'm sure the oversight must have been due to an aptitude I demonstrated for the classics, rather than an attempt to cool my passion for nature.

If nothing else, studying classics made me think in a logical way. In Latin each sentence has a subject, a verb and an object. It is simple and predictable. An accountancy qualification might have given me an insight into complex conventions, discounted cash flows and balance-sheet jargon. A degree in business studies could have shown me how to develop strategies, calculate return on investment and organize acquisi-tions and mergers. A qualification in food science would have provided me with a better understanding and management of the complex processes that take place in the production of bread and flour confectionery. In my early days of running Greggs, though, none of those would have been more useful than the simple, logical approach I had learned in my study of the classics.

In 1960, approaching my final year at St Catharine's College, Cambridge, where I studied Classics and Law, I had no idea what I wanted to do. I knew only that I didn't want to go into the family business. My parents had not encouraged me to con-sider it, and their quality of life, largely dictated by the business, did not appeal to me. Equally, I didn't think that what I was studying was likely to be of much benefit, whatever I chose to do. So, purely to pursue a less irrelevant subject, I switched to study law in my final year.

In the summer of 1961, thus equipped and still with no idea of what I wanted to do long-term, I decided to take a year out. In those days the possibility of spending months exploring Australia, South America or the East didn't exist so I decided to work in the business; I'd see if there was any way I could help my parents out of the endless slog, always being tired and under pressure, with not a lot to show for it. I hoped that a reduction in their punishing schedule would make them happier and more able to spend time doing things they enjoyed.

Both Mum and Dad were mortified that I should waste the opportunities that had cost so much of their sweat and money. Their dream was that I should find employment in one of the many large and expanding businesses that were then fashionable among young graduates. My mother expressly told me not to go into the business and both parents made every effort to dissuade me. They even drummed up a management trainee post, with a view to partnership, in Henry F. Dodds, Insurance Brokers, run by Harry Dodds, a lifelong friend of my father. In the event, a young John Henderson accepted the offer, and went on to manage Greggs' insurance and pensions matters for almost fifty years.

As a keen Freemason, who had recently been master of his lodge, Shipcote 3626, Dad devised a plan with Harry Dodds to bring me into the movement, the idea being that I would meet others who might knock some sense into me as to how I should spend my working life. Freemasonry held no appeal for me: I declined all invitations to attend meetings and remained resolute that I would join the business for a year. In the end my parents bowed to the inevitable and I duly started work on the same basic rate of pay as any other recruit. With both my parents firmly against my joining the business, even for a year, and my lack of any relevant experience or training, it was hardly a propitious start. However, I was quickly able to make a difference by being willing to do any job wherever there was a need – and that occurs regularly in a small business if someone is absent, equipment breaks down or a sudden extra order comes in. Whether it was packing cakes at six in the morning, manning a pie machine, standing in for one of the van drivers, serving in the shop or helping to cater for a wedding, I was up for it and always had a real sense of achievement from a job well done.

More importantly, I was achieving my primary objective of taking some of the pressure off my parents. After a while they stopped hounding me with adverts from the newspapers for accountants, surveyors or management positions at Procter & Gamble, and even took notice of some of the suggestions I made. The most important one was that they employ two part-time bookkeepers, one of whom would pay invoices, calculate PAYE and attend to all the administration my father did during the evenings and on Sundays. That meant he could be out with the vans, which was what he was best at and liked most, either building up the rounds or filling in for drivers who were absent.

My father was initially reluctant, and only agreed to the appointments on a short trial basis to see whether they would justify the expense. He soon discovered that the extra sales he was able to generate on the vans more than paid for the first assistant, Jean Tillmouth. Not only that, she reduced the pressure on his time and – though we had to whisper it around my father – did the job better than him.

The justification for the second part-timer, Jean

Potter, was even more immediate and remarkable. Although all the bakery goods, biscuits, sweets, cooked meats and cigarettes were ostensibly booked out to each of the vans, there had never been any calculation of the total value of goods taken, or reconciliation made with the cash each driver brought back. Dad suspected there might be some 'leakage', but nothing substantial. A 'good' salesman would do all right for himself and everyone else; a 'sharp' salesman would return more sales and profit for the business than a good honest plodder . . . or so he thought.

Mum suspected otherwise and she thought some of them were 'at it', given any chance at all, and in the hectic pell-mell rush of early morning in the bakery, there were plenty of chances. Boards of bread and trays of cakes were moving swiftly on top of heads, so it was difficult to see what was on them, and high-value items, like whole cartons of biscuits, cigarettes and cooked meats, were being taken out. This all happened in a short space of time and in a very small area behind the shop: twenty-four hours of production were concentrated into an hour's manic movement. If the goods weren't out and on the road by nine a.m., sales were missed and items left as waste at the end of the day.

Mum should have been in the front shop during this period but she couldn't rest until all the vans were out, looking for any excuse to disappear into the back and see what was happening, often going up and down the back staircase from which she could see what was being carried out on the boards and trays. She was always watchful, asking, 'What's this for?', directing operations and telling everybody what to do. The minute she saw a carton of cigarettes, for example, she checked that it had been charged out. I'm sure this contributed to her high blood pressure, and it was still to no avail: the charging out was a pretence, since no proper reconciliation took place between it and the cash brought back.

Dad was confident that his friendly *laissez-faire* approach was in everyone's best interest and only agreed reluctantly to have the check-out sheets priced up in the expectation that they would vindicate his methods. So, laboriously, we priced out and totalled all the products, a lengthy, mind-numbing exercise since it had to be done by hand.

When the sheets had been totalled and compared with the cash received, Dad refused to believe the difference in some of the van rounds. The calculations were rechecked and confirmed as correct. He assumed there must have been an error in stock-taking or credit calculation and that the deficits would be redeemed by a surplus the following week, but there was no improvement that week, or the week after. A good week's takings were in the region of £150 and the shortfalls ranged between 15 and 30 per cent of that figure. That accounted for a substantial part of the profit the business should have been making and to which Mum and Dad were fully entitled for all the hours and effort they put into it.

A battle of wits followed. The shortfalls came down but the outstanding credit total went up. So we put limits on credit, and stock levels started to rise. Stock levels were checked and returns of 'stales' increased, so these were checked each day. Gradually, via a much less affable process, reasonable balances were struck most weeks, and when they weren't, there was an investigation. Always an unpleasant procedure, it brought a salesman's honesty into question and occasionally led to dismissal.

That was Lesson Number Two: always make sure that cash returned matches goods despatched. In a retail bakery it is relatively easy to do, with little stock-taking required at the start and end of each week. Failure to do it regularly and systematically is not only poor business practice but also morally wrong: it puts temptation in the way of people who may be basically honest but find themselves under financial pressure and therefore succumb. Done once, it's much easier to do again, and even to justify – 'I work very hard for less than I deserve and it won't make any real difference to the business.' It's a slippery slope. The vast majority of people are scrupulously honest but, given the pressure and the opportunity, some may not be sufficiently strong to resist temptation.

Lesson 2: Always make sure that cash returned matches goods despatched.

My parents now set about work with renewed enthusiasm in the expectation that they would receive a better return. Even so, Mum continued to make her rush-hour trips up and down the stairs, because she knew that the only way some salesmen could continue to live in the manner to which they had become accustomed was to sneak out items that had not been charged to them, or to charge customers a higher than recommended price.

Fixing a price list in a highly visible part of the van would have been the next stage in what seemed a never-ending saga, but by then almost a year had passed and I had achieved my main objective of taking some of the strain from my parents and helping them achieve a better return for their efforts. Apart from helping out

with the hot cross buns, mince pies and other production pressures, I had not been allowed to get
involved in the little bakery behind the shop in case I
upset the manager. I had no ideas or ambitions to
develop the business and there seemed no point, since it
would add to my parents' pressures and uncertainties.
At only fifty-two, Dad wouldn't retire for a long time and
I wasn't prepared to wait till he did.

The only way forward was for me to find some other
employment, but I still had no idea what I wanted to do.
As I'd studied law in my final year, I decided my best
option was to sign up as a solicitor's articled clerk. On 7
August 1962, I started with Jimmy Chapman, a partner
with Maughan & Hall, of Lloyds Bank Chambers,
Collingwood Street, Newcastle. The change was more
than I could have hoped for. No more six thirty a.m.
starts in white coat and hat: now I caught the nine
o'clock bus in a dark suit and bowler hat to start work
at nine thirty. My stint in the bakery had been physically
demanding and at times unchallenging. Now I was
exposed daily to interesting and exciting challenges. I
was happy and fulfilled and, since I still lived with Mum
and Dad, could watch how their business progressed.

Within six months my career was mapped out: a
year in conveyancing, a year in company law and a year
in probate followed by qualification, then an early
partnership in an expanding and highly regarded law
practice. Dad was enjoying the administrative support
he now had and starting to think ahead. He applied for
a pension and life assurance policy with Sun Life
Assurance. He returned from the medical in high
spirits, having scored an A1 health accreditation.

Within twelve months, in early 1963, he had been

diagnosed with lung cancer. He was never told it was terminal – in those days they didn't tell you unless you pressed hard for the truth – but we were told after his second radiotherapy treatment. He had a period of a few months' remission, during which he believed he was getting better, and we made a few fishing trips together. The last was on a beautiful summer's evening when we fished the upper Pont near Eachwick, a few miles north-west of Newcastle. He was struggling to fish the small burn just a few yards from the car, but was still talking about soon being back at work. His emaciated outline against the beautiful summer sunset was unbearably sad, made even more so because he did not know what we knew. It has etched itself into my mind as my abiding memory of him.

As Mum nursed Dad at home through his last few months, protecting the rest of us, as much as she could, from the worst indignities of this cruel process, my newly acquired nine-to-five routine suffered a serious setback, with several hours' additional work at the bakery in the morning and evening. After Dad's inevitable but heart-breaking death in 1964, this hectic schedule continued for the remainder of my articles. Still grieving and no longer young, Mum needed my help. I gave it willingly, but I had decided that I should qualify as a lawyer before making any further decision about Greggs or my career.

2

JOINING GREGGS
Strawberry tart

*Modern transport and growing techniques have taken away
seasonality and excitement from our fresh food menu*

During the months leading up to my final exams in
1965, I worked under intense pressure. It was usual for
articled clerks to go to law school in Guildford for a
period of concentrated revision but my sessions at the
bakery prevented this. Instead, I revised late into
the evenings and split the weekends between Greggs
and study. There was also, of course, the emotional
turmoil that followed my father's death and, hanging
over all this, like a heavy weight, was the decision of
what I should do when I qualified. If I qualified. The
prospect of failing pushed me to the limit.

There was no prospect of my reverting to the career
I had aspired to while at Durham School – going into

the Church. My earliest religious connection and experience had taken place in the late 1940s, when a new church was built on the estate at Brunton Park where we lived, a few miles north of Newcastle. An old black Nissen hut had served the estate for the twenty or so years since the first house had been built, but when an energetic and charismatic new vicar, the Reverend Colin Turnbull, was appointed, he decreed that the old building was not a satisfactory place in which to worship God and inspired the local residents to build a new one.

Times were hard in those years following the war, but that did not stand in the way of the enthusiasm that carried the parishioners into several years of super-human fundraising and building. Dad became a churchwarden, I carried the cross on Sunday pro-cessions at the head of the choir and my brother Colin was the senior server at communion services.

Leading the choir into church was the closest I ever got to a musical achievement. All previous ambitions in that area had been dashed by my piano teacher's declaration to Mum that, in spite of endless practice, I was wasting his time and her money. (Any hopes that might have lingered where latent musical talent was concerned were finally extinguished when, at Durham School, in the house choir competition, I was put in the back row of 'growlers', who had to mime but not utter a note!) My church involvement also saw me reach the pinnacle of my acting career when I played the back legs of the horse in the church pantomime.

Eventually Mr Turnbull was transferred to St Luke's Church, Wallsend, and the parish returned to normal, but before I had time to conclude that it had been the singer not the song, I was sent to Durham School, where both Colin and I blossomed in the strong Church of England regime of chapel every morning and prayers every evening. We each in turn became head boy, in my case despite beatings for smoking, breaking bounds to drink alcohol and almost being expelled for blowing up the games' lockers when an illicit home brew of elderberry wine exploded. Maybe the authorities were ready to forgive a repentant sinner, or perhaps they thought the best gamekeeper was a reformed poacher. Either way, my religious experience from Brunton Park was nurtured and developed. I was strongly influenced by the headmaster, Canon Luce, who was then a leading theologian. His was a humorous and sceptical approach – he even resorted to logic based on what he called 'the twelve pillars of the New Testament': twelve actions and sayings of Jesus that I no longer remember but which took us as far as we could proceed with reasoning, then faith carried us over the gaps and doubts that remained.

By the time I left Durham School, my intention was to become a vicar, but then I went up to Cambridge and, in the heady mix of freedom, new friends, alcohol and the proximity of Newmarket racecourse, the pillars soon crumbled. Conviction gave way to agnosticism, which in time yielded to atheism. Ten years of building belief was blown away. Religious belief and conviction have remained very much at the centre of Colin's life, though, and have inspired many of the projects he has developed.

There used to be times when I envied my brother and others their faith, particularly a belief in life eternal, but not any longer. To me the very essence of life is its limits and challenges. We don't know where it will end, so we keep trying to do what we can while we can. At the same time, I do believe that Christian values and ethics remain an excellent basis for regulating our lives and behaviour. Without values such as 'love thy neighbour' and 'do unto others as you would have done to you', the communities we live in would cease to function effectively.

With the Church no longer an option and the suggestions my parents had made offering no appeal, my choice was either the business or the law. I really had no idea which route I would follow and changed my mind daily. I compiled long lists of the advantages and disadvantages of each, which were then amended, added to and rewritten. The family and I discussed all the alternatives for Greggs. Given the size and nature of the business, employing a general manager did not seem financially possible. Selling the business was. I tried to put it to the back of my mind until I had taken my final exams and, hopefully, qualified. But the alternatives went round and round in my brain, month after month.

During that time, we decided to look into selling the business. At the time, the main flour producers, Spillers, Allied Mills and Rank Hovis, were competing with each other to pay silly money for bakeries in order to guarantee outlets for their flour. This had a damaging long-term impact on the bread industry. Greggs bought its sliced bread from Graves of Chester-le-Street, an old-established family business that had been bought out by Spillers. The quantity of sliced bread we sold on our vans was significant and offered the only basis for securing a price from Spillers that would provide my mother with a reasonable standard of living. The offer they made was insufficient, and not improved by the suggestion of a management trainee position for me – I wasn't interested. I was twenty-five, had completed more than enough training and was ready for a real job.

With selling up out of the equation, I went on with my gruelling schedule of revision and sessions in the bakery. By June 1965 I was too close to my final law exams to take part in one of the busiest parts of Greggs' year: the annual ritual of 'Race Week' on the Town Moor, several square miles of common grassland on the north side of Newcastle, when large numbers of gypsies and travelling folk arrived to take part in the largest travelling fairground in the world, locally known as 'The Hoppings'. At the same time, horse racing traditionally took place at the Gosforth Park racecourse, culminating in the 'Pitman's Derby' on the last Saturday in June.

Every summer during Race Week, Dad had taken a van of cakes and savouries to the Town Moor to sell to the gypsies and travellers. The window of opportunity was small. Before ten a.m., they were still asleep in their magnificent caravans, polished chrome on the outside and Crown Derby china within. By midday they were too busy preparing their roundabouts and stalls for the Geordie throng who descended on them whatever the weather. It usually rained in Race Week, but managing your way through the resulting quagmire was part of the fun of the fair.

In that two-hour slot there were rich pickings to be had. The travelling folk were fantastic spenders and wanted only the best; they particularly liked fresh cream strawberry tarts. Like hot cross buns at Easter, strawberry tarts sold in huge numbers during the short season. They now sell in more modest numbers throughout the year and, to a large extent, seasonality has been extinguished from bakery products, fruit and vegetables by the year-round availability that modern transport and growing techniques have developed. As a result, our lives have lost some of their colour, interest and variety. In late May, the first home-grown strawberries were available in Kent. We were supplied by a circuit of producers and the source of the fruit moved gradually up through Lincolnshire, Yorkshire and into Scotland, as far as Dundee, returning south for a short second crop, beginning in Kent in July and ending in Devon.

When we were making our strawberry tarts, we were always searching for the crispest, shortest pastry and the perfect jelly to enhance the flavour of the strawberry but not slide off the fruit and make the pastry soggy. At the height of the strawberry season, when berries were plentiful and available locally, strawberry tarts were supplemented by meringue nests filled with strawberries, strawberry flans and strawberry sponges, all adorned with swirls and flourishes of fresh cream.

Each morning during Race Week, we made board after board of premium-priced strawberry tarts, with extra cream and strawberries, and took them to the Town Moor, where they were carried off on fine china plates into the burnished caravans, or grasped by the grubby little hands of children, who paused in their play just long enough to devour most of their prize, always leaving sufficient evidence on their cheeks to show off to less fortunate friends.

Trading from a mobile shop on the Town Moor was an amazing experience: the caravans, the Romany gypsies, the fattest woman and the smallest man in the world, donkeys with three legs and more Gypsy Rose Lees than you could count, including one who always had a long queue waiting outside her caravan. I supposed she must have been the real thing, but that was what they all claimed.

In that hectic two hours, with only a few strategic stops between the caravans, we took more cash than during a full day on even the best round. The van was emptied. Yet it was still as heavy at the end as it was at the start, for payment was made in copper (stored in large biscuit tins), which was what the fairground people received from their customers for rides, generally priced at a penny. Threepenny bits were quite common, sixpences weren't rare, but shillings were, and half-crowns were very special. Notes, either ten shillings or a pound, were rarely seen. The fairground folk retained them for themselves, stowing them beneath mattresses, in hidden recesses, or in safes in their caravans. They made it a high priority to get rid of their small change before they set off on their next journey, and we were glad of it, despite the mammoth counting and checking that had to be done before it was wheeled to the bank. The whole family could count, check and package into the appropriate little plastic bag or paper roll as fast as any bank clerk. It had to be done every Saturday night, when the van drivers checked in at home, so we were well practised in the art.

In 1965, in the last stages of preparing for my exams, I couldn't take my father's place in the annual strawberry-tart bonanza on Town Moor, so three of the van salesmen shared the task. I could only catch glimpses of the fair from the top of the double-decker trolley bus that I took to the solicitors' office in Newcastle each morning. The early caravans arrived the week before Race Week, and the less opulent group of raggle-taggle helpers and hangers-on congregated at the northern end of the Town Moor. By midweek every space on the moor was taken and it was full steam ahead with the erection of the waltzer, the big wheels and the other roundabouts and stalls. The next week the rain came, and the battle with the quagmire began. I watched every morning and evening for two weeks, and at each stage there was a long queue outside the caravan of the 'real' Rose Lee.

I am not superstitious, and reluctant to allocate supernatural powers to mortals, but why did one Rose Lee attract so many more customers than all the others put together? Each time I looked across from the trolley bus and saw the length of her queue, I became more curious about her powers and began to wonder whether she could help me to make a decision about my future.

Early on the final Sunday of Race Week I sneaked into the queue, head down to avoid being recognized. It moved quite quickly because, as I discovered, most opted for a five-minute palm reading at ten bob (50p). The alternative was a thirty-minute crystal ball gazing at a fiver, more than I earned in a month at the solicitors' office. Clearly that was out of the question, so the ten-bob palm reading it was.

When my turn came, I was seriously taken aback by the real Rose Lee's accuracy. She studied my palm and told me I had a brother and a sister, a parent who had died recently, that I worked in a tall building with many windows (I did), that I also had another job and that I was at a crossroads. She asked no questions, her statements were not in the least ambiguous and she got nothing wrong. I was so shaken that I made an appointment for the crystal-ball gazing the following evening.

The palm reading had been my first opportunity to see the inside of a gypsy caravan, but I had taken little in. It had all happened very quickly. The next evening I was more focused and, if not confident of Rose Lee's supernatural powers and a way out of my career dilemma, determined to get the best return from my investment.

When I went through the main door, I saw again what I had observed from the outside: opulence, fine china, cut glass, chrome but also real silver and a strong smell of lavender. On the other side of a second door, it was different, with dark drapes, two chairs, and a table with a fine paisley shawl covering what I assumed was the crystal ball. We took our seats and she gazed for what seemed like an age into the globe. At last she looked up and gave me a series of ambiguous statements, mumbo-jumbo and leading questions, which were totally unconvincing. I left disappointed, poorer and no wiser. To this day, I wonder how the two experiences produced such different results.

Shortly afterwards I passed my final exams and, with a degree of sadness, gave up thoughts of a legal career, for the moment at least. I knew it made sense: I could try the business for a couple of years and then, if it didn't work out, we could sell up and I could return to being a solicitor in Newcastle. However sensible and logical it might have seemed, for twelve long months I bitterly regretted that decision.

I had been a pipe smoker for some time, and my tobacco consumption increased exponentially under the stress of running the business, though the pipe did have its uses: whenever I was asked a question, I could puff away at it for a few moments while I searched for an answer. More worryingly, even though I had reduced my sporting activities and was eating more pies and cakes, I lost weight steadily from fifteen stone to twelve during my first two years.

With each day that passed, the challenges of the solicitors' practice seemed more attractive, and it soon became apparent that the premise on which I'd made my decision to take on Greggs had been false. It would not be that easy to sell the business. I had taken on new employees and developed future plans and ideas with them. I had made personal guarantees to the bank. Within twelve months I was trapped . . . but by then it no longer mattered. The pain had passed and, despite some very testing times, I never again regretted the decision.

3

THE OLD BAKERY AT GOSFORTH

Steak mince pie

Pie-eating traditions vary greatly across the UK. In the north-east the top-selling pie was always the steak mince pie, followed by the steak pie. In 1971 you could buy a steak mince pie for 5p

From the day my parents had bought the Gosforth premises, it had been obvious that the space behind the shop was too cramped for a bakery and despatch area that supplied more than the single front shop, but for the next three years, from 1965 to 1968, it was the foundation on which Greggs was built. The shop itself was twenty feet square and behind this there was a packing area of about the same size where the bread, cakes and pies were assembled on boards; in one corner there was a machine that sliced cooked meats to sell on the vans. A narrow passageway contained a hand-operated machine for pressing out pie bottoms, and a manual pastry roller, then widened into an area with a cake-mixer, a dough-mixing machine, some tables and an old coke-fired oven.

The overall impression was sepulchral. A small amount of natural light filtered through the windows in the passageway, supplemented by a few naked bulbs hanging from a ceiling that had darkened over the years with the emissions from the coke oven. The walls were brick and had once been white, but were now mottled and flecked with splashes from cake mixes, egg wash, gravy, jam and other ingredients that daily passed from container to mixer to the wooden benches where the bakers worked and eventually into the oven. Splashes and spills were frequent but most of these ended up on the concrete floor, which was pitted and eroded by energetic scrubbing at the end of each day. This un-appealing scene was redeemed by the ever-changing smells of the goods as they came out of the oven. Cakes, scones, pies and bread had their own distinctive aromas, so it was always a pleasant place to be.

There were two rickety staircases, one at the back of the shop, leading to a storage room and offices. The other was behind the oven and led to where cakes were iced and packaging stored. At the rear of the ground floor, wooden double doors opened on to a lane leading to Hawthorne Road, where the vans were loaded each morning.

It was difficult to know where to start, and Homer, Ovid and the law I had learned were no help at all. Developing van sales was not an attractive proposition: transport costs were rising and many of our potential customers were starting to use the new supermarkets in preference to buying from the traditional vans. The pork butchery at Longbenton was definitely not a candidate for expansion: I loathed it. When the butcher failed to arrive I had to deputize, and at six thirty in the morning, the reek of raw meat, mingled with black pudding and saveloys, turned my stomach. The nausea passed after a couple of hours and, seduced by the delicious scent of simmering pease pudding, I was usually enjoying a pork or ham sandwich by nine o'clock. What never went away, though, was the difficulty of working out whether the pork shop made a profit or a loss and the extent to which the wholesale meat traders saw my inexperience as an opportunity to offload on me their most fatty and gristly meat. There seemed little honour in the meat market. When the butcher was away, we got by, thanks to one of the van salesmen, John Mason, who had been a butcher and came to Longbenton in the evening after he had completed his round. Nevertheless I resolved to get rid of the business as soon as I could, as much because of the smell as the financial uncertainty.

The shop in Gosforth at the front of the bakery was clearly capable of doing more business, but it was in need of a refit, and even if the money had been available, neither I nor anyone else had any idea how to set about such a project. The only real option seemed to be to improve the bakery, which became our main focus in 1966 and 1967: a little overdue paint here and there, a new semi-automatic pie machine, a mixer for making the bread dough, an automatic pastry roller, and a gas peel oven. Each of these would repay the initial outlay quickly through labour saved, and I was happy to sign personal guarantees to the bank on the loans and hire-purchase agreements.

The Peerless semi-automatic pie machine 'blocked' (pressed out) the bases for the mince and steak pies; it also produced the shortcrust cases for strawberry tarts, peach melbas, apple pies, and mince pies at Christmas. Previously pie bases had been made one at a time, the operative placing a piece of pastry into the tin or foil, then using a lever to pull down a 'blocker', which pressed it into the required shape. The surplus was trimmed by hand and the pie base or pastry shell transferred to a baking sheet where it was filled and, if required, lidded. This was a slow process and no less than a marathon at strawberry-tart time and Christmas.

The shiny new machine, circular and about five feet in diameter, had five revolving recesses for the tins, or foils. The pastry was put into the tin and was automatically blocked on its way round. There were different shaped recesses and blockers for each product. A hopper, which filled the pie or tart, and a crimper, for lidding, were added later.

The new pie machine, the improved meat from a new supplier and the new seasoning we developed resulted in better quality and consistency, which soon led to increases in sales. We were also able to cope with the additional sales from the new shops that we were in the process of opening. The machine cost about a thousand pounds, which was repaid in a matter of weeks from increased sales and reduced costs. Without it, we would not have been able to develop our sales of mince pies and plug into the North Country tradition of eating lots of pies of varying shapes and sizes, depending on where you were. In Northumberland the favourite was the mince pie, followed by the steak pie. The former was

■ STEAK MINCE PIE ■

I large onion, chopped	I tsp Marmite
I tbsp olive oil	I tbsp Worcestershire sauce
I tsp dried rosemary	3 tbsp plain flour
2 bay leaves	2 beef stock cubes
Ilb 2oz/500g lean steak mince (90% lean)	Ilb 2oz/500g shortcrust pastry
I tsp English mustard	I egg, beaten, for glaze

1 Put the onion in a casserole with the olive oil, rosemary and bay leaves, and sauté for a few minutes until soft and translucent (not brown).

2 Add the mince and stir to break it up until browned. Add the mustard, Marmite, Worcestershire sauce and flour. Dissolve the stock cubes in 800ml boiling water, and add to the pan. Simmer for about an hour, stirring regularly. Allow to cool.

3 Preheat the oven to 200°C/400°F/Gas 6.

4 Dust a clean surface or board with flour and roll out one half of the pastry to line a 9in/23cm baking dish (1in/2.5cm deep) and the other half to make the lid. Put the cooled mince in the lined baking dish and brush the rim with egg.

5 Place the pastry lid over the mince. Crimp the edges with a fork or thumb.

6 Brush the lid with beaten egg and bake in the pre-heated oven for approximately 40 minutes or until the pastry is golden and crisp.

7 Serve with mashed potato and greens.

round and shallow, with shortcrust base and lid, filled with lean, coarsely ground mince and plenty of juicy Bisto-type gravy. The latter was deeper, more oval in shape, sometimes with a puff pastry lid and a stronger, more peppery gravy. Both types were difficult to eat warm by hand without dribbling gravy down your front, but they were soon leaving the little bakery in ever-increasing numbers.

At every possible opportunity, I toured the local high streets and shopping centres to check out the competition, staring endlessly through bakery shop windows. Carricks were the main retail bakers in north-east England, Rank Hovis McDougall had a strong presence and Crawfords (part of United Biscuits) had recently moved into the area with the purchase of a dozen shops from Fawcus of Whitley Bay. For a special treat, there were also the upmarket outlets of Smyths and Milburns, whose products, not to mention the prices they charged, filled me with envy. Each shop had its strong points and I gradually drew up a picture of what a new Greggs shop might look like: products like Milburns', a window like Crawfords', cream-cake counters like Carricks' . . . The most important feature, however, did not come from any of the bakers.

Supermarkets were flexing their muscles for market share and developing 'superstores', though 20,000 square feet counted as a superstore then, not the 50,000 to 60,000 required today, or the 100,000 for a hyper-market. This was a mighty battle, which raged for more than thirty years between some heavyweights. Tesco, founded by Jack (stack it high, sell it cheap) Cohen in 1919, had gone public in 1947 and was now expanding rapidly by acquiring and developing larger stores.

Sainsbury's, founded by John James Sainsbury in 1869, was at the forefront of pioneering larger self-service supermarkets. Asda had been formed in 1965 from the merger of *As*quith supermarkets and Associated *Da*iries. But in north-east England (and Scotland) the main players were Allied Suppliers and Fine Fare. The former was owned by James Goldsmith, with Presto and Lipton stores, Galbraiths and Templetons in Scotland, almost all later to be renamed Safeway.

This titanic struggle had more impact on UK high streets, shopping centres, out-of-town retailing and the way we shop than any other factor in the twentieth century. The battle centred on developing larger stores in which customers could buy all their food. The super-market owners also aimed to increase the frequency of visits by providing fresh fruit and vegetables, meat, delicatessen and bakery products, which would throw a knock-out blow to many traditional specialist food shops on the high street. The first of these stores I went to see was a Presto unit at Wallsend, a few miles east of Newcastle, which had a full in-store bakery producing bread, pies, cakes, the lot. I was astounded. This was real innovation. It was also theatre because there was continual activity as flour, yeast and other ingredients were mixed into dough, moulded into loaves, proved, baked and placed on racks to cool within sight of the customers, who soon snapped them up, attracted by the delicious smell of warm bread.

It was the first time I had seen one of the hot bread shops that were soon a feature of most large supermarkets and the high street. In-store baking was obviously here to stay. The exuberant and swash-buckling in-comer Don Miller, from Australia, was the front runner with his Hot Bread Kitchens chain, Sainsbury's made a good fist of it using frozen dough – a possibility that was never fully exploited by either the supermarkets, the baking industry or indeed Greggs – but in the end (as, arguably, with most things) Tesco did it best.

The in-store baking at Presto in Wallsend inspired me and seemed to offer Greggs an opportunity to do something exciting and different. Greggs would not be able to afford the money or the space in a normal retail shop to put in a full bakery, and in later years, when the idea was thoroughly analysed, high labour and rental costs, and the large capital expenditure, made it difficult to justify. But I wondered if the 'Pareto Principle' could come to Greggs' aid and provide 80 per cent of the benefit for 20 per cent of the effort and cost. Vilfredo Pareto, an Italian economist, had noticed in 1905 that 80 per cent of Italy's wealth was shared among 20 per cent of its population. His frequently ignored 80:20 principle is now used in the context of achieving 80 per cent of the benefit by focusing on the most important 20 per cent.

I also visited other family bakery businesses to find out what equipment they used, their production cycles and costing systems, and talked endlessly to the salesmen who sold ingredients, products and bakery equipment to Greggs about what was happening in the industry. Some, like Geoffrey Atkinson, were particularly helpful. He worked for Scobie & McIntosh, who supplied us with a range of racks, ovens and other bakery equipment. I spent hours, in those early days, asking questions, listening to whatever they could tell me about the industry and the players in it: who was doing well and who badly, what new products were being introduced and which techniques were being used. Our flour millers and other suppliers introduced me to successful businesses away from Tyneside. I established long-standing relationships with some, like Sayers of Liverpool, Birds of Derby and Birkett's of Penrith. I was a novice in the trade, but they were generous with their time, patient with my endless questions and even shared with me some recipes and tricks of the trade. If at first it was largely a one-way process, it soon became a two-way street, the small regional companies coming together in the face of the supermarket threat to our existence.

In retrospect, I think I was fortunate not to have any relevant training. Had I been an accountant, a food technologist or a skilled baker, I might have tried to build the business from that dimension, but I knew nothing and that made me, according to the Greek philosopher Sophocles, a wise man. He also remarked that success depends on effort, and I was determined not to fail for lack of that. I returned from my visits to other businesses clutching recipes for new products, specifications for equipment we might be able to afford one day but, above all, the realization that Greggs had to provide better-quality, more consistent products. I developed a passion for improving our products, and offering the best value for money anywhere; that was my Lesson Number Three, and remains the driving force in Greggs today.

Lesson 3: Offering best value for money anywhere.

The earliest baker I can recall was 'little Tommy' who worked the night shift and baked all the bread on his own. He was four feet eight inches tall, and had the biggest appetite I have ever seen. At the end of his lonely shift, during which the number and quality of loaves and rolls produced seemed more related to his mood than the order sheet (the reliability of the old coke oven was an easy excuse), he made a massive stotty cake about two feet in diameter, which he filled with ham and pease pudding or bacon and egg. He ate it sitting on the pastry table, little legs dangling, with a massive mug of tea made from a handful of leaves and Nestlé's condensed milk, as he traded insults with the day-shift staff about who was to blame for the mess in the bakery.

If Tommy (or the oven) had had a really bad night or, worse still, he didn't come in at all, there was an almighty scramble in the early hours to buy bread and rolls from our sliced-bread supplier or one of the other plant bakeries (the large automated bakeries which supplied the supermarkets and the retailers). These arrived golden brown, shining and uniform but the customers didn't like them. Tommy's loaves may have been funny shapes, some burned and some not baked enough, but the drivers knew who liked them well- or under-done, and they all tasted good.

Achieving improvement at that stage was not easy. Our premises and equipment, though better, were far from ideal but had to suffice for the time being. The biggest problem was our inability to retain staff for any length of time. Alan Johnson, a table hand, was an adopted Geordie from Hertfordshire and had joined Greggs in 1961. He rolled the pastry, made the sausage rolls and punctuated the day with enormous burps, which echoed round the bakery and could be heard in the upstairs office. Other staff came and went, but Alan stayed. He went on to various management positions in the company; eventually becoming transport manager at the Gosforth bakery and for the whole group. In every position he won the admiration of his colleagues for the quiet and conscientious way in which he dealt with all that life could throw at him. He retired in 1996 but retains his interest in the projection of wind and sound, now in the form of his support for the Northern Sinfonia Orchestra at the Sage, Gateshead. That's progress!

Alan was the mainstay of production, along with the bakery manager who, between purchasing flour, fats, fruit, sugar, seasoning, spices and a massive range of other mysterious ingredients, grudgingly made the cakes while reminding those around him of how useless they were. One day he suggested I see a young man whom he had interviewed and thought was a suitable baker. There were only two problems: he was asking for too much money and had long sideburns. I duly interviewed Kevin Rainey, who had turned up in motorbike leathers and was brimming with such self-confidence that he wanted twenty pounds per week, five pounds more than the going rate. I was taken aback but took him on anyway, in the hope that he might be able to provide that extra quality and consistency. He certainly did, but I was permanently concerned that he or Alan would leave. I could see that the bakery was not a happy place and reluctantly came to the conclusion that I had to discuss this with the manager.

He had always blamed the level of wages and the working conditions for the high staff turnover, but I had begun to wonder if he himself was not the cause of the problems. His attitude to life and work seemed to have been jaundiced by a long career at the hard end of a tough industry: he was hypercritical of the staff working under him, giving them an almost daily dressing-down for their real or perceived failings, and he didn't get on well with my mother, who sometimes challenged him. Their dislike was mutual, but her attitude to him may have been coloured by the fact that he had often been Dad's companion on the dog-racing and gambling escapades that were a source of friction between my parents.

For weeks I agonized over how to confront him. It was my first real experience of confrontation and I was frightened by it, particularly because he had been Dad's partner and had run the bakery on his own since it started. For more than ten years, almost nothing he did had been questioned. Perhaps he was right in his regular reminders to everyone that it was only his experience and efforts that kept the business going – Dad had certainly believed him, and no one else knew all the recipes. Whenever I found a reason to put off the dreaded task, the next day would provide another example of why something had to happen.

I have never been good at purveying bad news to the people it affects. In the end, I spent a whole day in the upstairs office, rehearsing the words and smoking pipe after pipe till my tongue was sore. That evening, after a whisky in most of the pubs between Gosforth and Longbenton, I went to his home, which was the flat above the pork shop, and talked to him and his wife, who also worked in the bakery. I had given no previous indication that change was necessary, but they accepted what I said without the surprise or anger for which I had prepared myself. We worked out a package, which included them staying in the flat until they found an alternative home.

A few weeks later I rid myself of another headache by transferring the pork business to the butcher who had been managing it for us. Our association soon ended as we no longer provided him with rolls for his sandwiches and neither did he supply us with meat, though I called in to see him occasionally and he seemed to do well for many years. The meat for Greggs' pies now came, lean and trouble-free, in stainless steel bowls from Arthur Temple, a well-known Newcastle butcher, who also became a good friend and fishing companion.

The day after my meeting with the bakery manager, I asked Alan Johnson if he would take on the role, Kevin Rainey becoming manager of confectionery with special responsibility for improving quality. In that capacity, Kevin spent time training at Spillers' Welfords bakery in Middlesbrough, which produced top-quality bread and cakes for Marks & Spencer.

As soon as the change in management had taken place, the bakery became a happier place. Existing products were improved, new ones were introduced and the staff, who had previously been lambasted for their shortcomings, were transformed into reliable, enthusiastic and creative participants. Until now, my main worry had been our ability to produce good-quality products consistently. Overnight we had taken a huge step forward and the focus soon shifted to how we could sell more of them.

I was regularly reminded of what a full-time commitment I had taken on, and how much it would impinge on my family life. On 10 April 1965 I had married Edith Wheeler at the parish church in Gosforth and we had bought our first home together in Kenton Bank Foot, a few miles west of Newcastle. I needed to find a good work–family balance, which was never easy in the baking industry. As the man in charge, I had to be in the bakery early in the morning, when most of the products were being despatched, to ensure that they were of the required standard and left on time. To be honest, I liked the bustle and excitement of this part of the day. My leaving home between six and seven each morning was non-negotiable, as was the occasional night-shift visit and my presence in the shops for part of each Saturday, the busiest day of the week.

Under such pressure choices have to be made. Cricket, rugby and golf were not too difficult to give up. Fishing was much harder, but I hardly went fishing at all for three years. This meant I could be back in reasonable time each evening, usually around six, and I also spent most of each weekend at home, but there were still times when business pressures stopped me winning Husband of the Year. A vivid example of this occurred on 20 April 1966, when I had been covering for an absent van salesman. Edith was heavily pregnant and, in spite of her protests, I set off to do the van round. There were no mobile phones in those days, so I was out of contact until I got back to the bakery at the end of the day, when I discovered I had missed the birth of our first child, a daughter we called Fiona. Our second daughter, Felicity, followed two years later on 30 June 1968, a breathlessly hot day when, thankfully, I was on hand, if not actually present at the birth.

The issue that most occupied my time was what to do about the travelling shops that had been the mainstay of the business up to that point. The two Jeans, the part-time bookkeepers who had been employed four years previously, were still paying the bills, calculating the wages and valiantly keeping up the war of cash reconciliation with the van salesmen. I suppose it might have gone on like that for ever, but I could see no great future in trying to develop the business through door-to-door van sales. Every long-term trend – increases in leisure time, disposable income, car ownership and social mobility, and the inexorable growth of super-markets – suggested that the traditional travelling shops and the roundsmen would eventually be following lamplighters and organ grinders into history.

Despite the difficult trading conditions on the high street, where supermarkets were providing ferocious competition for traditional bakers, I felt the future for Greggs lay in concentrating our efforts on retail shops, not vans, but it was a hard decision to make: our business had been founded on the vans and some of the driver-salesmen had worked for Dad for many years. They were part of the fabric of the business and almost part of the family as well. During the week they checked in at the shop and bakery at the end of the day but on Saturdays when they finished late between six and nine p.m. they reported to our home in Gosforth, where they usually had a cup of tea as they counted their takings and talked about the week's events.

There was no question of simply sacking them – they deserved much better treatment than that – but I needed to find a way to make that side of the business much less demanding of our time and effort. In the end we reached a happy compromise by leasing the vans at a low rental to the drivers, who then bought their goods from the business at a generous discount. In this way credit, stock and waste became their problem, not ours, and they paid their account before receiving any goods the following week. Simple. Most of them continued to make a good living from it for many years.

The first chance to expand the retail shop side of Greggs' business arrived almost by accident. One of the Jeans' husbands, Bob, was a surveyor at the Civic Centre and involved in the development of the council housing estates and shopping centres that were being built around Newcastle. The one at Newbiggin Hall, on the north-west side of the city, was close to completion. If Greggs was interested, he suggested, we should make an application for one of the shop units. We duly did so and were successful.

Excitement and panic took over. I had developed some thoughts about what a new Greggs outlet would look like, but had no experience of opening shops. The high-street shop in Gosforth had been bought as a going concern in 1951 and had not changed since then. We had almost a year before the shop at Newbiggin Hall was to open so I decided to open a low-cost, low-risk shop in nearby Salters Road to gain some experience. For a few hundred pounds – second-hand counters, a little paint and two pounds per week in rent – we learned many valuable lessons, in particular all of the processes involved in opening a shop, and how to operate an advance ordering system when the shop is distant from the bakery and staff are unable to pop in and ask for more of an item. It made a modest contribution for many years under the valiant efforts of Winnie Latimer, who ran it single-handed. Conscientious and friendly, Winnie set the standard for customer care in future Greggs shops.

The main focus was on what could be done in the Newbiggin Hall shop to buck the declining trend affecting retail and wholesale bakeries. Emulating the in-store bakery at the Presto supermarket would have been a possible solution if space and finance had been available, but they were not. Instead we fitted out the shop in a bright, modern style, with stainless-steel trays in the windows, a customer area in light oak panelling, similar finishes on the counter bases below the glass shelves, with blue Formica and stainless-steel racks behind the counters, and at the back of the shop, blue-veined tiles around a four-tray electric oven to bake pies, pasties, sausage rolls and pastries. All of the latter were made in the bakery and transported to a refrigerated container in the back shop, from which they could be baked fresh. Only a small amount of premium retail space was required for this, the manufacturing being confined to the bakery, but it would create the smell and 'theatre' of baking goods without the complexities and labour costs of full in-store baking where products are made from scratch.

Theatre! Pantomime was a more apt description from the outset. Customers arrived at the shop in much greater numbers than we had expected or Greggs had experienced before, all exchanging good-natured banter with the staff who were their neighbours. The bakery worked overtime, the Peerless pie machine was at full throttle and Alan's arms ached with all the sausage rolls and pastries he made by hand on the pastry table. For months I made trips between the bakery and the shop in a Morris Traveller – an old but normally reliable timbered Morris – taking whatever was needed to replenish the trays of pies and pastries that emptied as soon as they had been baked, and administering first aid to the staff for the burns they received as they took the trays from the oven. A burn across the forearm became the trademark of a good Greggs' shop assistant!

Jennifer Chalmers had been the outstanding applicant for managing the shop. She had management experience in department stores but she was looking for work that would involve less travel and we were offering her a job on the estate where she lived with her husband and two children. We were very fortunate to secure the services of someone so experienced, able and committed. Jennifer was dark-haired, glamorous and conscientious, but with a twinkle in her eye, and her enthusiasm rubbed off on everyone with whom she came into contact. Newbiggin Hall became the model for the early years of Greggs' expansion in the north-east and, in many respects, still remains the model today. It was of crucial importance that we got it right that first time. Jennifer brought together a great team, jollied the customers through the pantomime phase and introduced the systems needed for a busy shop. Most important of all, she brought into Greggs her experience and knowledge of how to sell. She went on to help with and supervise the openings of future shops, becoming sales manager and eventually a director of the Gosforth business.

We had exceeded Pareto's 80:20 ratio for Greggs at Newbiggin Hall, but was this a one-off, and what were the essential factors that had made it so successful? Was it the oven in the shop, the quality and value of the goods, or the friendly local staff who knew their customers personally? Or was it the shop's position at the heart of the local community, something we tried to nurture by supporting local events and organizations? That was the start of the community work that became a major focus of Greggs' future charitable activities and a vital part of the company values that I, and later my successors, kept at the heart of everything Greggs did.

Greggs has done what it can to help the communities where our businesses have been located. When the shop at Newbiggin Hall was opened in 1966, it was soon followed by a pie-and-pea supper for the neighbour-hood's senior citizens, a spontaneous way of saying thank you to the community for supporting our new shop so well. Pie-and-pea suppers for senior citizens became regular features in the calendars of estates and communities where Greggs opened shops, and we encouraged other local businesses, particularly off-licences, to support them. Some were modest local events with maybe fifty or sixty guests; others, like the one in Jarrow, were grander, with several hundred guests and the mayor donating the use of the town hall. All were great fun, run by the local staff who, as well as being waiters and waitresses, put on sing-songs (I was allowed to sing in those!), concerts and cabarets. Everyone had a brilliant evening.

The sensible way forward for Greggs was to try to repeat in each subsequent new shop as many as possible of the elements that had made Newbiggin Hall such a success. Over the next two years, shop openings at Forest Hall, Blakelaw, Kenton and Wallsend showed it had not been a one-off. Greggs had a formula that worked in the north-east, and enabled us to compete with the supermarkets: we provided very fresh, easily accessible products at competitive prices, served by friendly staff.

Back at the bakery, we employed more staff and squeezed additional small pieces of production kit into the increasingly inadequate space. The first floor at the very back, which had been largely used for general storage, was converted into a confectionery-finishing and despatch area. My sister Gay also joined the business. She had trained as a secretary, then worked for the NFU for two years, followed by two years as a veterinary assistant, and initially came to Greggs to help in the offices. She soon graduated to helping and troubleshooting wherever a need arose. Gay managed the new finishing area and despatch and, at the same time, learned how to be a personnel manager, which soon became her main role. She had had no experience in either of these disciplines and the only training she received (except for a one-day crash personnel session) was direct daily exposure to the needs and pressures of the business. She did both jobs admirably and her ability to develop excellent relationships extended beyond her own despatch department to the increasing numbers of staff in the bakery. She stayed with the company until 1977, when she left to have her first child, David.

My brother Colin also joined the business to develop the catering department. That had been Mum's main interest, but she was suffering from a bad back and needed to take things easier. Colin had been a science teacher at Durham School for three years but was interested in what was happening with the family business and welcomed the opportunity to take the strain from Mum. The catering side of the business had begun by chance. Customers who liked our products often asked Mum if she would cater for a family event, with sandwiches, canapés, sausage rolls and cakes for buffets, or ham, salad and trifle for sit-down occasions.

Some of the venues were far from suitable. Colin remembers one wedding reception in a Scout hut on a housing estate in Newcastle. When he opened the shutters, he discovered that many of the windows were broken. Another was in the Blue Bell at Shiremoor, a mining village near Newcastle, where we had to cater for eighty guests in a room that sat thirty, which meant serving ham, pease pudding and salad in three sittings.

The catering equipment, cups, plates and cutlery were stored at the back of the small shop in Salters Road but much of the preparation still went on in the family kitchen at 3 Linden Road and was transported by car to the event on wooden bakery trays. Sandwiches were made in stacks on the kitchen table, followed by rows of canapés. My mother found that a French stick, cut thinly, made a great base (in preference to Ritz crackers), which she buttered and then topped with slices of tomato and egg, swirls of cream cheese in a variety of flavours, prawns and pâté, all garnished with parsley – simple, colourful and delicious. Mum had established quite a team of people to help prepare, serve and wash up. They coped with all eventualities and had a lot of fun in the process.

Colin tried to take some of the workload away from Mum and give her more free time. Apart from the catering, she continued to work in the Gosforth shop and had taken an interest in the new shops. If Jennifer Chalmers wanted a meeting of shop managers, for example, Mum liked to host it in her own kitchen, insisting on baking sultana scones and Victoria Sandwich cakes, rather than having them sent from the bakery.

When an opportunity came up to lease the Assembly Rooms on Gosforth high street it seemed the ideal way to release the pressure on the family kitchen. The Assembly Rooms were on the upper floors of the Victorian buildings on the north-west side of the high street, with the entrance sandwiched between two of the standard shop units that occupied the ground floor. There was a dance hall on the first floor, a bar and kitchen on the second. The Assembly Rooms became the catering headquarters with three different functions. All of the outside catering was prepared in the kitchen. The bar was upgraded, and during the day we opened a café called the Piccolo, serving morning coffee, lunch and afternoon tea.

We used the dance hall as a function room for private parties, but every Saturday night there was a public dance that developed some notoriety. The participants, or at least the male ones, tended to spill out of the pubs and rugby clubs between nine and ten p.m., by which time some of them had lost control of their dancing steps, among other things. Nonetheless, many couples in the north-east found their eventual partner at 'Gos Ass', as it was known, and it became a local institution. However, the 'Swinging Sixties' had brought with them a heady mix of liberation from old strictures, testosterone and alcohol and Saturday nights became nightmares, sometimes ending with fighting when the police were called. We needed to move on, but had to develop new business to replace the revenue the dances had generated before they could be stopped.

The weddings, parties and general catering business continued to expand. The excellent multi-skilled team, mainly part-time, enjoyed the variety of challenges and its members were happy to work late. Colin added some new elements to this traditional business. On Mondays, to improve cash flow, he started a folk club with the High Level Ranters and many other local groups coming to play and built up a regular audience who liked beer with their music.

The most exciting new development was the production of chilled, ready-made meals for re-heating in canteens when a company did not wish, or was unable, to provide conventionally cooked food for its staff. The potential of this market had been greatly increased by the arrival in 1967 of the microwave oven, which was capable of heating a meal in a few minutes. The dishes were made in the Assembly Rooms' kitchen and transferred to vending machines in staff canteens. This aspect of the business grew very quickly and offered huge potential, but by now Colin wanted to return to teaching and I was too busy running the bakery to take on anything else. So, not without some reluctance, we sold that part of the business to a local caterer, who made a big success of it.

Although he had returned to teaching, Colin remained a director and was actively involved in the company, which meant there were now four of us in the business: Mum, Colin, Gay and me. It was at this point that Greggs the Bakers, as the company was now called, faced a major decision. We had a successful retail trading formula and there was potential for many more shops in the north-east where this could be applied, but the existing bakery could barely cope with demand from the current shops.

The only way forward was to create additional production capacity, but this posed a serious problem. The modest profits we'd made to date had been used to improve the existing bakery, putting down deposits on equipment and fitting out new shops. I was already personal guarantor for several hire-purchase agreements and the twenty-one-year lease of the shop at Wallsend at an annual rent of £850, by far the highest rental we had paid to date. The potential liability was almost £18,000 – four times the value of the new four-bedroom house Edith and I had bought at Kenton Bank Foot.

I had swallowed hard when I signed that guarantee but I need not have worried. It was an amazing success from the outset. The manager, Jennie Huggins, was a Geordie stalwart, an inspiration to staff and customers alike, achieving sales levels that fired our ambition. The landlord had been hard-nosed in insisting on a personal guarantee but he paid a steep price for it: the annual rent remained at £850 throughout the term of the lease. By the 1980s, it was Greggs' lowest rental anywhere, only a fraction of its market value.

The sum we needed to acquire a site, build and fit out a new bakery was likely to exceed £100,000, which was, at that time, a very large sum of money. It was much more than I was willing to borrow and guarantee. The only item of real value in the company was the shop and bakery building, but its value had always been seen as my mother's pension fund, and thereafter as an inheritance to be divided between her three children. However, she looked at the situation and decided that if her children wanted it now, they could have it and use it to help fund the cost of a new bakery.

This was a massive decision for us all. I had a great

affection for the old bakery on Gosforth high street. It had been an important part of our lives for as long as we could remember, just a stone's throw from our home and seeming almost part of it. We had all worked there as children at busy times, and been friends with many of the staff. It was difficult to imagine life without it. I had spent the first few years of my working life there, learning about the bakery industry and carrying out most of the jobs it entailed, from creaming cakes early in the morning to cashing up in the evening but the financial implications were even greater than the emotional pressures.

I wasn't sure that I wanted the personal responsibility of guaranteeing an adequate income for my mother and an inheritance for my brother and sister, but Mum, Colin and Gay encouraged me to go ahead. At each stage before and after this, I received 100 per cent support and encouragement from within the family. That made a huge difference to me and enabled me to get on with developing Greggs. It was undoubtedly the most important example of their support, and it's difficult to see how the new bakery could have been built otherwise. It allowed the expansion of the business to continue, and us to take advantage of trading opportunities as they occurred, developing the momentum that made Greggs what it is today.

4

STOTTY MANIA
Stotty cake

*In the early 1970s Greggs revived the forgotten north-east
tradition of stotty cake. Tyneside went wild for them, with
shops selling 500 a day, more than we could produce*

Until this point, the Greggs board of directors had continued its relaxed pattern of one meeting per year and
production of a sparse record to comply with legal
requirements. Any discussions or decisions about the
business took place not in formal board meetings but
over coffee or supper, as happens in many small family
businesses. This changed in 1968 when the share
capital of the company was increased from £2,000 to
£10,000, to reflect the increasing size of the business
and to make changes in the shareholdings within the
Gregg family to reflect our responsibilities and levels of
investment. Neil Calvert, for whom I had worked while

I was doing my articles, arranged it. He was probably the best company solicitor in Newcastle and did a remarkable job for Greggs over the next twenty-seven years.

From then on, the minutes included a much more detailed record of major decisions taken as the board began to play a vital behind-the-scenes role, approving major decisions, revenue budgets and capital expenditure. The directors were still all family members – Mum, Colin, Gay and myself – but I felt it was important that they took part in decisions and that proper records were kept. We all had a lot at stake in the business. I had given up my career as a solicitor and it was now my future; Mum was totally reliant on the company for income, having given up her life interest in the Gosforth property; and Colin and Gay had given up their entitlement to the proceeds of the sale of the property to enable the new bakery to be built.

We appointed Peat Marwick Mitchell as auditors. Alan Wardropper, the partner in charge, had been recommended to me as among the best accountants in Newcastle. He became general financial adviser to the company and its shareholders, a position he carried out to excellent effect for thirty years. He lived in Gosforth and, with shared interests in golf, cricket and the countryside, we became good friends. However difficult the problem, Alan could always explain the issues and set out the options clearly. He liked to keep things simple, avoiding the complexities that financial advisers revel in today. The board now had structure and formality, with agendas, budgets, discussion papers and decisions, plus the best legal and financial advice available in Newcastle.

The new bakery was built in 1968 at Christon Road, Gosforth Industrial Estate, on land owned by Gosforth Council to the north-east of the town. Surrounded by housing, it was just large enough for about ten modest factories or warehouses, and Greggs eventually occupied more than half of those units. The original bakery provided 7,200 square feet of production area with 1,800 square feet of offices above, at a cost of £50,000. In retrospect, this seems a small investment for such a substantial building but it was then ten times the cost of a decent four-bedroom house.

The walls were brick and cladding up to a pitched asbestos roof, lined with plastic-coated plasterboard. The interior walls were finished with white gloss paint and the floor covered with quarry tiles. Compared to the specification of the bakeries Greggs builds today, it was modest and utilitarian, but at that time, in comparison to what we had been used to at the old bakery, it was utterly amazing, state-of-the-art and *enormous*. Our major concern was how we could utilize all the space and fill the cavernous oven: trays of bread and cakes were loaded into it at one end, then carried through on a moving belt to emerge perfectly baked at the other. However, the increased production capacity was rapidly absorbed by a steady stream of new shop openings. Between 1968 and 1970 we opened shops at Longbenton, Shields Road, Walker, Chillingham Road, Four Lane Ends, Newcastle City Centre (Grainger market), North and South Shields, Morpeth, Cramlington, Ashington, Gateshead and Jarrow. They were all clustered around Newcastle and Gateshead, which enabled several daily deliveries of freshly baked goods to each one, and kept down transport costs, which were starting to escalate. Petrol had reached the giddy height of 5s. 3d. a gallon (28p, or 5½p per litre). At this stage there was a significant element of wholesale business in bread and cakes, with Fenwick's, Bainbridge's and Binns among our customers; we also supplied lunch to Askham House School, the preparatory school in Gosforth where Colin and I had been pupils.

The new bakery and the rapid shop expansion programme soon used up the proceeds from the sale of the Gosforth property, but we could fund continued growth without substantial borrowing because of an unusual working-capital position in our expanding retail bakery business. Normally, as a business expands, it requires additional capital to fund stock, work in progress and debtors. In Greggs' case there was little or no stock or work in progress, no debtors because we received cash for products used and did not pay for materials for weeks or, in some cases, months but always on agreed terms. This positive cash inflow, with the directors taking modest salaries and the shareholders no dividend so that all profit was retained for investment in the business, was a key factor in allowing Greggs to expand without accumulating large quantities of debt.

We needed a 4,500 square feet extension early in 1970 (by which time there were already twenty shops), and the size of the bakery was doubled the following year, when another 13,500 square feet were added, filling the site to capacity. The cost of the building, plus the plant and machinery in it, was £150,000. Two-thirds of this extension was a bread bakery with a daily production capacity of 100,000 rolls and 20,000 loaves. Other features included an eighteen-ton flour container, or silo, air-conditioned additions to the confectionery and savoury departments, a deep freeze of 3,500 cubic feet, a staff canteen and changing rooms with showers.

New machinery included a Tweedy 140 high-speed bread-mixer, which could mix 280 pounds of dough in a five-minute cycle, a special gas-fired travelling oven, which could bake 1,600 loaves an hour, a Winkler plant, which hammered out 8,000 bread rolls an hour, and an Oliver Douglas board-washing machine. The latest extension was opened by Councillor George Trice, chairman of Gosforth Council, which had been very supportive of the initial development and each extension.

All these developments came as a shock to the residents of South Gosforth, many of whose gardens backed on to the bakery site. Their leafy suburban outlook was replaced by the back of an industrial building and silos for storing flour, with vans coming and going twenty-four hours a day. This was a minor nuisance, compared to the disruption caused by the building of the Metro line, which divided the bakery from the houses in 1980, but the residents were generally not pleased and we were in regular negotiations on how we could lessen our impact. One particular neighbour was always phoning to complain, demanding that we close the windows to keep down the noise of the music or machinery, or do something about the smell of whatever we were making; it wasn't until years later that we discovered that the man's wife had been working in the bakery! We tried to meet the householders' complaints as far as we could, because we wanted to be good neighbours and have them on our side, but it wasn't always easy.

In time, an extensive tree-planting scheme made a big difference, but there were still occasional incidents, such as the night when a safety valve blew on the flour silo, causing an explosion. It was a windy night and clouds of flour were blown over the neighbouring houses. By dawn, it looked as if Christmas had come early and there had been a snowstorm. It took all the hygiene staff from the bakery and most of the window cleaners in Newcastle to sweep up the drifts of flour and clean all the houses, windows, gardens and cars. The neighbours also had to put up with the smell of two tons of cheese and onion mixture being cooled for the pasties, nice in small doses at lunchtime but not in that amount at six thirty a.m. We never did find a satisfactory solution to that.

One other occasional source of grievance was the exuberance of our night-shift bakers. In summer the 'Confect' department often finished work at about four a.m. and would take advantage of the light summer mornings to have an impromptu game of football before they went home. The yells of delight as a shot flashed into the net or of derision as a butter-fingered goalie made a complete hash of a save were not what the local residents wanted to hear at that time in the morning. We had to impose a curfew on football.

The expansion of the bakery had created continuing management pressures and we made a succession of new appointments to bring in the expertise Greggs needed. In 1969 Peter Owen Ward joined as general manager, leaving the Spillers Coast Road bakery, which was supplying sliced bread to Greggs as we lacked the specialist equipment at the Gosforth bakery to produce it. He was an impressive man in his early thirties, who had moved quickly to a senior position at Spillers. I felt we needed the benefit of that management experience and was prepared to offer a directorship and shareholding to secure it, but sadly his appointment did not last a full year.

Although I tried not to interfere on a day-to-day basis, we were still relatively small and Peter preferred the challenges and structure of a larger business. He felt limited by Greggs, by my presence and the close relationship I had with many of the staff. There were no disagreements or hard feelings on either side, just sadness that it had not worked out. In that short period, though, Peter made major contributions to several areas of the business, the most important of which was the introduction of a weekly profit and loss account. In his last months, when he already knew he would be moving on, he strove to leave this legacy, which he regarded as an essential part of managing a bakery business. I can still picture the smile on his face when he had achieved it. Since then, Greggs has produced a profit and loss account every single week – Lesson Number Four: react quickly to what is happening with sales and costs. The weekly profit and loss account became to the Greggs manager what charts are to the mariner.

Lesson 4: React quickly to what is happening with sales and costs.

If Peter's appointment did not work out for the longer term, others did. At the start of 1971 John Gardener was appointed wholesale sales manager and Brian Wildblood quality control manager. Both were from Allied Bakeries, where Brian had been group production manager for the north-east, and John regional sales manager of Carricks' two hundred shops in the north-east. A keen Scottish dancer, John had prodigious energy, and could out-dance his younger colleagues at any social event. Brian had considerable production experience and was a chief examiner on breadmaking and confectionery for the City and Guilds awards.

Ramsey PR were now handling our public relations and doing a remarkable job at promoting Greggs in the north-east. They took a close personal interest in everything that happened, converting it into news stories and features, which the local media gobbled up, whether it was a new bakery extension, shop openings, new products or celebration cakes to mark local events. In 1971 they published the first *Greggs Gazette*, which appeared thereafter two or three times a year and captured all the personal stories and individual achievements of staff and some customers, as well as providing an opportunity for the company to get across any major messages regarding expansion, investment and strategy. The stream of articles in the local press and the regular appearance of the *Gazette* played a major part in developing pride in the business among its employees, and awareness of Greggs among the public.

Peter Feather was noting these newspaper articles from a quiet backwater in residential Gosforth, where he lived with his wife, Audrey, and their two sons. Some ten years older than me, he was a highly successful entrepreneur, but shunned publicity and the limelight. He had previously built up a successful chain of wine shops, and we met at Newbiggin Hall, where he was involved in opening Newsfare, the local newsagent-post office, as part of another small retail chain. He was very aware of what was happening on the high streets and shopping centres in north-east England, and approached me to find out whether I was interested in taking on a partner. We immediately got on well together.

In spite of daily support from management and staff, encouragement and advice from family and professional advisers, my role still seemed at times a rather lonely one. There were decisions in which I needed help, areas where we were short of experience and, most of all, a lack of knowledge about where all this expansion was heading. Peter had built up successful retail businesses and had a remarkable knowledge of property and trading locations; he saw the strategic opportunity available to Greggs in and beyond the north-east, and nurtured a desire to be involved in taking a company to the stock exchange. He was also cautious and a good check on my enthusiastic optimism. He joined Greggs in 1971 and was executive property director for ten years, and a non-executive director until 1988. Today he still takes a very active interest in Greggs.

The business was going from success to success. By 1971 Greggs had first-class production facilities and an increasingly experienced and professional management team. Shop openings continued to exceed expectations, with the little electric Chandley ovens baking prodigious numbers of pies and pastries. John Gardener was pushing hard to capitalize on the lunchtime queues by introducing sandwiches, which Greggs did not sell at that time. Sandwiches were a major focus of our competitors, particularly Carricks. With dogged Scots determination, he bent my ear at every possible occasion about the sales potential Greggs was missing, but I didn't want to detract from our savoury sales: first, they were very profitable and one of the pillars of the business, but also the period between eleven thirty a.m. and two thirty p.m. was already frantically busy and I was reluctant to increase pressure on this critical period. Of course, he was absolutely right about introducing sandwiches, which we did a few years later to meet customer demand, and they are now a very big part of our business.

In February 1971 Greggs won the *Newcastle Journal* Top Shop Award in the independents section, and was also overall winner across all three sections: independents, national companies, and department stores. There were fifty-seven entries, which included most of the major national multiples, and Greggs attracted 50 per cent more votes than any other entry in any category.

By now the number of our employees had increased to more than three hundred. At the bakery, many came from the mining communities around Ashington, which had suffered from the decline in the coal industry. Ashington had been the capital of coal mining in the north-east. In 1800 it had been a sleepy rural village, but from 1847 the Ashington Coal Company had exploited the rich seams in the ground below. The process mushroomed in the 1920s and by 1934 production had peaked at more than three million tons of coal per year from a workforce of 3,600 men, directly and indirectly supporting the total population of almost 30,000. By 1970, the pit was in serious decline as the richer seams of 'black diamonds' had been exhausted, though it was another eighteen years before the final closure, by which time only 350 were still employed there.

The Ashington Coal Company had been, by the standards of the time, a benevolent employer. It provided good-quality housing for its employees, and encouraged them to develop interests outside their work. During the 1920s and 1930s there were two operatic societies in Ashington, plus the Priestman's Institute and the Workers' Education Association, all of which encouraged intellectual and artistic pursuits, the latter spawning the now famous Pitmen Painters.

With the coal industry in decline, more and more former miners were forced to look for alternative employment, and the men who came from these communities to work for Greggs proved reliable and hard-working, many staying with us for twenty years or more. Bob Barrass joined Greggs in 1971, aged twenty-two. His father had been a miner, one of a family of ten, with five brothers, who all worked for the Ashington Coal Company either 'down pit' (below ground) or 'on bank' (above ground), and five sisters who all married men who also worked 'down pit' or 'on bank'. Bob's mother had three brothers who worked at the colliery. The whole family lived in the same neighbourhood so whenever Bob went 'up street', 'down street' or into 'next street' he was always going 'home', where the doors were never locked and there was always a pot of tea on the go. Bob broke with family tradition and worked for Greggs for thirty-five years, mainly as bread and night-shift manager; he had to retire early in 2006, at fifty-seven, to have a heart triple bypass. He still happily tends his allotment.

The money at Greggs might not have matched what miners had earned down the pit, but the work was cleaner and less dangerous, the shifts less anti-social and the employment secure and regular. Some, like Bob Barrass, were promoted into supervisory and management positions, and many graduated to the night shift where, with minimum supervision, they got on with producing bread rolls and scones. As well as being reliable and hardworking they followed the recipe, weighing each ingredient carefully and sticking to the specification – unlike more flamboyant bakers who liked to guess or estimate, had their own ideas about the best recipe or process, and were confident that, with their skills and training, they could handle anything unusual that occurred.

Greggs was winning the hearts of the north-east. People like a success story and there weren't many in the region at that time. Our products were fresh, local and good value. In spite of the inflationary pressures of decimalization in 1971 and escalating wage increases, in 1973 steak mince pies were still only 5p, six sultana scones cost 7p, large chocolate cakes 9p and jam dough-nuts were three for 5p. A large loaf was 10p and a small loaf 6p, which Greggs reduced to 7p and 4p respectively for miners' families in Ashington and other areas affected by the coal strikes of 1972 and 1974 – the first times the miners had downed tools since the General Strike of 1926. We reduced the prices not to signal support for the strike but to help families who were hard hit by it and struggling to survive with virtually no money coming in.

In June 1974 we embarked on another initiative to help those who were struggling to make ends meet. Although perfectly edible, misshaped bread rolls, scones and cakes, and day-old bread had previously been binned as waste and fed to pigs. We were concerned to end this waste and to offer something to those who were worst affected by the soaring inflation of that era. We opened a 'seconds' shop in Westgate Road, offering at half-price day-old bread, pies and cakes, with surplus or misshaped products from the bakery. It proved a very popular move, and was usually sold out by lunchtime. It attracted significant publicity: the Soviet newspaper *Izvestia* ran an article citing the queues as proof of how people in the capitalist West were starving and forced to queue for rations!

Although Greggs was doing better than could possibly have been forecast or imagined, I was concerned that the marketing advantage we had established over our competitors would not last. It depended on well-located outlets, close enough to the bakery for multiple daily deliveries, friendly local staff, shops that became part of the local community, and baking savouries and pastries in store. More supermarkets were developing in-store bakeries and the national bakery chains of Allied Bakeries and Rank Hovis McDougall had already developed significant sandwich businesses. I was convinced they would start developing in-store bakeries and copy other aspects of Greggs' business, but they continued to focus more on sandwiches and catering.

Perhaps the difficulties faced by the industry made management too introspective, or they were too preoccupied with the problems of catering, or the industry was dominated by manufacturers who did not understand retailing, or perhaps their bakeries were too focused on the needs of wholesaling to supermarkets and not strategically located to accommodate multiple deliveries to small bakery shops. In the early 1970s I did not have the benefit of such knowledge. Instead I was convinced they would copy Greggs and that we needed therefore to develop our in-store baking formula by making and baking bread on site. Freshly baked loaves with that mouth-watering aroma would stop our customers going to the supermarket or one of our competitors.

We chose Shields Road, Byker, a densely populated area in east Newcastle as the trial site. Instead of a full in-store bakery, we installed a Chandley peel oven, a small bread-mixer, a prover and a stainless-steel table. It was a limited one-man operation, producing small quantities of crusty bread and fresh rolls to supplement the range of freshly baked savouries and pastries. Most of the bread would still come from the bakery, but the smell of freshly baked loaves would give the shop another marketing advantage and Greggs would learn more about in-store baking. For this to work, we needed a skilful craft baker, and found one in George Stogden, who lived in nearby Longbenton. Aged fifty-nine, he had spent forty-five years in bakeries and was a real crafts-man of the old school, conscientious, always on time, respectful of everyone. I agreed with him the bread and roll recipes he would use, though in George's case they probably weren't necessary. He had a magic touch that meant everything came out perfectly.

George's fresh loaves and rolls were soon selling well and everything was in line with expectation until the day he asked if he could make some stotty cakes. Some customers were asking for them and it seemed worth trying. Traditionally, it had been customary for women in Tyneside and in the surrounding mining villages to bake their own bread. From a mixing of dough they made enough loaves in tins to last for the next few days and any surplus was rolled out flat and round and baked as a stotty cake on the oven bottom, hence its other name 'oven-bottom cake'. Before the

Second World War they were commonly to be seen cooling on house steps or windowsills. They were ideally eaten faintly warm, with plenty of butter. In more recent years they seemed to have fallen out of fashion – or perhaps memory – but the stotty cakes at Shields Road touched a chord in the Geordie psyche and sparked a remarkable revival.

Stotty cakes have to be eaten fresh when they are delicious. It is interesting to wonder why they fell out of favour. Perhaps they had simply been forgotten after the war, when home baking declined. Perhaps mass-production in plant bakeries had destroyed their essential qualities. (In later years we tried to mass-produce them on a pizza line at the Gosforth bakery and almost killed the goose that laid the golden egg.) Perhaps the small craft bakeries failed to capitalize on a marketing opportunity. We certainly couldn't have planned the revival that began at the Shields Road shop with George's stotty cakes. The results were amazing. Queues began to form and persisted throughout the day. There were fights if anyone was thought to have jumped a place or if the shop assistant sold the last one or two, leaving a short-tempered customer to wait for the next batch.

It was an opportunity that had arrived by chance and was embraced by a young business passionate about quality and freshness, and by customers looking for a distraction from the normal pressures and bad news that assailed them. Greggs was trying to manage serendipity. Following the Shields Road opening, though, we simply couldn't cope with the demand for stotty cakes. We put a separate pie oven in the shop, virtually stopped bread and roll production so that

■ STOTTY CAKES ■

2lb/900g strong plain white flour
2 tsp salt
2oz/55g butter, cut into pieces
3 tsp dried yeast

1 tsp sugar
10fl oz/300ml lukewarm water
10fl oz/300ml lukewarm milk

1   Mix together the flour and salt in a large bowl and rub in the butter until it resembles coarse sand.

2   Mix the yeast and sugar into the lukewarm water and milk and leave until the yeast has dissolved.

3   Make a hole in the centre of the flour mixture and add the liquid, stirring from the centre with your hands. Work the mixture into a firm dough, and then knead well for about 10 minutes until the dough is smooth.

4   Dust with flour and place on a floured board. Cover with a clean teatowel and leave to rise in a warm place for about 1½ hours, until it has doubled in size.

5   Turn the risen dough onto a floured board and knead lightly to let out the air and to make the dough pliable again. Cut into pieces of about 12oz/350g. Roll into balls and rest for 10 minutes under a teatowel.

6   Preheat the oven to 220°C/425°F/Gas 7.

7   Roll the pieces out into 7in/18cm rounds. Cover with a teatowel and rest for another 10 minutes.

8   Place on a floured baking sheet. Make a hole in the centre of each cake with your finger. Bake on a high shelf in the preheated oven for 12 to 15 minutes, turning after 8 or 9 minutes. (If you have an Aga or solid base oven bake the stotties on the oven bottom.)

9   Eat warm with butter. Stotties are great for sarnies and when split make a good pizza base.

George could concentrate solely on stotty cakes, and employed a second baker. Then we opened another in-store bakery at nearby Chillingham Road, manned by Pat Whelan, another stotty stalwart. We opened more in-stores wherever there was space, but still it was not sufficient. Fuelled by more excellent publicity from Ramsey PR, demand spread across Tyneside like wildfire. Shops without in-store bakeries required stotties to be sent from other shops to meet popular demand. An eighty-year-old man in Jarrow even claimed that the stotty had aphrodisiac properties, which certainly can't have hurt sales in our shop there.

To the fury of Longbenton housewives and their husbands, the local shop sold 500 stotties a day during the week, but on Saturdays it was allocated only 200 because demand was so high elsewhere. One irate husband phoned the shop manager, Lillian Sutherland, and said, 'Tell your boss it's not fair. Saturday is the one day of the week when husbands are at home and can enjoy a stotty cake as it should be – warm. Better still,' he added, 'organize a petition and we'll all sign it.' She did, gathering 400 signatures in a few hours and 800 altogether. Longbenton's stotty allowance was increased.

In the same year, 1970, Ramsey PR organized a major coup when they secured Miss World, Eva Rueber-Staier of Austria, to open the new shop in Ashington, which also featured Greggs' largest in-store oven to date. The plan was for a gleaming Rolls-Royce to drive her and me from Newcastle to Ashington and we had organized a champagne and stotty cake reception for staff and customers. However, the Rolls-Royce broke down en route and we had to wait for half an hour to be rescued. Many men would have thought that they'd died and gone to heaven if they were offered half an hour with Miss World in the back seat of a Rolls-Royce but I was too preoccupied with trying to get the car moving or finding an alternative way of getting her to the shop to appreciate my good fortune.

The waiting crowds had accepted the delay with good grace, sipping champagne and nibbling freshly buttered stotty while they waited, and when we arrived, Eva charmed the audience and performed the opening with aplomb. As a battery of cameras flashed, she was presented with a cake, decorated with an icing-sugar portrait of herself and scenes of Northumberland life, then ate a stotty, washed down with champagne. Greggs' stotty cakes received a whole lot more publicity, which they probably didn't need since demand already outstripped supply. We couldn't produce enough in spite of the in-store bakers working overtime, even doing without the occasional tea breaks.

We also designed a new product based on a stotty cake, cut in half horizontally, covered with tomato, cheese, ham and other toppings, then flashed through the oven. We offered a prize to the customer who could come up with the best name. The winner was 'Stotza', the only problem being that this was suggested by more than half the entrants! Perhaps more interesting was the suggestion that won second prize: 'Cushie' (from Cushie Butterfield, made famous by the Geordie song named after her), but we struggled to find a third prize, and in the end grudgingly awarded it to 'Gizza Pizza'!

Jack Ramsey and Yvonne Purvis of Ramsey PR continued to work with Greggs until 2002, a remarkably long relationship between a company and a PR agent, the norm being closer to between one and three years. Their work with Greggs earned them the Sword of Excellence awarded by the Institute of Public Relations for the best long-term PR campaign. Jack and Yvonne maintained their close personal interest in everything that happened in Greggs, continually dripping stories into the local media, from staff getting married to celebration cakes made for special occasions. Such cakes might not have been very profitable and many bakers don't make them today, but they provided great photographs and personal interest stories, and kept the cake decorators very busy.

Our confectioners, Cyril Ward, Bert Hutchinson and Margaret Eagan, produced novelty cakes made of moist layered genoese with raspberry jam and butter cream, or chocolate cake with ganache, or best quality fruit cake, covered with royal icing, fondant sugar icing, marzipan, in green, red, black, blue, yellow, or whatever was required. They came in all sorts of weird and wonderful configurations, including a policeman's helmet, a football pitch, a town hall, a cricket bat and even the Grand National, but perhaps the strangest of all was a cake in the shape of a coffin, covered with chocolate and with gold braid as handles. On each occasion, the proud creator and his or her cake appeared in the local papers with a story of how long it had taken to make, what ingredients had been used, how it had graced the celebration and how it had later been sent to the local hospice, hospital or other worthy destination to be eaten.

Our confectioners also produced dummy wedding cakes with blue or even black icing, which were intended simply as arresting items to put in our shop windows. It was believed that passers-by who stopped to stare and wonder at the unusual wedding cake would then notice the appetizing confectionery surrounding it, and the sales figures certainly seemed to bear out the theory.

However, the stotty cake remained the flagship for Greggs, and in 1972 George Stogden received an award for baking his millionth stotty. The two millionth arrived even quicker – within seventeen weeks – because Greggs was now selling 60,000 each week from fewer than forty shops. We had always prided ourselves on our roots and began a poster campaign in Geordie, with subtitles like 'Gerrastottykyekheorhinny' or 'Stotty an' broon . . . noo y'taakin'', which would have been incomprehensible to anyone but a Geordie.

Stotties entered every area of our lives. When my sister, Gay, got married, the apprentices from the bakery formed a guard of honour and she and her new husband left the church beneath an arch of stotty cakes. In March 1973 the prime minister, Ted Heath, was the guest of honour at a reception at the Civic Centre. The star item on the menu was not leg of Cheviot lamb, not Northumbrian sirloin of beef, not salmon from the Tyne. The lord mayor, Alderman Arthur Grey, wanted Heath and the other guests to relax and enjoy themselves in true Geordie style so they ate warm buttered stotties to the strains of 'Blaydon Races', with the PM expected to join in the chorus, not easy with a mouthful of stotty, even if you know the words!

By special request, before HMS *Andromeda* set sail from Newcastle in 1976, a tray of our stotty cakes was piped aboard for its hungry Geordie crewmen. Two Royal Air Force pilots also benefited from a special delivery while serving in Oman. Any stotty cakes we had sent them would have been stale by the time they got there, but we did the next best thing: we sent them a recipe and enough ingredients to bake a few dozen instead.

In 1978 we produced a six-foot diameter stotty, claimed to be the world's biggest ever, and in 1983 we commissioned the world's first ever machine for mass-producing stotty cakes, though generations of Geordie engineers would have been spinning in their graves because no British company could supply it and we were forced to import it from Holland. That same year, to mark Greggs' one hundred millionth stotty, Nicholas Soames, the former food minister, and Neville Trotter, the local MP for Tynemouth, hosted a celebration at the Houses of Parliament and an early-day motion was tabled, congratulating Greggs and recommending the introduction of stotty cake to the various catering establishments in the Palace of Westminster.

Greggs also sponsored a number of athletes, particularly those in field events, who required a calorie-rich diet. Scottish hammer-throwing champion Chris Black needed 8,000 calories a day as part of his training regime for the Los Angeles Olympics, and received 1,000 rolls, 200 pies and 350 loaves. We also sponsored a nineteen-stone Northumbrian policeman, Peter Gordon, who, while training for the discus event at the same Olympics, munched his way through 2,500 meat pies, 1,000 cream cakes, 400 stotties, 200 custard tarts and 200 wholemeal loaves, the latter his sole apparent concession to what a modern dietician might regard as an appropriate diet.

Those heady times from the late 1960s to the early

1970s were, from my perspective, the most exciting and exhilarating period in Greggs' development. I was proud of what we had achieved, establishing a culture of endeavour, pride and loyalty, with people working together for the benefit of the business, staff and customers, unhampered by the selfishness that seemed to be damaging society and industry around us. Without any conscious effort, we had established a set of values that would be a significant element in Greggs' future growth.

However, although we couldn't yet see them, clouds were gathering on the horizon, and Greggs was soon to taste the bitterness of the industrial unrest that shook Britain throughout the 1970s. In addition, we would discover the difficulties that expanding into new geographical areas could bring. More lessons were about to be learned.

5

GLASGOW
Bridie

*Scotland's spicy alternative to the pasty. The name derives
either from their popularity at weddings or from Maggie
Bridie, who sold them at Forfar market*

During the fifty years or so leading up to the 1970s,
there had been major changes in the flour milling and
baking industries, which would contribute to Greggs' expansion, though at the time I was not aware of them or of the
opportunities they offered. After the First World War there
had been over-capacity in the milling industry and competition was fierce. To be viable, millers needed to operate
continuously, twenty-four hours a day. There was inadequate demand to achieve this and many mills were closed
down or amalgamations forged, notably in 1920 between
Vernons and Spillers, which became Spillers Milling. Rank
and Spillers were the dominant firms in the industry.

In 1928 the two firms set about reorganizing the industry at the request of the National Association of British and Irish Millers. They introduced a Millers Mutual Association (MMA) and allocated each mill a quota. If they wished, millers could sell their quota to the MMA. Their mills were then 'silenced', a euphemism meaning 'destroyed', and the MMA reallocated the quota to one of the surviving millers. In ten years forty mills were silenced, and mergers and takeovers further reduced the number of milling firms from 300 to 200.

Thanks to the efforts and charisma of James Rank, the eldest son of Joseph Rank and head of the MMA, the millers played according to the rules laid down for them, the industry returned to profit and he was hailed as its saviour. Such a system, with fines for exceeding quotas, was soon regarded as interference against competition and made illegal, but it laid the foundations for the modern UK milling industry, regarded as the most efficient in Europe.

Until the outbreak of war in 1939, the industry concentrated on expanding the market for its products. Although there were some plant bakeries by then, there was no such thing as a loaf of standard specification, and certainly not a sliced and wrapped one. Most were produced by small bakeries, which were members of the National Association of Master Bakers (Greggs is still a member today).

All this changed when Garfield Weston, son of a Toronto baker, entered the British market. He had already developed a substantial business in Canada and the northern USA, and in the early 1930s he started to manufacture biscuits in the UK, then to acquire bakeries that he formed into Allied Bakeries. Except for the period of the Second World War, when import controls forced him to use flour from UK mills, all the flour used in his bakeries came from Canadian mills. As a result, both Rank and Spillers lost significant volume and feared that even more of their flour output could be lost to Canada in the future. In order to secure a substantial part of their remaining market, the two companies entered the baking industry and began buying major bakeries. In 1962 Rank acquired Hovis McDougall to become Rank Hovis McDougall (RHM). Garfield Weston responded by stepping up his own acquisitions and the three major baking groups – RHM, Spillers and Allied Bakeries – entered into fierce competition for the remaining significant independent bakeries.

Britain had begun negotiations to join the European Economic Community (now known as the European Union). Weston feared that he might face a levy or control on purchasing flour from Canada if the UK became a member, forcing him into dependence on RHM and Spillers for his flour, so he started buying UK flour mills. By 1963 he had acquired twenty-eight, sufficient to service his bakeries and more.

The milling companies had invested massively during this period to take out surplus capacity, merging, acquiring and modernizing mills, then purchasing bakeries, but there was considerable competition to acquire them, which resulted in full and sometimes inflated prices being paid. The net effect of this on the retail baking sector in the early 1960s, when Greggs started to expand, was that the companies owning multiple retail bakery shops had over-invested in the rush to protect market share and there wasn't enough left in the kitty for the further investment required. To achieve a return on this investment, they attempted to improve margins and cut costs by closing bakeries. This resulted in loss of morale and a further decline in sales, which in turn led to more closures.

The underlying objective of the large bakery companies was to sell flour, which would make their mills more profitable, and the best way to achieve that was to sell large quantities of sliced bread through supermarkets. Their retail bakery businesses were not a high priority for senior management, nor properly understood by it. Although we didn't grasp it fully at the time, all of this created an opportunity in the retail bakery sector, which Greggs was able to take advantage of.

If we were going to expand on a national basis, however, we needed a more strategic approach. Alan Wardropper, at Peat Marwick Mitchell, recommended that we commissioned the consultancy arm of his company to produce a comprehensive report on the issues Greggs needed to address as part of our expansion plans. The consultant they sent was Janol Scott, a short, dark-haired Scot with a disarming smile, a sharp mind and a wealth of experience developed over many years as a senior consultant. He recommended a management structure with a head office and independent local management team for each geographical area, and gave us job descriptions for the key members of this structure. He set out the format of a budgetary control system, with quarterly comparisons, plus cost-accounting processes for controlling ingredient costs.

With the weekly account Peter Owen Ward had

introduced, this provided a systematic control for investigating variances from budget, and differences between businesses. Most of this was new to me and far removed from the day-to-day excitement and hurly-burly of the expanding business at Gosforth, but I knew it was important and found time to question every aspect of it to make sure the recommendations would fit well into Greggs. Although I had great respect for Janol, this was Greggs' and my future, not his. It was worth the effort because ultimately that report provided the control systems and management appointments which guided Greggs for the rest of the century.

Since Peter Feather's appointment in 1971, we had taken a more strategic approach to shop openings. Peter was quickly able to decide where future shops should be opened on Tyneside and Teesside. In Teesside we aimed to develop the business via a suitable satellite bakery there, producing bread rolls, scones and cream cakes, which had to be very fresh and locally produced, while savouries for baking in the shops and longer-life products would be delivered from the main bakery in Gosforth. Endless debate took place over the next two decades about exactly where this satellite business would be located, how big it should be, what items it would produce and how it should be managed. In the end, the satellite concept was realized much later – in Edinburgh.

The main expansion plan was to replicate what had already happened on Tyneside over the last ten years in another geographical area. In conjunction with local estate agents in each area, Peter carried out surveys of competitors and suitable trading locations in Glasgow, Leeds and Manchester. Peter McKendrick, of Sanderson

Townend & Gilbert, had done a great job for Greggs in its expansion to date but we thought it was necessary for Greggs to have a local agent in the new conurbations, with a detailed knowledge of suitable trading locations and a good network of contacts. This local presence, with keen local management and regular visits from Peter Feather, offered the best chance of securing quick and effective penetration into a significant number of new retail locations.

In addition to Peter Feather's surveys of competition and trading situations, Neilsen Marketing data revealed that on the consumption of bread and flour confectionery, Scotland, and Glasgow in particular, was well ahead of the north of England, which was in turn ahead of the midlands and south. There did not appear to be any significant competitors in Glasgow, Leeds or Manchester to deter us, but the deciding factor was the extra bread and flour confectionery consumed by Glaswegians. So Glasgow it was: from there, we could supply 80 per cent of the five million people in Scotland. We chose Graham Webster as Greggs' property agent in Scotland, and Webster & Co still act for us today. Maclay Murray & Spens were appointed solicitors (affectionately and unfairly referred to as 'Delay, Worry and Expense'), and the professional team was in place.

Greggs' management needed changing and strengthening to cope with the geographical expansion. To begin with, the Gosforth business needed its own structure. Kevin Rainey became managing director in 1973 and noted at once that 'The weekly meetings seem to take longer these days, now that I'm in the chair.' Alan Johnson was put in charge of the bakery, Jennifer Chalmers of the shops and my sister Gay was head of personnel, all promoted from within, which was Greggs' policy whenever possible. They received little management training but their natural ability and plenty of on-the-job experience more than compensated for that. I withdrew from Gosforth to focus on the expansion into other areas and the development of the business as a whole.

To complete the team we made an outside appointment. The size and complexity of the bakery equipment Greggs needed was increasing rapidly and we required an experienced bakery engineer. We found one in Sid Gledson, who had worked for several large bakery companies in the north. He was older than the rest of the management and liked a drink, a smoke and a party, none of which stood in the way of him making a huge contribution to Greggs.

In 1973 we interviewed someone who was as cocky as Kevin Rainey had been when he had first approached Greggs. John Bailey had qualified as a confectioner, but when he applied to Greggs, he was offered a job as a van driver. He walked out of the factory, but then telephoned me to tell me exactly what he thought of that job offer. I was sufficiently intrigued by his self-confidence to call him back in for a further interview, then offered him a job as a confectioner. Within five years he was the bakery manager.

A head office was now required to steer the good ship Greggs. It was felt that its team should be located separate from the Gosforth bakery and we secured the lease of the first and second floors of 1 Lambton Road, Jesmond, a modest Victorian terrace house close to the bowling green. The team comprised Peter Feather (property director), Brian Wildblood (group production manager) and John Gardener (group sales manager); in 1972 we recruited Malcolm Simpson as financial controller. He had qualified as an accountant with Peat Marwick Mitchell and, after gaining suitable experience, joined Procter & Gamble on Tyneside, where he was rapidly promoted. He saw Greggs as a risk worth taking at that stage in his career, preferable to the possibility of being moved around the country, away from his family, roots and Newcastle United Football Club. Malcolm was, and is, an ardent believer in market forces, but he also believed that accountants should be involved, not just in producing figures but in developing plans and strategies based on them, and playing a part in implementing them. Malcolm became financial director four years later and consistently pushed that belief to the limits of which he was capable.

Ken Middleton, a handsome Scot with a dry sense of humour and such a gloomy demeanour that he became known as 'McDoom', was appointed group personnel manager following a successful career with Kellogg's. As a child he had learned Hindustani when his father was a major in a Sikh brigade in India, but now had to learn another new language: Geordie. Ken was able to bring to the company the expertise and experience needed for an organization of several hundred people, including around forty managers and supervisors. My sister Gay was pleased to be relieved of this role to focus on the Gosforth business, which was where she most enjoyed being, leaving Ken to develop general company policies, management development areas and a strategy for dealing with increasing union militancy, which, if not yet evident in Greggs, seemed to be closing in from all sides. In 1971, there had been a major postal strike. In

1972, the government had declared a state of emergency over the miners' strike and there had also been a national dock strike. In 1973 there had been an enforced three-day working week to conserve electricity supplies.

The expert knowledge and experience that Ken Middleton brought to the business fascinated me. Of course there were the mechanics of salary scales, wage structures, contracts of employment and all the systems and procedures without which a sizeable organization could not function effectively, but much more interesting to me was the question of how best to motivate people and provide maximum job satisfaction, from a thorough induction programme to regular feedback on achievement and ways of removing dissatisfaction before it festered.

Some companies seemed to be run as if there was a continual war of attrition between management on one side of the barricade and the employees on the other, with daily activities carried out in an atmosphere of mutual suspicion, distrust and often open hostility. This seemed to me to be no way to run any company, and was contrary to the Greggs approach, which aimed to make everyone feel that we were all part of the same team, pulling in the same direction. Ken Middleton now gave that drive added focus by introducing me to Herzberg and Maslow's 'hierarchy of needs'. Herzberg had concluded in 1959 that factors such as company policy, supervision, working conditions and salary were 'hygienic' factors rather than motivators. Absence of such created dissatisfaction but their presence did not motivate or create satisfaction. What did, were achievement, recognition, the work itself, responsibility and advancement.

In theoretical terms this was new to me but the thrust of it reinforced and complemented what had been taking place in Greggs over the past decade. It had always seemed common sense and in line with decent values to treat everyone as equals, to inform them about and involve them in decisions, to share profits, to push decision-making down the structure and to give people more responsibility whenever possible. It was in stark contrast to what was generally happening in industry. Here the focus increasingly seemed to be on confrontation between management and unions, investment in automation, mergers and acquisitions, redundancies and generally reducing the importance of people as individuals.

Learning about Herzberg was important to me. It was evidence that the principles on which Greggs had been developed were sound, and it brought into focus the need to ensure that these principles were built into the future fabric of Greggs so that they could not be eroded by growth or changes in the business. It became one of our key priorities to ensure that people were valued, achieved satisfaction from their jobs and were proud to be part of Greggs.

Ken brought in many new schemes to achieve this: briefing groups, expanding profit-sharing into share ownership, and formalizing and giving structure to some of the processes that already took place. Take the management rota he introduced: in accordance with this, each manager had to spend a day of every month 'on the job' – selling in the shop, baking, driving a van, and so on, a day in each department of the bakery and the offices. This kept managers in touch with other employees, their working conditions and the processes that were used, and showed them just how demanding and repetitive many production-line jobs were. Managers were always more sympathetic to complaints about the stress and/or tedium of certain jobs after they'd experienced the work for themselves.

Ken also introduced Anniversary Awards to recognize employees' service at five-year intervals. Five years is a long time to give to a company, and those evenings gave employees with five, ten, fifteen, twenty and twenty-five years' service the chance to get together, reminisce and enjoy a sociable evening. As the business increased in size and it became more difficult to maintain close personal relationships with staff, those get-togethers helped people to recapture some of the excitement and the ethos of earlier days.

Under the new personnel regime, the informal chats I had with managers became biennial written appraisal reviews, now known as 'personal development plans'. In 1977, ahead of its time, we tested three-hundred-and-sixty-degree appraisals, in which the performance of bosses was reviewed by the managers reporting to them. I can remember my first such review, conducted by Ken after long and detailed consultation with the head-office team. It was very short: 'Reaction to good news – bad. Reaction to bad news – good.' Initially I was puzzled and upset, interpreting this as criticism that my reactions were predictable and unresponsive, which was probably correct, but later I rationalized it into a more favourable assessment: when things are going well, people need checking to stop them becoming over-confident, and when things are going badly they need encouraging rather than criticizing. Above all, a good appraisal system encourages you to appraise yourself, both personally and as a manager. It makes you think hard about yourself. Mine told me that I avoided confrontation, which is sometimes, though not always, the best way forward. I put off passing on bad news. I could be impetuous in making decisions and I contained my emotions and reactions so that people didn't know whether I was pleased or not. The main outcome was that I needed to be aware of these factors and try to do something about them.

Managers at Greggs had never had reserved car-parking spaces, their own canteen or other privileges. All this was now covered by a written single-status policy statement. So, what was then modern personnel theory and practice slotted seamlessly together, with one unfortunate exception. As a young boy helping in the bakery, I had always been called by my Christian name. This continued until I came into the business, when my mother decided that I should be shown the respect she believed my education and position warranted: she wanted me to be known as 'Mr Gregg'. She was universally referred to as 'Mrs Gregg'; 'Elsie' would have been unthinkable. I was only interested in everyone getting on with their job. Mum was determined, but just as she was beginning to achieve a reasonable number of converts, along came the single-status policy, which decreed that everyone should be known by their Christian name. I became Ian again, at least to most people. This was also ahead of its time and I think was seen as a positive reflection of equality and informality. Certainly I preferred it.

With a head office now in place, we needed a management team to develop the Glasgow business. Gordon Thompson, a young and successful general manager for

nine years with Rank Hovis McDougall, was appointed
managing director in Glasgow and supervised the
recruitment of a number of other managers. This represented a huge amount of change and additional resource
in a very short period of time – I feel tired just thinking
about it now! But we had a head office, a management
team to continue the original business in the north-east
of England and a team to develop the Glasgow business,
all of which was in line with Peat Marwick Mitchell's
consultancy report.

During the 1970s, Greggs took on more senior
managers, who were appointed to the main board as
soon as they had earned their spurs; in due course,
Malcolm Simpson, Ken Middleton, Gordon Thompson
and Brian Wildblood all became directors. The prospect
of a position on the main board undoubtedly helped us
to recruit some excellent candidates. During this
exciting and formative period in Greggs' development,
the main board was the forum for all major strategic
and operational decisions. I was both chairman and
chief executive but reported to the board, which met at
least quarterly and more frequently when required. It
worked effectively, providing excitement and interest to
all involved and a structure within which I felt account-
able but not stifled by rules and procedures.

Joining Greggs was initially something of a culture
shock for the young managers who had left larger companies, such as Kellogg's, Procter & Gamble and
Allied Bakeries. They had come to Greggs for more
responsibility and greater challenge, and they got both
in measures that exceeded their expectations. They
were not so pleased, however, with the lack of 'perks'
they had thought would go with their senior positions.

Ken Middleton and his wife, Sandra, a strong-minded feminist, never forgave me for the poky little flat in which they were confined while they waited for their new house to be ready. After their first night there, I collected Ken at six the next morning for two days in Glasgow. He was glad to leave the flat, and Sandra's wrath, to resume an executive lifestyle. He had been promised a coffee break en route and clearly envisaged something considerably grander than my shared cup and flask in a lay-by on the A74.

Following a long day in Glasgow, we returned to the Central Hotel, owned by British Rail, in the centre of the city. Here, Malcolm had negotiated a rate of ten pounds per night for spacious, if dated rooms, with a large shared bathroom up the corridor (en suite would have been an extra five pounds per night). I really liked the huge baths, big enough to swim in, and the enormous rubber balls on chains that served as plugs and, of course, I liked the price. Peter Nichols, one of the first apprentices at the new Gosforth bakery, who eventually accumulated forty-five years' service, came to Glasgow with me on several occasions and also stayed at the Central Hotel. As he says, 'We never needed an alarm clock, because the trains were in and out all night, so we never got to sleep!' It was difficult for our new managers to complain too much at first, but in time, they persuaded me to introduce arrangements that were a little more appropriate to their managerial status, even extending to en-suite facilities.

Our intention was to proceed in Glasgow on a green-field basis: we would start by building a new bakery and opening shops as quickly as possible. We had acquired an excellent site on Southcroft Road, Rutherglen, on the south-west outskirts of the city, close to the motorway system, which would make it easy to service the whole central belt. The grand plan was to invest £700,000 over five years, creating 400 jobs. We signed a contract for £165,000 with Taylor Woodrow and ordered appropriate plant and machinery. We applied for a loan of £140,000 from the Department of Trade and Industry, which was turned down, but then secured the required finance by a variety of loans and lease arrangements, including £50,000 from our millers, Hudson Ward, and a similar loan from our bank, National Westminster. All was proceeding more or less to plan, with frequent sorties from Newcastle up the M74 to look for suitable shop sites.

On one such trip, Peter Feather, Brian Wildblood and I were looking at possible sites in Bellshill, a strong working-class area a few miles east of Glasgow. We had left Newcastle early and by midday were ravenous. Lunch on these occasions was always a selection of products from a convenient baker's shop. That day, the most convenient was Price Bros, a business that traded from about forty locations in and around Glasgow. We had looked at it as a possible acquisition but quickly decided it was unsuitable: the shops were run down, the products moderate and the bakery at Shettleston dilapidated and badly located.

But we were hungry! You have to try competitors, and here was an opportunity to learn more about Scottish bakery products, many of which were very different from those eaten in the north of England. Strawberry tarts were made upside-down with the strawberry on top, butter cream instead of fresh cream, and much sweeter jelly, but the savouries varied most.

■ BRIDIES ■

2 tbsp olive oil
1 onion, finely chopped
1 tsp dried thyme
12oz/350g lean steak mince
   (10% fat)
1 tsp mustard powder

3fl oz/80ml strong beef stock
   (1 whole stock cube)
½ tsp salt
freshly ground black pepper
1lb 2oz/500g ready-made puff pastry
1 egg, beaten

1   Preheat the oven to 200°C/400°F/Gas 6.

2   Heat the olive oil in a frying pan and fry the onion and thyme gently for 2–3 minutes, until soft and translucent.

3   In a bowl combine the mince with the mustard powder and beef stock. Add the fried onion mixture and season with salt and pepper. Mix well.

4   Roll out the puff pastry on a clean, floured surface to ¼in/5mm thick and cut out four 6in/15cm diameter circles.

5   Place a spoonful of the mixture into the centre of each pastry circle. Brush the outer rim of the pastry circles with beaten egg. Fold the pastry in half over the filling, to create a semi-circular pasty shape and crimp the edges together well to seal.

6   Brush the pastry with beaten egg and make a small hole in the top with a sharp knife.

7   Transfer the bridies to a preheated baking tray lined with baking parchment and bake in the preheated oven for 40 minutes until golden.

8   Eat warm.

Instead of pasties they sold 'bridies', which had been invented by a Forfar baker around 1850 and named either after a Maggie Bridie, who had sold them in Forfar market, or on account of their frequent presence on wedding menus. They are generally made with puff pastry, no potato, and contain more spicy seasoning than pasties. The most popular pie was not mince or steak but the Scotch pie, traditionally made with mutton (but now other meats are used) and well seasoned with pepper. The shell was made from thin, hot-water pastry, which was dried or cured for at least two days before it was filled with meat and lidded. The curing process meant it could be baked without a tin or foil, in the same way as traditional hand-raised pork pies, giving the pastry a special crispness.

We bought our pies, bridies and sandwiches, and ate them as usual in the car, but what really surprised us was the excellent service we received from the shop staff. Price Bros' business might be going down the pan, but Margaret McCaig, the shop manager, and her team were proudly keeping their part of it in shape. We came out of the shop with more products than we had planned to buy, puzzled that such apparently good staff should continue to work in these unsatisfactory conditions. We visited several other Price Bros shops that afternoon and continued to be surprised by the quality and attitude of the staff. Serendipity had set a trap to upset our carefully laid plans for a green-field start-up.

Of the forty shops that Price's traded from, more than half were in desirable trading locations. It would take us several years to build up a portfolio of shops like that, but if we could take the staff, shops and bakery from Price Bros for nothing and save them the redundancy and winding up costs, we could advance Greggs' rate of expansion by several years. Because there would be substantial production volume to move into the new bakery, we might also escape some of the losses we had estimated (probably severely under-estimated) in the early years.

So, that was how Greggs started in Glasgow, thanks to 'wee Margaret' from Bellshill. At that stage, though, we had not learned that you can't buy a bad business cheaply enough. This should have been Lesson Number Five for us, but it took a few more occasions before we had learned it properly. We did not foresee some of the problems that lay ahead. Would the originally planned green-field start-up have avoided them – or made them worse? In the end Greggs has never carried out a green-field start-up – except in Belgium some thirty years later; we wound it up after six years as it hadn't expanded sufficiently to be viable.

Lesson 5: You can't buy a bad business cheaply enough.

We were young, energetic and confident that the success on Tyneside could quickly be replicated on Clydeside. We would transform production quality by transferring from the ramshackle remains of the bakery at Shettleston to the modern, up-to-date bakery and equipment at Rutherglen. By weeding out the hopeless trading positions, applying a coat of paint and refitting or tidying up the remaining sites, with a steady stream of new shop openings, we also aimed to transform sales volume. David Spark, of Ainsworth Spark, had won the contract for developing a new design and image for the shops – he had beaten off strong opposition that included

Terence Conran's London-based design company. It included the complete redesign of shop fascias, interiors and corporate image, and its value was £2,500. My mother balked at such profligate and unnecessary expenditure and voted against the award of the contract, the only example I can find or recall of a split board decision. She was in a minority of one and outvoted, which she took in good spirits.

We were bursting with ideas and confidence, not just about better products and increased sales. We were certain that the substantial investment, new management and commitment to a future on Clydeside would release new levels of energy throughout the business, and we had a secret product with which to wow Glasgow. The product range was to be based on local tradition, with bridies not pasties, mutton not mince pies, sausage rolls with a beef-based filling rather than pork, and Eiffel Towers – fairy buns dipped in raspberry jam, turned upside down and covered with coconut. There was one exception: we felt the stotty cake had a taste and a texture that were perfectly suited to Glasgow taste buds. To make it even more attractive, and to appeal to Scottish nationalism, we renamed it the 'scottie', but attempting to transfer bakery products from one region to another is notoriously difficult. The scottie failed, in spite of our best marketing efforts, which wounded our corporate pride. The pain, though, was slight in comparison with what happened twenty years later when McDonald's succeeded in selling lorry loads of Big Macs to Parisians!

Before any of that came to pass, however, we had a massive setback in Newcastle. My mother had now officially retired, but although she enjoyed the rest and free time, she missed her involvement in the business. In 1971 she had spent a week behind the counter of our new shop in Gosforth, 'just for old times' sake', proud of the progress the business was making and happy to be there. In December 1972, though, she was ill, appeared to recover, then collapsed. I was called back from a weekend away but by the time I got there she had lapsed into unconsciousness. I sat with her all night but she never came round. I was unable to say goodbye or to thank her for being the best mother anyone could have wished for. She died the next morning, 15 December 1972, aged just sixty-two.

Mum was gone, yet she lived on inside each of us. She had been our guide, friend and inspiration, and her light continued in the company. Customers in the shop said how much they missed her, and everyone was aware of the part she had played because at every stage she had been active and involved. As if reflecting this, the business has continued to be more about the female than the male. Men have dominated senior management but most shop staff are women, most customers are women and in the bakeries, apart from in bread-making, driving and delivering to shops, women predominate.

Although most things continued unchanged after my mother's death, they seemed different. Something was missing and nothing could fill the void. It was a time to keep busy but it was difficult to stop reflections, both happy and melancholy, flooding in. Mum and Dad had died so young, which was sad enough, but their life together had not been happy, which made it worse.

As a family we had not discussed things openly. There were many questions I wished I had asked but now could not. Was there anything we could have done to make life happier for them? Were there things Dad might have wanted to do? What had they thought were the causes of their differences and disagreements? Would they have been happier apart? We were left to draw our own conclusions. As the eldest I felt some responsibility: I had always tried to prevent confrontation arising and compensated by helping rather than speaking my mind and risking additional stress. Now they were gone and would not witness what became of the business they had started.

Whatever our feelings about our loss, the show had to go on and, while awaiting the development of the new bakery at Rutherglen, our first priority was to progress the Glasgow business by making the best job we could of the old one in Shettleston, where the buildings were falling apart. When it rained, water streamed in through the roof. When it was hot, the temperature and humidity rose to intolerable levels. During the summer months, it was often so hot and humid in the bakery that the night shift worked topless, which was neither hygienic nor an appealing sight. The equipment was ancient and unreliable, having had little in the way of maintenance for many years, but worst of all was the hygiene. There were layers of dirt everywhere, providing a paradise for pests and rodents. It could have been a nineteenth-century sweatshop from a Dickens novel that had somehow escaped the notice of the local authority's public health inspector. Perhaps they had issued warnings but hesitated to close a business that was providing employment in an area that had little going for it at that time. Like much of Glasgow and the surrounding areas, it was transformed in the following twenty-five years. We took photographs of the conditions we inherited to defend Greggs against any renewed interest from, or prosecution by, the local authority, but its representatives were supportive, understanding and appreciative of the improvements we were making.

Such improvements were hard-earned. I always liked to be involved directly in any new venture, whether a shop, a bakery extension and in particular our first new bakery, although 'new' in this case was a misnomer. I put in some early-morning stints there on a few night shifts with Brian Wildblood and some volunteers – at least I think they were volunteers – from the Gosforth bakery to check that the quality was right and that everything was running as it should. In addition to checking production quality, we also needed to spring-clean the bakery from top to bottom. Over several weekends, Colin, Gay and I led expeditions of cleaning parties across the border to remove the grime from the premises and equipment. While Gordon was finalizing his management team, we put plans in place for shop refits, new shop openings and advertising, all of which had to be held back until the business had transferred into the new bakery and production had settled in there. This took a further six months, and passed without any major mishaps.

The time came to reveal the metamorphosis, like a butterfly shedding its chrysalis, of the crumbling old remains of the Price business into a young, vigorous reproduction of the Gosforth phenomenon, resplendent in its corporate livery. All the managers involved expected progress to be quick and dramatic, and the burden of delivering this fell on Gordon. He accepted it willingly and without hesitation. He was an idealist, young, ambitious and somewhat disillusioned by the state of the baking industry in Scotland, who saw the opportunity of developing a successful and exciting business. He had spent some considerable time absorbing and discussing both ethos and practice with the Gosforth management, and could see no reason why what had taken place on Tyneside over the previous ten years should not be replicated on Clydeside. The markets were similar, the competition was not strong and, *per capita*, consumption of bread and confectionery was higher. Greggs now had the precedents, the systems and greater resource than ever before, and this convinced everyone that success, though it might require great effort, would come quickly.

In most respects our plans unfolded according to expectations. In December 1972, Mrs Belle Hutchinson, wife of James Hutchinson, provost of Rutherglen, unveiled a plaque to mark the opening of the new bakery. The improvements to the product range, specifications and quality were significant. Product shortages due to equipment breakdown became largely a thing of the past. New Greggs of Rutherglen fascias, refits and new shops began to brighten up local high streets. The management team was settling in and improving processes. Staff were generally keen and enthusiastic as the investment around them began to deliver better working conditions and job security.

However, although sales improved, they did not reach anywhere near the level of the Gosforth shops. This was easier to understand in the old Price conversions, where it might take some time to shake off the image of the past, than in the new shop openings, which

everyone had thought would achieve similar sales levels
to Gosforth. We needed them to achieve those levels
because shop rates were 80 per cent higher in Scotland
than in England. In addition to this, in our inexperience
and naïvety, we had seriously misjudged the difficulties
of developing a run-down business into a successful
enterprise. We had underestimated the number of day-
to-day decisions, which can be crushing in their detailed
complexity but do not arise in an established business
where good governance and management have built
solutions into the fabric.

Gordon was a proud man and all too sensitive to the
differential between Gosforth and Glasgow sales levels.
His chief strengths as a manager were planning and
long-term strategy rather than dealing with the daily
minutiae that bombarded him. The head-office team
helped as much as they could but the buck stops in just
one place, and in any case, their attentions were about
to be diverted elsewhere.

6

LEEDS
Bread cake

The Leeds business introduced Greggs to more unfamiliar products. Bread cakes weren't cakes but bread rolls and might be also called barm cakes, tea cakes or baps, depending on where you were. Confusing!

Peter Feather had identified a small and expanding business, Thurston Parfitt, on the outskirts of Leeds, which had twelve shops and was about to build a new bakery at Bramley. The timing was not ideal but the opportunity could not be ignored. It was a family business, founded by Harold Thurston, who had later been joined by his brother in law, Geoff Parfitt. The Thurstons were keen to retire and Greggs bought out their interest, with part of the Parfitts', leaving them with a 25 per cent stake, to be purchased later by Greggs at a value linked to the profitability of the

business. It had good-quality products, a good reputation and was profitable and well-managed, with Geoff
Parfitt, the managing director, Marie, his wife, as sales
director, and Eric Mallinson, the bakery manager, who
remained a strong presence in the business until his
retirement in 1998. They all possessed more than their
share of traditional Yorkshire qualities: pride, tenacity
(or stubbornness) and a wish not to spend more than
was absolutely necessary. Prior to this we had believed
the Scots led the world in the matter of parsimony but
soon discovered they were mere apprentices to
Yorkshiremen – as the old joke goes, Yorkshiremen are
like Scots but without the generosity! Together they
made an effective team, which steadily moved the business forward without a large input from the centre.

In Glasgow we had changed the trading name from
Price to Greggs, but in Leeds we had no wish to change
a name that carried with it goodwill and customer
loyalty. In fact, very little changed with Greggs' arrival.
It was our strategy that each business should be
independent, a separate limited company with its own
management, product range and profit-sharing. Given
the pride and independence of the local team, any other
approach would have created problems.

Local autonomy, however, was a two-edged sword. It
encouraged initiative, ownership, responsibility and
creativity, but it also fostered resistance to good
practices, new ideas, marketing initiatives and anything else that had not been 'invented here'. Our
head-office team learned an early salutary lesson about
the difficulty of achieving change and conformity with
best practice. At this stage the benefits of local
autonomy outweighed the disadvantages, and the

head-office team had to be satisfied with achieving the
odd local concession as the directors reinforced their
independence, eventually earning the (possibly
deserved) title of 'Robber Barons'. They were strong
characters who liked to make their own decisions, and
they resented anyone from head office telling them what
to do, whether it was how much to charge for a
doughnut, to use butter or margarine in their sandwiches, or to carry out personal development reviews
once or twice a year. Later, as Greggs grew, the disadvantages of being unable to capitalize on the benefits
of integration and scale, and the inability to maximize
marketing opportunities, began to shift the balance.

However, when it came to finance and management
accounts, Malcolm Simpson had insisted from day one
that everything, without exception, should take place
according to Greggs' systems and format. No local
version was ever suggested, not even in Leeds where
Geoff Parfitt was an accountant by training, a reflection
of Malcolm's authority and presence (which he modestly
and consistently underestimated).

In the Thurston' shops, a customer would not have
been aware of any change in ownership. In October
1974 there was little mention of Greggs when the mayor
of Leeds, Councillor Joan De Carteret, opened the new
£250,000 bakery at Bramley. Thurston's was the local
baker: although shops were fitted and refitted in a style
that reflected some of the Greggs' livery and we introduced the baking of savouries and pasties (and later
frozen dough and rolls) in the shops, the presence of the
crinoline lady, a traditional feature of Thurston's livery,
was a ubiquitous reminder of where the power still lay.

As at Gosforth, there were several families who

could boast generations of relatives in the Thurston business. A notable example was Mick Duffy, who had started as an apprentice in December 1969 and retired as bread production manager after a total of forty years and seven months. This might have been longer had he not been dismissed by Harold Thurston – a stickler over quality and standards – for having long hair like his heroes in the Human League. He was later welcomed back after a suitable hair-cut. Mick's mother, Lil, worked from time to time in the canteen, and his younger brother, Eddie, was a driver for ten years. Eddie's wife Sue also worked in the bakery for fifteen years, as did his other younger brother, Danny, and his sister Elizabeth Jowett. Mick met both his wives in the bakery, Elaine who worked at Thurston's, then Caroline. Oh, yes, and his daughter was a Saturday girl.

As well as having its own individual characters and families, the Leeds business also had its own products. More pork pies were eaten in Yorkshire than on Tyneside and in Scotland, although the number was lower than it was further south, in the midlands, where pork pies predominated. Yorkshire curd tarts were new to us – a shortcrust pastry shell filled with the fresh curds left from cheese-making, currants, sugar, eggs and a touch of nutmeg. Bread cakes were, of course, not cakes but bread rolls, and the variety of bread rolls was confusing. In Tyneside and Scotland, tea cakes were sweetened and made with currants. In Yorkshire these were known as currant tea cakes to distinguish them from plain tea cakes, white and brown. And in some areas tea cakes were called barm cakes or baps, which might be turned in the oven like stotty cakes to become oven bottom cakes.

■ BREAD CAKES (or white rolls) ■

1lb 2oz/500g strong white bread flour,
   plus extra for dusting
1 tsp salt
1oz/30g butter, cut into pieces

2½fl oz/75ml lukewarm milk
8fl oz/225ml lukewarm water
2 tsp dried yeast

1   Mix the flour and salt in a bowl, and rub the butter into the flour until the mixture resembles breadcrumbs.

2   Combine the lukewarm milk, water and yeast, and stir until the yeast has dissolved.

3   Add the milk/yeast mixture to the flour mixture and mix together well with your hands. Form the dough into a ball.

4   Using floured hands, knead the dough on a clean, floured work surface for 10 minutes, until the dough is smooth.

5   Return the dough to the bowl, dust with flour and cover with a clean teatowel. Set aside for 1–1½ hours in a warm place until the dough has doubled in size.

6   Return the risen dough to a floured work surface and knock the air from it. Rest the dough for 10 minutes.

7   Divide the mixture into ten parts and roll each into a ball. Flatten each slightly with the palm of your hand and transfer to a lightly floured baking tray, placing them close together. Cover the tray with a teatowel and set aside for another hour, or until the rolls have doubled in size again.

8   Meanwhile, preheat the oven to 220°C/425°F/Gas 7.

9   Dust the rolls with flour and bake in the preheated oven for 8–10 minutes, or until golden brown and cooked through.

Back at the centre we made further moves to strengthen the central management team. Graham Randell left Storeys of Lancaster to become head-office marketing manager. A tall, genial character with a strong sense of social responsibility, Graham had also worked at Kellogg's where he had met Ken Middleton, who, with assistance from Malcolm, persuaded me that Greggs needed a marketing manager. I didn't know what a marketing manager did (I'm still not certain) which greatly surprised the Institute of Marketing when I made this confession to them in 1984, having been invited to speak at their annual conference in Newcastle!

As I didn't understand what marketing was, it was obviously difficult for me to direct Graham effectively, but even if I had been able to do so, the Robber Barons would have ignored him. After two years of valiant endeavour, he left to pursue a successful career with Surridge Dawson, retail newsagents. He rejoined Greggs much later in his career, eventually becoming managing director of the original business at Gosforth.

There were now several senior managers in Greggs who had worked in large businesses like Procter & Gamble, Kellogg's, Allied Bakeries and Rank Hovis McDougall. They had experience of turning ideas into businesses, developing brands and creating management structures that would accommodate growth. From time to time we talked about these and other issues facing Greggs, but there were always so many day-to-day pressures that we were never able to do justice to them. The only solution was to lock ourselves away from everything for as long as we felt the business and our families would allow: a Saturday and Sunday at the Hydro Hotel, Peebles, in the Scottish Borders.

In a beautiful setting on a thickly wooded hillside overlooking the upper Tweed, the original Hydro had been a huge Victorian-Gothic spa hotel. The turreted and pinnacled original had been destroyed in a fire in the early twentieth century and had been rebuilt with balconies and steeply pitched pantile roofs, giving it the look of an elegant French château. However, we had little time to appreciate the opulence of the hotel or the beauty of our surroundings for we spent most of our time closeted in a conference room, in the most exciting and intense period of creative planning I have ever experienced. After two days in this feverish, fertile hothouse, we returned home exhausted but exultant that we had created a new vision for Greggs.

This vision was for a fresh food store, not dissimilar to Tesco Express or Sainsbury's Local, but with in-store baking and catering, and with less emphasis on commodities and self-service. The preferred size would be 3,000–5,000 square feet, about five times the size of our existing shops. Pride of place would go to our traditional baked goods and savouries. This would be augmented by several other activities, chosen according to the size of the premises and the local market but to include:

- in-store bread baking, which was appearing in more and more supermarkets and also in specialist shops, like Don Miller and other chains. Our limited experience around Newcastle with the stotty cake had been encouraging and this seemed a natural development.
- delicatessens offering a range of cooked meats,

salads and general delicatessen, which seemed a natural partner to our existing business. Birds of Derby, the bakery business I admired above all others, already did it to great effect. Sayers of Liverpool also seemed to succeed with this extended range, and so did Braggs in the midlands.

- sandwich bars, which were already an important part of most bakers' shops but Greggs had been slow to develop.
- catering: teas, coffees, cakes, sandwiches and light lunches, which again were well established in many bakery shops and seemed a logical extension.
- ice cream, which would help to make up sales in hot weather when pie and savoury sales slumped.

This all made good strategic sense. It would considerably broaden our 'offer' – what we made available to the public – and help us to compete with supermarkets. It would allow us to take on shops of sizes and in locations we could not consider from our traditional narrow base and enable us to employ higher-calibre local management. We wrote up the proposals, drew sketch layouts, established product ranges, estimated capital costs (frightening), made profit forecasts (probably optimistic) and bound it all together in a glossy Peebles Plan folder.

Apart from proving where we had been that weekend and what we had been doing, the Peebles Plan was ultimately to achieve very little. Other than a couple of limited attempts at catering and delicatessen, none of our grand plans came to pass. Years later, in 1985, we acquired a midlands business that sold delicatessen products, and in 1994 we bought a retail chain of bakery shops with catering, but by then no one could even find a copy of the Peebles Plan!

While it did not have the strategic impact for the company that we had intended, the weekend served a personal purpose, for which I remain grateful. I loved the beauty of that setting on the upper Tweed valley, and later found a holiday home in the area. Tweed Cottage, Dryburgh, was Edwardian, and had once been the gardener's cottage to the Dryburgh Abbey Hotel. I also acquired a share in the fishing rights to the stretch of the river that bordered its two-acre garden. It was intended for family holidays but I used it mainly for fishing trips with friends. When I could get some time off, there was nothing I enjoyed more than fishing for salmon on the Tweed.

Arthur Temple, the butcher who supplied Greggs' Gosforth bakery with meat for many years, also had a share in the fishing rights and became one of my fishing buddies. We drove up to the Tweed together regularly. He was a mischievous but engaging character and was never happier than when he was catching salmon. His fishing stories were legendary. He made me laugh and helped me to relax. In fact, getting away for a day's salmon fishing was a wonderful antidote to business pressures and preserved my sanity. Arthur was a loyal and generous friend. Years later, when he was terminally ill with cancer, we went up to Tweed Cottage together one last time. By then he was not fit enough to go on the river, but he could sit on the terrace and watch it. He died a few weeks later.

Our failure to implement the Peebles Plan at the time might have been due, in part at least, to a lack of courage, but a more charitable, and probably more accurate, explanation lay in Greggs' determination to focus on one area and do it well. We were learning Lesson Number Six – 'Stick to your knitting' (or what we knew and were doing already) and keep things simple. We were fully stretched with our bakery shops, and later found that shops with delicatessen sections were more profitable when we phased out the delicatessens and gave our undivided attention to our original business.

Lesson 6: Keep things simple and stick to your knitting.

We were just completing a £200,000 investment plan at the Gosforth bakery to automate roll production with a Winkler plant, to modernize meat and savoury cooking with a massive pressure cooker (which, no doubt to the irritation of our neighbours, doubled the whiff of cheese and onion in the locality), and to increase bread production from 300,000 to 500,000 loaves per week. At this moment, with an immaculate sense of timing, the Bakers and Allied Workers Union went on strike. Their strike, in September 1977, was in response to a dispute between the union and the federation of Bakers, which represented plant bakeries. Greggs had not been involved – until we doubled bread production, which brought in the pickets. We negotiated a way forward whereby Greggs would not exceed normal production but would be allowed to produce, through volunteer labour, an extra 20,000 small loaves per day to be sold to pensioners at cost (3p) for an hour between four thirty and five thirty p.m. every day in each of Greggs' shops in the north-east. At this time, bread was an important part of the diet in the north of England – much more so than it is generally in the UK today, when bread consumption has roughly halved. Older people suffered in particular, frequently missing out in the scramble to secure a loaf, which took place early each morning. Some people hoarded more than they needed so that many regular Greggs customers were unable to secure their daily bread. The public were angry, and the newspapers, radio and television full of stories of frustration, inconvenience and even suffering. The 20,000 small loaves helped a little and it was difficult for the union to refuse this extra production.

By 1974 Greggs had moved, in the space of two years, to a business with three operating divisions and a management structure to fit. At the end of the year the Gosforth business had forty-three shops, continued to make good progress and was the main profit generator. Glasgow had thirty shops, all now in the Greggs livery, and was making progress, albeit still at a much slower than expected rate, and was still not achieving profitability. Leeds had twenty shops and was making reasonable profits in line with expectations.

Most weeks I drove up and down the A74 to Glasgow once and sometimes twice. Until then, I had run an Austin family saloon, which had been fine for getting round Newcastle, but was far from ideal for motorway driving. I had witnessed some horrendous accidents and, worse, had returned home late at night on occasion and been unable to remember parts of the journey, having almost fallen asleep at the wheel. If I was going to continue covering hundreds of miles a week, as well as running the company, I owed it to my family and to Greggs to find a safer car and recruit a driver. In that way, I would ensure that I arrived at my destination alive and in a suitable frame of mind to make coherent decisions and deal with any problems that might have arisen. The car with the best safety reputation was the Rolls-Royce and, without researching it – there were too many other, more important issues – I ordered one. There was a waiting list of at least two years and, as a result, nearly new models sold for a substantial premium over the price of a new car. I told myself that if I decided I didn't want it when it arrived, it could be sold at a profit.

I cannot imagine what folly drove me to this decision, because it was totally out of character. A few days later, I decided I would sell the Rolls-Royce when it came, and in the interim bought a Mercedes, which more than adequately met the requirements I had of a car at a fraction of the price. I also employed a driver, Les Reay, whose sister, Betty, had been one of my mother's regular helpers at catering events. While Les drove me to my destinations, I could prepare for meetings, dictate notes or even sleep if I was tired. Les was cheerful, reliable, enthusiastic and always great company. He not only reduced my workload but also became a good friend and fishing companion. He enjoyed a drink as well, and on one or two occasions while we were away in Scotland, we reversed roles. I took the wheel and drove us back to our hotel, while Les, slightly the worse for wear, snored peacefully on the back seat. He remained with Greggs until his retirement in 1989, proving himself an invaluable help both to me and to my successor.

My cunning plan to sell the Rolls-Royce had taken

no account of changing economic conditions. In the two years between order and delivery, the UK economy went into a severe downturn, which reached its nadir at the moment I took delivery of the car. From being an appreciating asset, it was now a total liability – you could hardly give away a nearly new Rolls-Royce – and I started to panic. Not wishing to provide the unions with a trump card in the annual wage negotiations, I decided that the only solution was to hide it somewhere until the economy turned the corner, when it could be disposed of without too much embarrassment, financial or otherwise. The huge silvery-green machine just fitted into the garage of our Gosforth house, where it lurked for several long months, like some monstrous dragon that might burst out from its prison for all to see, until a kind man from Harrogate relieved me from this daily terror. I had been the owner of a Rolls-Royce for six months but had never even sat in the driving seat, let alone taken it out on the road.

As Greggs grew and became more profitable during the seventies, I began to want to invest some small part of this profit for the benefit of the north-east. My child-hood had been spent with jam jar and fishing net in pursuit of anything that moved in the streams and ponds around Newcastle, which led me to consider wildlife and environmental projects.

At weekends I often spent time with my daughters at Pets Corner in Jesmond Dene on the north-east side of Newcastle. There, a scruffy collection of bedraggled ducks, rabbits, hamsters and miscellaneous un-fortunates of the animal kingdom all lived in dusty (or muddy, if it had been raining) squalor, without foliage or

natural protection. My daughters loved it, as did everyone who visited it, but I wondered why Newcastle City
Council did nothing to make it better, and daydreamed
about the improvements that could so easily have been
made. In my mind I planned how they could be implemented and what extra enjoyment and education
visiting children might derive from the experience. Also,
it would be more in keeping with the Jesmond Dene
that Lord and Lady Armstrong had left to the people of
Newcastle in the 1850s, with its seventy-eight acres of
landscaped terraces and secluded walks.

When the last slice of carrot and breadcrust had
been eaten, Fiona, Felicity and I would stroll through
the Dene along the polluted Ouse Burn. As we ambled
along, I imagined children fishing with nets in the
shallow stretches and with rod and line in the deeper
sections above the dam, where week after week, year
after year, I strained my eyes in vain for a glimpse of
any fish that might have survived in the murky water.
At Gosforth Park, near the racecourse three miles north
of Newcastle, there were similar walks past overgrown
and neglected ponds, which, with some funding and
volunteer effort, could easily have been restored and
opened up for people to enjoy.

However, such plans remained no more than day-
dreams: I was too busy at Greggs to take on any other
commitments and there were no ready-made, off-the-
peg models available then. Wildlife trusts and other
voluntary organizations were not knocking at the door
with the worked-up proposals and projects they offer
today.

In the north-east there was no Community
Foundation to co-ordinate or support local social and

environmental projects. All I and Greggs were able to do was react to the increasing number of miscellaneous requests for funding that came in the post. This was frustrating, since none of them really matched my aspirations. Also, we had no way of properly assessing the requests and no procedures in place to ensure that any money we donated was used for the stated purpose. In line with our values, we continued to support local community and charity projects, and in my quieter moments, I continued to dream of a day when we could put such support on a proper professional footing, and greatly increase our funding and involvement. That day was still a long way off.

7

MANCHESTER
Parkin

Another new regional product for Greggs, parkin is mainly associated with Yorkshire, but it also sells well in Lancashire, along with treacle toffee at Hallowe'en and on bonfire night

1975 and 1976 were intended as consolidation years, strengthening each of our businesses, updating and improving market intelligence about other possible trading areas. The most obvious choice was Manchester, Lancashire, which would consolidate our presence across the north of England.

Peter Feather had already completed surveys of suitable trading locations and competitors, and established that the local competition was fiercer than in Glasgow and Leeds, with several strong Warburton companies and other independents, in particular Greenhalghs. Sayers were also present on the west side of Manchester and had blanket coverage of Liverpool and the west of Lancashire. It all required careful analysis and planning, but suddenly we were approached to buy the main Price Bros business, based in Manchester. It had more than a hundred run-down shops and a rambling, ancient bakery in Parrot Street, Clayton, on the banks of the Ashton canal. The products were of poor quality and the company was on the verge of having to close down, but the retail staff appeared generally good, and more than half of the shops were in desirable trading locations. With the scars from acquiring the Glasgow business still far from healed, this had a worryingly familiar ring to it. Had we learned Lesson Number Five, that you can't buy a bad business cheaply enough?

Buying Price's main Manchester business was a great opportunity for Greggs because we would more than double our number of shops, many in good locations, at a very low cost, but it was also a huge risk because of the run-down nature of the business and equipment, and the losses it was incurring. We had not yet turned round the position in Glasgow and had only very recently acquired Leeds.

Prior to our board meeting on 15 June 1975, my brother Colin and I had been in favour of proceeding, with Peter Feather and Gay against. Unwilling to use my chairman's casting vote on a decision of such magnitude, I had negotiated an alternative deal with Price Bros: to pay £10,000 for an option to buy after one year at £120,000, less any losses incurred in 1975. This would give us time to assess the business in more detail and also to build up the resources we thought were needed.

We approached Industrial and Finance Corporation (ICFC) and began negotiating with them to purchase a stake in Greggs and provide loan facilities. They then conducted a full appraisal of the risks and opportunities that the Manchester business offered. On the basis of these discussions, they took a 15 per cent stake in Greggs and agreed to provide loan facilities of up to £250,000, later increased to £400,000.

These were two huge decisions for Greggs: to more than double the number of shops in the business and sell part of the company to an outside shareholder. However, the flipside was that an external financial institution, with a record of shrewd, profitable investment, had approved the project and we had the additional security of its funding, with greater knowledge about Price Bros, gleaned during the option period. The more cautious members of the board were won over and a unanimous decision was taken to go ahead.

None of that prepared us for what was to come. We had looked around the bakery but, as young optimists, we had focused on the opportunities and had not fully appreciated the task of bringing the sprawling buildings to an acceptable standard. We were buying the remnants of what had once been a major force in the bakery industry. Before the outbreak of war in 1939, Price Bros had been a household name in the north of England and Scotland. Its reputation for excellent bread had been unsurpassed, but the ravages of war and the upheavals that had taken place in the milling and bakery industry after 1945 had brought the business to its knees.

Here and there I saw vestiges of the excellence the business had once aspired to. It had developed and

■ PARKIN ■

5oz/150g medium oatmeal
7oz/200g self-raising flour
1 tsp baking powder
4 tsp ground ginger
2 tsp nutmeg
1 tsp mixed spice

8oz/220g soft butter
4oz/110g soft dark brown sugar
2oz/55g black treacle
7oz/200g golden syrup
2 large eggs, beaten
2 tbsp milk

1   Preheat the oven to 140°C/275°F/Gas 1, and grease an 8in x 8in/20cm x 20cm cake tin at least 2in/5cm deep.

2   Combine all the dry ingredients in a large bowl.

3   In a large heavy-based saucepan gently melt the butter, sugar, treacle and golden syrup until the sugar has dissolved. Do not allow the mixture to boil.

4   Gradually add this mixture to the dry ingredients, and stir to mix thoroughly.

5   Add the beaten eggs a few tablespoons at a time. Finally, add the milk and again mix well.

6   Pour the mixture into the greased tin and bake in the preheated oven for 1½ hours until firm and set and dark golden-brown.

7   Remove from the oven and leave to cool in the tin. Once cool, store in an airtight container for a minimum of 3 days. It will keep (and improve) for several weeks.

8   Parkin is delicious on its own or spread with butter. It's also great as a pudding with stewed rhubarb and custard or with toffee sauce and fresh cream.

maintained a great reputation for parkin, which was more generally associated with Yorkshire, but Price Bros made huge quantities for sale in the autumn, with treacle toffee, particularly for Hallowe'en and Bonfire Night. Whenever possible after Easter, the bakery made parkin in eighteen-by-nine-inch wooden frames on baking sheets. The slabs were wrapped in greaseproof paper and stored until the autumn, which improved the quality; the sticky oatmeal texture was protected by 'cutting' the slabs in the shops with a fork, not a knife. The customer indicated what size she wanted and a fork was inserted along that line and the piece broken off.

Huge quantities of parkin were stored in every part of the crumbling buildings that surrounded the potholed yard. At the front was the office and administration block where the directors had continued to dine, the maintenance block, which housed a vintage Rolls-Royce and a custom-built Rolls-Royce delivery vehicle. The rambling confectionery bakery and despatch, where the old vans parked each morning, was on the left; the tall and gloomy bread bakery stood on the right, and on the other side, flanked by the canal, was the plastic tray and waste storage area.

In addition to bringing these buildings and the machinery in them up to standard, we were then assailed by another problem, over which we had no control whatsoever: the summer of 1976 was the hottest in the UK since records began. The temperature approached 30°C on most days in June and July and reached as high as 36°C on occasions, and the heatwave, with a serious drought, continued without a break until well into the autumn. Every day began clear and cloudless with the temperature soaring, and ended in a brilliant red sunset, followed by a humid night, and it continued day after day, week after week, month after month. Cream cakes melted, pies and sausage rolls were left uneaten and customers deserted bakery shops in search of ice cream, lettuce leaves and cold drinks. Staff in the bakery and shops (without any air conditioning) were hot and exhausted. Over apparently endless months, we endured a repeating nightmare of counting and dealing with mountains of waste products, trying to lift morale and improve trading performance in near impossible conditions.

I had already developed a dislike for hot spells in the summer, because of their effect on business, but that summer was indescribably difficult. To this day a thermometer reading in excess of 20°C drives me into a condition between depression and melancholy, as I recall the salt tablets, which were the best we could offer to our employees in those impossible temperatures.

Those conditions were a very extreme example of the way in which weather always looms large on the Greggs horizon, Periods of heavy rain can be just as damaging to sales as extremely high temperatures. If it's raining hard, customers stay at home unless it's absolutely necessary to venture out. That's bad news for all retailers but for most the probability is that the customer will return to make their purchase of a shirt, a pair of shoes, a can of baked beans or a mobile phone the next day or the day after that. Pies, cakes and sandwiches that fail to sell are lost for ever. The customer makes do with something else and, worse still, the product is not available for someone else to purchase the next day because the one-day shelf life that applies to most of Greggs' products means that whatever is not sold that day is thrown away, a demoralising 'double whammy' of low sales and high waste. Even when the weather is settled and dry, with moderate temperatures, the retail baker still walks a daily tightrope, trying to balance the risk of running out of products, and disappointing customers, with that of over-producing and facing the mounting cost of waste.

In the midst of all this, we appointed a managing director to the Manchester business. David Rees was from Wales, young and full of enthusiasm with a successful record in the baking industry and an amazing vocabulary of swear words, some of which I had never heard before. Those I did know were often used in unusual ways or placed in the middle of an ordinary word or phrase, like 'sausage-effing-roll' or 'sliced-bloody-bread'. Manchester offered a great opportunity for the practice and development of these Welsh oaths!

Despite our failure to turn around the trading situation in Glasgow, we were confident that we would succeed in Manchester by applying the same formula; it was just a matter of time. The rationale for both acquisitions – good shop locations, decent staff and the ability to develop the business more quickly – was precisely the same. Manchester was a replica of Glasgow but on a much larger scale. We had the run-down shop premises, dilapidated production facilities, and another chapter from a Dickens novel, examples of which we photographed once more for defence against any enthusiastic public-health inspector.

We set a similar programme of improvements in motion. There was a small bakery at Chorley, which we closed. (Chorley and Eccles are part of the greater Manchester sprawl and gave their names to Chorley and Eccles cakes, the former being made with short-crust and the latter with puff pastry.) We also closed some of the more distant shops around Blackpool and in Derbyshire so that we could direct more attention and focus to the main body in the Greater Manchester area.

The ambitious programme of minor and major refits proceeded as quickly as we could manage it. We spent huge effort and resources on improving production efficiency and product quality, by making new appointments and borrowing managers from other parts of the company. We strengthened the management team, too, but there was one aspect of Manchester that was different from anything Greggs had experienced before: the attitude of some employees. The first thing we did was to invite all employees to the Belle Vue Conference Centre where I explained how Greggs would invest in the bakery and shops, providing them with both security and opportunity. This provoked no response other than stony stares of disbelief. On the other hand, the promise and display of new shop overalls raised a cheer.

At our first staff Christmas party and dance, I spent some time preparing a speech that would be both encouraging and amusing. The only reaction was an increase in the level of background noise as most people got on with enjoying the hospitality. I gave up after a few minutes. Before the Greggs takeover of Price Bros, there had never been any dialogue or effective communication between management and the workforce, which evidently had no idea how to react to this strange interloper who was trying to turn their world upside-down.

A proportion of the workforce at the bakery,

particularly the bread bakery, was more militant and 'difficult' than any we had previously encountered. Manchester had a full and formidable union presence. Ken Pritchard, the shop steward in the bread bakery, was from Liverpool and, despite a stammer, could speak very fast and for long periods without drawing breath, which made it difficult for others to get a word in, but he had a great sense of humour and liked a drink. The branch secretary, Alan Rowe, was quieter and a deep thinker, who was always several steps ahead of everyone else. He had a wry wit, which he practised on everyone, and a sharp brain, which he later put to good use in managing the stores. Les Shannon, the shop convener, was a highly skilled cake mixer, a union man of the old school, imposing, statuesque and honourable.

At first, they ran rings round the Greggs' management, who, through lack of relevant experience, had no idea how to manage the situations that arose. To survive the many years of neglect that the Price Bros business had suffered, employees had developed their own systems of shift patterns and tea breaks. They even had their own back-up systems for coping with staff shortages, including a pool of casuals who met at a nearby pub and were called on to make up staff shortages on the night shift.

Endless unproductive meetings were required to make any changes to working practices, particularly in relation to the tea-break system in the bread bakery, which I never properly understood, and to the pool of casuals from the pub, whom we wished to replace with full-time employees. The union team defended the status quo as though their lives depended on it, and Alan produced arguments against each change we proposed. There were no written agreements and procedures, just custom and practice, which gave the union team full opportunity for inventive improvisation. When they had started to wear us down, Ken would come in with long monologues, his strong Scouse accent and stammer increasing in intensity as he became more excited and sensed the end of the meeting approaching without his having given any ground. 'OK,' he'd say, trying not to smile. 'Let's meet again in another month . . .'

Greggs had no experience of implementing change with employees whose attitudes had been hardened over years of not being listened to and having to work in appalling conditions. They simply did not believe what we said at the outset and remained suspicious, although we delivered on our promises as quickly as we could. It would be fair to say that these attitudes were in the minority, but it was a powerful one, and slowed our progress.

The majority of employees were pleased to see investment, change and improvement, and were happy to give Greggs a chance, including many who always gave their best and rose to the challenges and opportunities that we offered. In the past, Bill Duffy, the bakery manager, had seen and even taken part in personnel disputes that had been settled by fights on the wasteground behind the bakery. A proud man in his middle forties, Bill had come up from the shop floor in this tough environment and his features could sometimes betray how hard life had been, but he had an infectious smile and an incredible sense of humour. He welcomed our more consensual approach as much as the new equipment we provided, and became part of the Greggs' team, eventually transferring to the Leeds bakery with his wife, Carole, a brilliant cake decorator.

Dick Ward, the despatch manager, was built like a prop forward, with the face of a boxer. He was like granite on the outside, but soft in the middle. With help from his wife Ann, Dick strove to meet the daily challenges thrown up by an antiquated fleet of vehicles, often 'breathing hard into the ears' of his drivers. Don Brooks stood firm in despatch, a gentle giant, moving racks and products to meet the needs of the shops, whatever difficulties presented themselves. He was a fellow fisherman and we would exchange fishing stories as he pushed the racks forward. He later caught his first salmon with me on the Tweed.

Manchester also had more than its fair share of families in the business. Eric Gill was a senior operative in the cake department and had met Pauline, his future wife, at Price Bros. Four of their six children worked for Greggs at some stage in their lives and two still do: his youngest son Lee works as a bakery operative and is the DJ for charity events, while Mark started with us twenty-two years ago as an apprentice mechanic and is now the retail manpower planning manager.

And the Vasconcellos family can claim equal representation. Kay Vasconcellos worked in the Manchester bakery in despatch and her sons, Aldo, Alan and Tony, with their sister Julie, followed her. Today, Aldo is a bakery operative with thirty-four years' service and Tony is hygiene supervisor with thirty-three years' service. Their other sister, Trish Coyle, is manager of the Oxford Road shop.

Extensive family links existed in the business when Greggs took over. The families lived close by, mainly in areas like Clayton and Droylsden. Times were hard and working conditions far from ideal, but strong bonds and a sense of camaraderie united people. They lived close to each other, worked together, supported each other through whatever life or the bakery threw at them, drank and partied together. Their only real point of divergence was whether they supported City or United. Memories and traditions went back to when the canteen had been a stable, horse races had taken place round the yard, and hearses had stopped in the yard on their way to bury a former worker so that everyone could pay their respects. Some horses had done daily bread rounds for so long that they could complete them without human supervision, stopping as they reached each calling point.

It was difficult for an outsider to understand the strength and depth of this culture. We arrived expecting our investment and proposed changes to meet immediate and universal approval. This was a mistake, because many did not want change and grew tired of hearing how good the Gosforth business was and how they should strive to match it. Despite the shop-refit programme, investment in the bakery and equipment, the improvement in product quality, the Manchester business continued to trade at a loss. By the start of 1977, the shortfall had grown to an eye-watering £11,000 per week, a sum that exceeded the profit made by the rest of the business. Glasgow was still making a small loss and Leeds a small profit. All the profit generated by the continuing strong performance at Gosforth was going straight down the drain in Manchester.

We were running out of options. There was no money for further investment. The loan facility from ICFC had been used up and further borrowing would have been difficult against this background, but the longer we delayed the decision about whether to cut our losses and close down the Manchester business, effectively ending our longer-term aspirations, the more we were putting the rest of the business at risk.

In 1977 the British economy was going through a difficult period. Millions of working days were lost due to strikes, inflation was rampant at almost 16 per cent and unemployment rising. Britain was disparaged as the 'Sick Man of Europe'. To try to minimize unemployment, the Labour government had introduced a scheme known as Temporary Employment Subsidy (TES), by which a business that was considering redundancies could receive a grant for each worker it continued to employ until it had weathered the difficult times.

Malcolm Simpson, who had been appointed a director in 1975, with Gordon Thompson and Ken Middleton, put together an application for TES in respect of the workforce in Manchester. Although the situation there seemed to make it an ideal candidate, we were by no means confident, and it was an enormous relief when we were awarded a grant of £4,000 per week for six months. It was a last-gasp opportunity.

With luck the general economic climate would improve during that breathing space, but what else could we do to turn around the trading position? The buck always stops at the top and we reluctantly decided that David Rees would have to go, even though, in fairness, he had largely been following an agreed strategy and we couldn't criticize any of his decisions. I had been with him most weeks and I wasn't sure I could have done any better, but there had to be change. I decided to take overall control myself, with help from the head-office team, although I was still managing director of the Gosforth business and also needed to spend time in Glasgow and Leeds.

The scene was set for an *annus horribilis* for me and senior Greggs' managers. Throughout the summer of 1977, which seemed endless, I spent three gruelling days a week in Manchester, and there were more board meetings than at any other stage in Greggs' history – 1 and 22 June, 20 and 26 July, 11 August, 11 September, 14 September, 12 October and 9 November. Simply re-reading the minutes thirty-five years later gave me palpitations, with each meeting involving major decisions, applications for more TES (which were refused) and looking at critical cash flows.

As if that was not enough, in September Greggs was drawn into a strike without notice and in respect of a grievance that had nothing to do with us. The dispute was between the union and the federation over payment for bank-holiday working. Greggs was not a member of the federation and had its own agreement with the union. The amount in dispute was £100,000, which seemed a ridiculously small amount to bring most of the bread industry to a halt. Greggs' bakery at Gosforth was picketed and our shops in the north-east closed, cutting off the life blood of the business, further stretching Greggs' already very depleted financial resources and presenting a horrible dilemma. Some of our bakery staff were union members who wanted to support their colleagues, and we did not want to encourage our non-union staff to work, which might have created long-term divisions and conflict between them and the union staff.

We had seen and read plenty about pickets and

picketing on TV and in the newspapers, but that was no preparation for coping with their physical presence outside our premises and the threat it posed to our business. Much of the picketing we had seen and heard of was unpleasant and sometimes violent, and I suppose that might have happened at Gosforth too, but we maintained good relations with the pickets, explaining our position and at the same time trying to understand theirs. Tea and other refreshments helped the process but the most important thing was to respect the pickets as individuals who were doing what they believed was right.

The strike forced many bakers to impose a system of rationing on their customers. Trying to break the impasse and move negotiations forward, I arranged a £100,000 promise from major independent bakeries, and when, after three further days, no progress had been made, Greggs negotiated a return to work without pickets for its non-union staff. During those three days there had been a lot of anger at several levels in the business. Management was furious at being drawn into a dispute not related to Greggs at a time when the company was in severe difficulties, and many non-union staff were angry at being unable to work. It was a potentially explosive situation that could have done long-term damage to our industrial relations, but somehow Ken Middleton steered us through these events without inflicting hard-to-heal wounds. We continued to work constructively with the union, including asking officials to open extensions in Glasgow and Newcastle. Two years later Ken concluded a single agreement with the Bakers' Union, allowing existing employees to remain non-union but making union membership a condition of employment for new employees. Such an arrangement was known as a 'post-entry closed shop' and would now be illegal.

For Greggs to pursue such an agreement when there was so much unrest throughout the industry was controversial. Many businesses had closed-shop agreements, which had been forced on them by a vote of employees, but whenever possible other businesses tried to keep the union out. Some within Greggs and others in the bakery industry thought we should adopt the latter approach. But this would have created a negative relationship between management and the union. Instead, Greggs chose to offer union membership to all new employees and to develop a constructive relationship with a single union.

We survived and had started to turn the corner. The Manchester loss had started to decrease and we could see a way forward. Most importantly, we had the man for the job – 'Cometh the hour, cometh the man'. In November 1977, John Thomas joined Greggs to sort out Manchester. The original contract was for three days per week but this was soon changed to full-time. Although not a large man, John had a huge presence. He had begun his career as a tax inspector and, without exception, he greeted everyone with a firm handshake, fixing them with a clear, penetrating gaze from behind his dark-rimmed glasses. He was the outstanding applicant from an extensive advertising and head-hunting exercise, having been through the tough school of Allied Bakeries. After Fred Acres, of Acres the Bakers, the 'axeman' of Allied Bakeries, had hacked his way through business after business, ruthlessly cutting costs in pursuit of an elusive improvement to the bottom line, John had been sent in to rebuild the business, which he had previously done admirably at Whittakers of York and Hagenbachs, re-establishing them as proud and profitable enterprises.

He had a tougher and more confrontational management approach than Greggs' but that was needed in Manchester to root out some of the old practices and bring about the change needed. As well as having expertise in all aspects of the industry (production, wholesale and retail), he was as fair as he was determined and ambitious. He set the highest possible standards for himself and others. He was something of a cross between a terrier and a Rottweiler, never giving up until what had been agreed was achieved.

Greggs has had some great general managers and managing directors, but I don't think any of them could have turned around the Manchester business in the way that John did – I know I couldn't – and Greggs was fortunate to find him at that time. His ability, experience, ambition to succeed and toughness made the difference. John dismissed people during his time at Greggs, but when the boot went in, the recipient was expecting it and knew exactly what the reasons were.

John saw merit in elements of our approach that were new to him, including our more consensual style of involving people, profit-sharing (whenever that might come to Manchester) and share ownership. The combination of these with his previous experience proved to be a formidable blend in turning around Manchester and in establishing (when he eventually got round to it!) his own successful business, Thomas of York, which now has more than thirty bakery shops.

The 'Winter of Discontent' still lay ahead, with the

industrial chaos that saw transport paralysed, bins unemptied, mountains of rubbish in the street, bodies left unburied and regular power cuts during one of the coldest winters of the century, leading to the downfall of James Callaghan's Labour government and the election of Margaret Thatcher. For Greggs, though, it seemed that the crisis was already over. With confidence returning, we went back to building and expanding the company, but the nature and scale of the business had changed from those heady days of just five years before, when we had taken Tyneside by storm without really having to try. The economic climate and industrial relations, the skills and experience required to manage a much more complex business were all very different now. And those five years, especially the time I had spent in Manchester, had taken their toll on me.

8

CONSOLIDATION
Eclair

*Eclairs sold well everywhere. A box of four was the nearest
Greggs came to corporate entertainment for its directors*

1978 saw the start of a five-year period of consolidation,
my first priority being to reduce my day-to-day management overload so that I could focus on managing the
business as a whole. John Thomas's arrival had freed
me from routine responsibility in Manchester, but I
needed to appoint a managing director for the Gosforth
business. I should have been done it two or three years
earlier but we had hesitated to make any changes to a
business that was generating 80 per cent of Greggs'
profits and funding the investment in Glasgow and
Manchester. Change is always a threat, and though I
was probably overstretched and unable to give Gosforth
the full-time attention it required, our record at finding

managing directors was not good and we had decided
that we couldn't risk it, particularly when the Gosforth
business seemed able to run itself.

There had been remarkable employee stability. Few
people joined the company at any level then moved on
quickly, and it was common for employees to stay with
us for a long time, even their whole working lives. So
many staff members had been there from the start as
apprentices or juniors and had then been promoted to
shop managers or supervisory posts in the bakery that
endless strands and links held the business together.
Many families had more than one member working for
us, like the Hutchinsons, Burt the cake decorator and
his wife Ann, who was the leader of the number-
crunching comptometer operators weekly calculating,
with amazing accuracy, the charge-outs to all shops.
Paddy O'Neill worked for Greggs in various management positions for almost forty years and, not satisfied
with having two brothers in the business, also persuaded his wife June to become an assistant manager in
the Cramlington and Greenmarket shops for eighteen
years. Paddy swears his son would have joined Greggs
too, if he hadn't answered the call to the priesthood! At
the Gosforth bakery today, the four senior managers
and twelve of the twenty supervisors all started in the
apprentice scheme. Lillian Patterson, the PA at
the Gosforth bakery, had twin sons who worked in our
shops and became shop managers.

There were many other long-serving employees in
the bakery who had been through the three-year
apprentice scheme that Kevin Rainey introduced in
1972. This was extended across the other businesses but
at Gosforth at least five new apprentices were taken on

each year. There was huge competition to be chosen as Apprentice of the Year and the scheme produced a steady stream of supervisors and managers: Peter Nichols, who became a head of department in 1974, Ian Connell, who won three times in a row and went on to be bakery manager in the midlands, and Robert Walby, who won twice, and became bakery manager at Gosforth. Eventually a woman, Jeanette Schofield, won for the first time in 1981 and again in 1982, just to reinforce the point.

Not that the life of an apprentice was all hard work. Unofficial pranks and rituals were common. New apprentices were ceremoniously baptized in one of the capacious sinks, and a variety of treatments was administered to those getting married. One bridegroom was held down and had his feet and ankles painted with green food colourant. It proved impossible to wash off, and he went green-footed to his wedding night, which must have been a rather alarming sight for his bride.

The original Gosforth business, where success and excitement had come in such abundance, where I knew the people so well and where home and family were, occupied a special place in my heart, and I was reluctant to give up the part of my job that I liked best. I had poured much of the last fifteen years of my life into it and the emotional bond was enormous. I had been involved in the acquisition and fitting out of every one of the shops, in the development of each extension to the bakery and the specification of every piece of equipment; I had tasted every product many times in the search for improvement and excellence; above all, I loved the people, who gave so much and asked for so little in return. I loved being in the bakery in the bustle of the early mornings. I loved being in the shops when they were busy, the office, vans, stores, in fact wherever people were getting on with their jobs.

Each year we had a huge party, a dinner dance for 1,200 employees, and almost everyone was there, from the bakery and all the shops. The only place that could accommodate such numbers was the Mayfair Ballroom in Newcastle. Many of the women had been up before six a.m. to prepare their husbands' bait and kids' breakfast, and had been in the shops from before eight until six p.m. They then put on their best dresses, wined, dined and danced to Abba's 'Waterloo' and 'Dancing Queen' until about two o'clock in the morning. It was deafening, intoxicating and the most impressive display of corporate confidence and invincibility. How proud I felt! But I also felt an awesome responsibility for these people, their families and the part Greggs played in their lives.

Colin, Gay and I always used to go the party and we stayed right to the end. After being up till two in the morning, it was a struggle to be in the bakery first thing the next morning, but I always made sure I was there. We'd usually be missing a few of the staff on the morning after the dance and one or two of those who did turn up weren't always in the best shape. I can remember one man working on doughnuts falling asleep and finishing up face down in a pile of them, but on the morning after the party, I was willing to turn a blind eye to things that would normally have called for a stern word.

Despite my close involvement from the start and the close relationship I had with the staff, I had to be free to concentrate on the whole business, not just the Gosforth bakery, which needed its own full-time managing director. Greggs now had a suitable candidate in David Parker, then thirty-two, who had joined the company two years earlier. He originated from the north-west of England but had spent several years in Nairobi with a bakery and milling company. He was a rugby player with an imposing and athletic build, the good looks of a 1970s film star and a Cary Grant dimple in his chin. David's background and lifestyle in Kenya might have raised concerns about how well he would relate to the ethos and no-nonsense culture of the Gosforth business, which was quick to reject anyone with a haughty or grand attitude, but he settled in well and quickly established excellent working relationships. His wife Pat also took a keen interest in everything that happened.

In addition we made several important management appointments to strengthen both production and sales. The most notable of these were Neill Hastie who was appointed production director at Head Office, Wighton Clark who became sales director in Scotland, and John Van Bedoff who joined the Gosforth business as chief engineer.

In the midst of this, Greggs received an approach about the business from Nicholas Horsley and Chris Haskins of Northern Foods. They were a formidable pair, a couple of years older than me, the former tall, intellectual, thoughtful and reserved (as a good Yorkshireman should be), the latter stocky, brusque, full of Irish humour and natural inquisitiveness. They were at the height of their partnership, which transformed the Horsley family business from a local Yorkshire dairy company into the largest manufacturer of high-quality chilled foods in Britain, and the owner of other major food manufacturers. It also had an excellent reputation for quality, with Marks & Spencer its main customer.

A few years earlier I would not have considered an offer at any price but the events of recent years had eroded my confidence and determination. Apart from issues of personal financial security, I never again wanted to be faced with the prospect of putting large numbers of people out of jobs, which had been a very real possibility in the Manchester business. At a board meeting in May 1979 we appointed Hambros Bank to advise Greggs in the negotiations.

We provided the necessary accounts and forecasts and held several meetings with Nicholas Horsley and Chris Haskins. Both were radicals and members of the Labour Party (Chris later became Tony Blair's rural tsar) and related well to the Greggs values, as did the Quaker background of the Horsley family. They could have provided resource and security and I would have been happy to work for them. I was prepared to consider surrendering some independence in return for being relieved of some of the worry and responsibility, but within a month they decided they didn't want to proceed. They had considered but now rejected the possibility of developing a retail arm for their company, fearing it might create conflict with their wholesale customers. They also saw Greggs' manufacturing facilities as fragmented and labour-intensive, and I suspect they were unsure that we had Manchester on a profitable long-term route.

It had been an unsettling few weeks and I was both disappointed and relieved by the outcome. We made a firm decision not to pursue any other possible sales of Greggs but to settle down and focus on our original plan to develop the businesses in Glasgow, Leeds and Manchester to the profitability levels achieved at Gosforth. That would give us the option of becoming a public company quoted on the stock exchange and would require other changes, including to the main board.

By the end of the seventies, as more senior managers joined Greggs, it became impracticable for them all to become board members. The interests of some also lay primarily with their separate businesses, rather than with the company as a whole, so no further divisional managing directors were appointed to the main board. When Brian Wildblood succeeded Geoff Parfitt as managing director of Thurston's, and Ken Middleton became managing director of Glasgow, each resigned from the main board. They understood why they should do so, but went with considerable reluctance from positions they had enjoyed and which carried some status.

In 1979, a second institutional shareholder took a stake in Greggs, the pension fund of the National Coal Board. It seemed an appropriate link to our early days in the mining villages of Northumberland but also a strange bedfellow, given the industrial unrest the miners had caused, but their fund was regarded as a respectable institutional investor, almost separate from the activities of its members. At the same time ICFC increased its shareholding. This added to the stability and stature of the business and would provide access to future funds, if needed.

Not unnaturally, those shareholders wanted a non-executive director (NED) on the board to watch over their interests. The Greggs board was also keen to have someone who understood the City and would look at decisions differently from the executive directors, who were more involved in the day-to-day running of the company. Hambros sent up a candidate for our consideration. He was experienced and qualified, and Greggs would have fitted well into his portfolio of non-executive directorships. He would have made a contribution, got on well with everyone, and the institutional shareholders would have been happy, but he did not have the acumen and business flair the Greggs board was looking for.

Not without some embarrassment, we declined on behalf of our institutional shareholders and Hambros despatched another candidate north, then a third and a fourth. I began to fear we would be regarded as both obstructive and disrespectful, a little upstart outfit from the north spurning the City's finest, chosen by the mighty Hambros. Fortunately we chanced on a compromise. Stephen Curran, the manager of the Coal Board's pension fund, had been attending board meetings until an NED was appointed. He seemed to have all the qualities Greggs wanted. He was tall, with longish dark hair and glasses, smart suits and the suave air of a successful young man in the City, and he was different from the rest of the Greggs board: we were close to and cared most about the people, the products and the north of England. He was analytical, hard-nosed and primarily interested in return for investors, but he was also very shrewd and a good strategist. Everyone was delighted with what turned out to be a brilliant appointment for Greggs. Lesson Number Seven: Don't compromise. Hold out for what you want.

Lesson 7: Don't compromise. Hold out for what you want.

An NED from the City created a new and necessary dimension to the main board, someone whose primary concern was the return for shareholders and who was familiar with how the City worked. It was important that such a voice was present and listened to, without being allowed to dominate the agenda. Stephen admirably fulfilled this requirement and remained on the Greggs board for a remarkable twenty-seven years, which must be something of a record in the City, where the stock exchange ceases to recognize NEDs as independent after they have served ten years. Maybe it was the difference in Greggs' values compared to the City's that interested him, or the box of fresh cream eclairs and cakes he carried home after board meetings, the nearest Greggs got to corporate entertainment – or perhaps it was the lavish board lunches, when directors were offered a selection of Greggs' sandwiches, pies and cakes with a cup of tea. How many NEDs can boast the skill of being able to cut a cream slice without all the cream squidging out?

The company was now making progress across most fronts. A key element to this and future progress was the management development programme at Appleby Castle in Cumbria. This was the headquarters of Ferguson Industrial Holdings, a builders' supply merchant. The chief executive was Denis Vernon, who had qualified as a solicitor in the same building, but with a different firm, in Newcastle as I had done, and whose parents had also owned a small bakery business in Newcastle. After qualifying he had joined Ferguson, which he had expanded and floated on the stock exchange. Denis was passionate about the importance of training, and the facilities at Appleby Castle were brilliant. For many years Greggs carried out all its management development and training there with Ferguson Industrial Holdings staff and outside consultants.

Greggs' management development was centred on a new approach known as 'Results Through People'. Managers were expected to take part in three development courses, from basic through to advanced, and others to develop particular or specialist skills. Apart from the excellence of the facilities and the high level of commitment to it, one special feature set it apart from other management development schemes. The courses were usually attended by representatives from each of the Greggs' divisions, which provided an excellent networking opportunity and, most important, the managing director of any division represented had to attend at least the final day of the course. This ensured that, when delegates returned to their division, the person in charge of the business was aware of any conclusions reached at the course, which meant there was a better chance they would be adopted into the business. How many 'road to Damascus' moments are gradually eroded by people and events not touched by the experience? We wanted to change that.

Appleby Castle was magnificent, with its twelfth-century keep, the moat populated by a wide range of unusual waterfowl and beautiful grounds that were a centre for rare breeds. The managers worked hard by day and often played hard at night. On one occasion, two of the Gosforth managers went down into the village for a couple of beers before dinner. When they came back, two of the others had got into the suits of armour standing just inside the doors and scared the pants off them. A bit of self-discipline was required because there were cupboards and cupboards full of booze, and Denis Vernon used to say, 'Just help yourself, lads.'

Back in Glasgow, progress had remained slow. After seven years of hard work and commitment, Gordon had not achieved the success he and Greggs were looking for. We had become good friends and, with other Greggs' senior management, I had enormous respect for his intellectual ability, his integrity, his sense of humour and his seemingly endless commitment to making the Glasgow business successful, but he was ready for a change, a return to a larger business where, away from the daily cut and thrust of retail bakery, he could make better use of his management and strategic skills. We discussed a package, which included a further period with Greggs, while he sought another position.

A few weeks later, I received a call from his wife, Dorothy. He had been driving home, felt the onset of a severe headache and pulled into a lay-by. There he had suffered a brain haemorrhage and died. I was utterly devastated that this kind, conscientious man should die so young, leaving behind a wife and two children, and was worried that the pressures of managing the Glasgow business, without the benefit of success, had contributed to his condition. I was assured that it would not have done but I couldn't be sure, and the nagging doubt stayed with me for a long time.

Gordon's death was not the only tragedy. Our excellent young accountant, Ian Walker, had died from cancer, also leaving a young wife and children. His successor was soon in Barlinnie prison for embezzlement from Greggs. He had set up a fake account and was diverting money into it, though fortunately the sums involved were not huge and soon detected. He was arrested by the police at the bakery and marched right through it as an example to everyone.

Our Glasgow production manager and engineer also left the company to start their own pizza business. All that remained of the management team were Jean Dunsmore, the personnel manager, and Cathy Scott, the sales manager, with help from me on one or two days a week. Morale at the bakery was very low and there was an expectation that the Glasgow business would have to close down. In fact, we never seriously considered this, but convincing people that Greggs had a long-term future in the city was not easy when capital was still in relatively short supply and it was difficult to justify further investment until what had been spent to date started to show a reasonable return. However, the truth was that more investment was required. We needed to improve production capacity and efficiency and convince everyone that Greggs was in Glasgow for the long term. The board was persuaded to invest further in plant and machinery, in particular a new Winkler roll plant, and to continue shop openings and refits.

That was enough to stop the rot and we started rebuilding the management team. Before the search for a new managing director got under way, a surprise offer came out of the blue from Ken Middleton, our personnel director. Frustrated by the advisory nature of a head-office role, determined to prove that the motivation principles he preached really would work if passionately embraced, and keen to prove himself in a testing line-management role, he asked to be considered for the Glasgow post.

As yet, he had shown no financial acumen or

business judgement, so there was a distinct risk that Greggs might lose a good personnel director and acquire a moderate general manager. But if Ken was willing to put his career on the line I felt he should at least be given a chance. I was more than willing to help and so was John Thomas, if and when Manchester permitted. So Ken became managing director of Greggs of Rutherglen, and I continued visiting regularly to offer what help and advice I could.

Two key positions now needed filling. We had to find a new personnel director to replace Ken, and a successor to Peter Feather, who retired as property director in 1981, though he remained with us as an NED. He had been the architect of Greggs' shop-selection strategy and, for the last ten years, had personally travelled the high streets and shopping cen-tres of the north of England and Scotland. We had benefited enormously from his experience of other retail businesses, his strong entrepreneurial flair and innate unwillingness to accept anything other than an excellent deal. Without him, we thought, the shop-site selection might lose some of its cutting edge.

Eventually we found a candidate, John Hambleton, who filled the role admirably for several years. He joined us from Leicester where he had been senior development surveyor for the British Shoe Corporation. He was young, energetic and very ambitious, and his cheeriness and humour added much colour and enjoy-ment to our Head Office. He quickly established good relationships with local management and estate agents so that our shop-acquisition programme maintained its momentum. He was later succeeded by John Rook who, with his assistant Ashley Ritchie, developed the property, management and acquisition function into a formidable unit that now employs fifteen people.

Ken Middleton's role had been vital in maintaining surveys and developing the good employee relationships and values that had existed within Greggs from the outset. For almost ten years he had valiantly worked at building these into the structure of Greggs' four autonomous businesses. Now that the business was embarking on further expansion, maintaining good industrial relations and high levels of motivation were more important than ever. Ian Edgeworth was appointed personnel director and filled this difficult role for more than twenty years. He had originally taught mathematics in Birmingham before moving into personnel management with Hepworth, Wilkinson Sword and, finally, Glaxo. He, too, was young and ambitious, a keen cyclist, with a great and unusual sense of humour and the ability to relate to people at all levels.

9

GOING PUBLIC
Chocolate cake

Did you get a share of the cake? When Greggs floated, the share price was £1.35. Today it is the equivalent of £50

The continuing pressure of all the changes and events that had taken place had left me badly in need of a break and I took a three-month sabbatical, leaving John Thomas in charge. I returned unsure of how things had progressed in my absence and how I would feel about my own ability to manage and develop a business that, over the previous ten years, had grown so much in size and complexity.

On the first count, 1 needn't have worried. Under John Thomas's leadership, with 100 per cent support from the head-office team and Malcolm Simpson at the fore, the business had progressed well. Everyone had enjoyed the fresh challenges my absence had created.

This was my first experience of distancing myself from Greggs and finding it had done better without me. Over the next twenty years, as I moved into a part-time and then a non-executive role, each step away seemed to result in an increase in Greggs' achievements and performance.

There were a number of possible conclusions that could be drawn from this, some of which are not good for one's self-confidence! I had had no training or management development as preparation for running a business of this size. I definitely preferred the hands-on approach that a small business allowed, rather than the strategies and planning that a larger one required, but I reassured myself that our progress was based on the values and principles to which Greggs had always adhered, and that putting distance between myself and the business had its advantages. I was more able to see the wood from the trees and focus a fresher mind on the main issues facing Greggs. Moreover, my absence created space and opportunity for others to take on more responsibility.

Whatever doubts I had about my ability to manage Greggs I could put to one side because of the support and encouragement I received, and the need to deal with a number of pressing issues the business faced, in particular the question of whether to remain a private company or try to obtain a quotation on the London stock exchange.

The advantages of going public were straight-forward: it would provide a route to future funding in the form of equity and loan capital; it would enhance the company's standing and covenant – its perceived ability to meet future rental payments and other requirements in the leases of shops. This was important because land-lords preferred their premises to be occupied by companies of substance, increasing both rental security and property valuation. Going public would also increase the opportunity for employees at all levels to become shareholders and to be given share-based incentive schemes (some of which could, over time, deliver life-changing sums of money), and it would enable Greggs' shareholders to achieve a better spread of investment and a ready market for their shares.

The disadvantages of being a public company were the multitude of regulations and governance procedures that would need to be observed and the risk of an un-welcome takeover resulting in loss of control of the company. Most worrying to me was the pressure it might put on us to take decisions based on the short-term requirements of external shareholders and the stock exchange rather than on long-term profitability, especially if it threatened any erosion of Greggs' traditional values. From my personal perspective, this was an enormously complex and difficult decision, which senior managers and the board debated and dis-cussed over several years, without reaching a firm conclusion. Was it better that Greggs should be subject to the market and financial pressures of the City, how-ever short-term and capricious they might be, rather than the whims and fancies of private shareholders? I had no reason to be concerned about the current family shareholders, who were committed to Greggs for the long term, proud of its achievements and its prominence in the north of England and conscious of its responsi-bilities to its employees, but what about future generations? As a solicitor, I had seen some fine family businesses wound up as a result of family disputes, the inability to attract the right managers and the difficulty of finding the money to pay taxes due when a major shareholder died. Did I really want future family shareholders to be faced with the responsibility for such major issues, particularly when I had always been clear that I did not want future generations to feel under any pressure to be involved in the business?

Eventually, after debate, soul-searching and changes of mind, we made the decision to go public. Our priorities were now focused on meeting the criteria required for a public quotation, the primary one being to show a record (and hold out future prospects) of profit growth. Greggs needed to show a steady improvement in Manchester to meet this requirement. The decision to buy the Manchester business had been a bad one, in my opinion, and it had reached a point beyond the ability of normal effort and investment to effect a recovery. Temporary Employment Subsidy had been a lucky break but, as its title suggested, it was not a permanent solution. The resolve and determination of the Greggs board to make it work had resulted in our continuing to invest long after normal criteria would have suggested abandoning ship, and John Thomas had provided a much greater degree of commitment and effort than expected, though on occasions it had driven him to exhaustion and the brink of despair. Yet still neither John nor I could countenance being beaten and were determined to keep going until we had turned the business around.

A further factor that marked the difference between failure and success was the stream of able and experienced managers we were able to recruit from Allied

Bakeries, all looking to escape the despondency that pervaded it as it strove to achieve better profitability through relentless cost-cutting. Greggs did not have to entice these managers away. They kept knocking at our door, regardless of the problems and uncertainty we faced in Manchester.

On the sales front, Mel Gerson was in his late thirties, a tireless sales dynamo. He left Hagenbachs, came to us and set about establishing the required standards and sales results throughout all the Manchester shops, which necessitated a stream of major and minor refits. Greggs had no in-house resource at that time to manage this workload so we recruited a company-wide shopfitting manager, Chris Smailes, again from Hagenbachs. He was thoroughly experienced in all aspects of shopfitting and design and, in his spare time, loved to cruise the canals on his narrowboat with his wife Annie and two sons.

These and several other appointments came as the result of a single advert in the *Wakefield Express*: 'Would you like a share of the cake?' That newspaper was chosen because Wakefield was the headquarters of Hagenbachs, once a successful independent bakery but now a struggling satellite of Allied Bakeries. The effect of this advert, and the subsequent exodus from Hagenbachs to Greggs, became a talking point and concern within Allied Bakeries and led to other people joining us, most notably Stephen Greenfield, previously chief executive of Sunblest, Northampton. Tall and dark, with a serious demeanour, he was determined but friendly, and one of the young rising stars of the bakery industry. The objective was for him to help John Thomas improve profitability in Manchester and take over from him as quickly as possible, so that John could focus on his own business in Yorkshire.

Little by little, step by step, we cranked up the Manchester business performance until in 1984 we were able to say in our prospectus offering shares to the public:

> In 1976 the company took advantage of a further opportunity for expansion by acquiring Price Brothers (Bakers) Limited, which was by then operating mainly in the Manchester area. Although this company had been trading at a loss and had suffered from a lack of investment, it was attractive to Greggs because approximately fifty of its retail outlets were in good locations. Considerable managerial and financial resources were invested in this business and a trading loss of £326,000 in its first full year of operation under Greggs' ownership was turned into a trading profit of £305,000 by 1980.

That was true (it had to be) but, given the events of those eight years, it was also the biggest understatement I have ever been associated with!

Performance in the Gosforth business improved too. David Parker had proved a safe pair of hands, and Laurie Rotin, who had achieved amazing sales growth in Manchester, moved to Gosforth in 1981 and had a similarly immediate and electric impact. Laurie had much more than his share of optimism, energy and enthusiasm, and was the most remarkable salesperson in my time at Greggs. He continually pushed managers and shop staff to the limit, but they respected him because he asked even more of himself, and everyone could bask in the glory of the sales increases that followed him. He soon became half of another Greggs husband-and-wife team. Theresa had started as a part-time relief clerk before being promoted to office manager and assistant accountant of the Gosforth business. Laurie had obviously been watching her closely at work because he proposed to her on their first date. Some years later he suffered a stroke and was prevented from working again. Theresa continued part-time but looked after Laurie in a manner that won her admiration from all quarters. She received regular support from Laurie's friends and colleagues at Greggs, in particular Paddy O'Neill, Bob Shiels and Phillip Peng, a great example of Greggs' values at work in every aspect of the business.

Under Ken Middleton's direction, the business in Scotland moved forwards steadily, and was boosted by a major extension to the bakery, opened in May 1983 by Michael Kelly, the charismatic provost of Glasgow and promoter of the city under the slogan 'Glasgow's Miles Better': the city had shed its dour old image, in preparing the ground for the Garden Festival in 1988 and becoming Europe's City of Culture in 1990.

In Yorkshire, Brian Wildblood oversaw further sound progress as Greggs moved towards chalking up the profit record required for going public.

The statement in the prospectus document showed a steady rise in turnover and pre-tax profits for the five years from 1979 to 1983, with turnover nearly doubling from just under £19.7 million to more than £37 million and profits almost trebling from £598,000 to £1.74 million.

With the rest of the UK to aim at, in addition to improving profitability in the existing businesses, future growth did not pose a problem, and we felt able to say:

> The Directors also believe that there is considerable potential for expansion on a geographical basis into the Midlands and the South of England. Surveys of major conurbations have been carried out and although no firm plans have been made, the Company expects to establish a presence in one of these areas within the next twelve months. The autonomous divisional structure operated by Greggs will allow such new divisions to be acquired or set up with minimal disruption to the trading operations of the existing divisions.

We also needed to demonstrate that we had a management team who could deliver this growth, but I was not sure I could do this, or that I wanted to. I also felt it would be less than honest to go public and soon afterwards to change the managing director (although nowadays managing directors and CEOs come and go at short intervals, often carrying away rewards out of all proportion to effort expended or value added to the company). On the other hand, because I had been the managing director who had developed the business, any change would create uncertainty in the minds of potential investors. However, I was not everyone's idea of a thrusting business executive – the *Newcastle Journal* once described me as 'a business tycoon as mild-mannered as a village curate' – and in any case, best practice suggested that, in a public company, the roles of chairman and chief executive should be separate, so we now took the decision to bring in experience from outside.

Some of the senior managers did not feel change was required, and if it was, that an internal appointment would be more appropriate. I was not convinced that any of our existing managers had the ability and experience to take Greggs forward. Instead, we had an opportunity to appoint an executive who would bring in new ideas and experience from a larger organization. In spite of considerable pressure from some with aspirations for themselves (which I applauded) and others who simply did not want change (which I understood), I was determined not to compromise. There was too much at stake. Greggs was now a substantial business employing almost four thousand people (at least two-thirds being part-time). Greggs had an excellent track record and ambitions for the future. This was a one-off opportunity to strengthen top management.

I had met Mike Darrington on a number of occasions in his capacity as managing director of Sayers of Liverpool (part of United Biscuits). He was two years younger than me and shared the same passion and similar ideas for changing the retail baking industry. We got on really well from the start and I saw in him the qualities and experience we needed. He'd been commercial director at UB, but was ready to run a business, and when UB were looking for someone to turn round Sayers, its loss-making subsidiary on Merseyside, Mike had been quick to volunteer.

Sayers had about 120 shops, most of which were good sites. At one time the company had had a very good name, but things had gone badly wrong and it was losing money hand over fist. When Mike had taken over in 1978 he had faced a very difficult task because it was not a happy place. There were many problems and morale was at rock bottom.

Trying to get a feel for the business and identify the major problems, he had gone into the bakery during different shifts, talking to the employees and, more important, listening to them. One of the key moments was when he went to talk to the evening shift on despatch – the last stage before the bread and cakes go out on the vans. The products didn't look very good to Mike, but he thought, I'm not a baker, and they must know what they're doing, but then asked, 'What do you think of the products?'

The reply came back, 'They're all right.'

'But would you buy them yourself?'

'No. They're all right, but they're not that good.'

'So you're sending them out to our customers,' Mike said, 'even though you don't think they're good enough to buy them yourself? There's a big lesson there. In future, if you don't think anything's good enough to go out – if you wouldn't buy it yourself – then you tell the bakers it's got to be made again.' Mike's attitude was always that he'd rather someone be disappointed because they couldn't buy a product they wanted than be able to buy it but be disappointed by it and not come back.

His reputation had been made during his five years at Sayers where, ironically, he had tried to persuade his bosses that Greggs was a very good model for a bakery business and that they should buy us while the company was still small. His bosses didn't listen . . .

When he had first arrived at Sayers the employees

were expecting him to shut the place down, but he got them all together and said, 'I'm sure we can get this place back on its feet.' He told them what he wanted them to focus on, of which improving the quality of their products was the most important, and made a pledge: 'Over a period of time we will require less people working here, but if you work with me, I promise that I will bust a gut not to make a single one of you redundant.' He got them working together, the quality improved, the costs went down, the sales went up and they made Sayers profitable. They did it without making anyone redundant, and in the late 1970s on Merseyside, that was quite an achievement.

Mike and I used to meet up on occasions, and because we weren't rivals – Sayers was on Merseyside and Greggs was in the rest of the north – we discovered that we shared a lot of the same ideas, values and enthusiasms. Without that, I don't think I would ever have persuaded him to come to Greggs, because he was already very successful, had held a number of important positions with United Biscuits and had bright future prospects. He was being developed for great things by Sir Hector Laing, then the chairman.

However, he wanted to build a business and he couldn't do that at UB. As he said to me, 'Building is always a lot more fun than maintenance.' So, I knew there was one person out there who fitted the bill and I thought he would be interested in the opportunity, but the appointment took place only after appropriate advertising, interviews, assessment of other available talent, and Mike's extensive investigations into Greggs' history and prospects. Eventually, we decided that Mike had the requisite experience and ability, but it was a huge decision for me and Greggs to hand over to him. Above all, I had to be sure that he would continue to nurture the values on which Greggs had been founded. It was an equally massive decision for him. Whatever our own potential, we were asking him to abandon a successful career and great future prospects with a leading UK company, to join a relatively small and unknown business in the north of England and Scotland. I was delighted when he decided to do so.

Mike's fascination with bakeries had started early. In the late 1940s, when he was six or seven, he used to stay with his grandparents in a small village in Somerset. Next door there was a baker's shop. Mike and his younger sister used to go there early in the morning and the baker used to let them help him, mixing flour, kneading dough and all sorts of things that Health and Safety would never allow now. At the end, the baker would give them a loaf of bread, warm from the oven, to take back to their grandparents' house for breakfast. Any warm fresh bread is nice, but a really good-quality loaf that's still warm is heaven. Mike's never forgotten that experience – his eyes still mist over when he talks about it.

Even though he was on track to get a scholarship to Cambridge, he didn't go to university, deciding that he wanted to start in business. He looked at going to Harvard Business School, but couldn't get the funding and instead qualified as an accountant and went to work for United Biscuits as a group exports accountant. In the early 1970s, aged thirty-two, he finally got to Harvard on a four-month course, sent there by United Biscuits because he had been earmarked for future promotion.

One of United Biscuits' customers was Marks & Spencer. In the 1960s and early 1970s, M&S were keen on quality and the standards they set were extra-ordinarily high. They really were sticklers and didn't mind if it cost them more money: they just wanted the best. Customers knew they would enjoy the products they sold and were – still are – happy to pay a few extra pence for them. If it's a treat, you want it to be a nice treat, not a disappointment. This was a lesson that Mike was passionate about and strongly reinforced at every opportunity. Lesson Number Eight: quality is everything.

Lesson 8: Quality is everything.

That lesson was reinforced when, during his time with United Biscuits, Mike was involved with a crisps company, some of whose products were supplied to supermarkets as own-label crisps, but others marketed under the unimaginative brand name 'Crispy'. When UB took over KP Nuts they decided that as everyone had heard of KP, they'd rebrand the crisps as KP. It became the third main crisps brand, behind the 'Big Two': Smiths and Golden Wonder.

There was also a small crisps-making business in the west midlands called Walkers and Mike found that whatever KP did, whatever price promotions or any-thing else they put on, they couldn't beat Walkers in the west midlands. Intrigued, Mike investigated and dis-covered that Walkers were absolutely committed to quality; it wasn't enough that their crisps were good, they wanted them to be brilliant, and they would go to any lengths to ensure that they were.

One year there had been a very wet growing season.

The quality of the potato crop was poor and all the manufacturers knew there would be a shortage of potatoes. They all had long-term supply contracts, but when the potatoes started to come into the storehouses, they were not up to specification. KP, Golden Wonder and Smiths reacted by lowering their specification and accepting potatoes they would normally have rejected. Walkers rejected all the sub-standard potatoes. They then told their customers, 'We can't get enough decent potatoes, so to ensure that you still get a top-quality product, we're not taking on any new customers, and for the next six months, existing customers will only be getting 50 per cent of their usual supplies.'

For those six months they made only half their normal sales and took a big hit in their profits. Meanwhile the big three manufacturers gleefully bought the sub-standard potatoes that Walkers had rejected and made a lot of money selling them, but as soon as the new crop came in and the supply situation returned to normal, their customers deserted them in favour of Walkers, which carried on expanding year after year and is now the leading UK brand. Once more, quality is everything.

The other interesting lesson Mike learned from the 'crisps wars' was that, although the retail price of all the brands was the same, the big manufacturers were only making about two per cent profit on turnover, whereas Walkers were making ten times that: 20 per cent. They had much smaller sales volumes then, but they were making more money. They paid great attention to detail, their production lines were smooth and efficient and there was very little waste, but the major reason for their level of profit was that they wouldn't give big discounts: they knew that every retailer had to have their product because that was what the customer wanted. Everywhere they expanded, they immediately became the leading brand, because their quality was so good that customers chose Walkers in preference to any other brand.

The success of Warburtons in baking bread told a similar story. Most large bakers then would buy whatever flour their miller produced. Warburtons not only told the miller what wheat they wanted their flour made from, but even which farms in Canada or America to buy it from. In that way they got the taste, texture and consistency they wanted. It worked for them, because in every single blind tasting test, Warburton's bread won. From being a very small bakery, they've become the dominant force in the industry.

A pie-maker taught Mike another valuable lesson. The company made pies for all the big supermarkets but, perhaps surprisingly, he told Mike that the best ones he made went to Aldi. There were two reasons for that, he said. Aldi wanted top quality and didn't screw him on the price. They wanted to pay a fair price, but they also wanted him to make enough money to stay in business and keep supplying them. All the other big supermarkets were continually screwing him down on price, and in the end, he said, 'You can't keep dropping the price without the quality suffering – you can't get prime beef for the price of scrag end.' The quality standards for the big supermarkets were governed by the need to have it cheap, and over the years they've contributed to wrecking the market. Supermarket buyers prove their worth to their company by the extent to which they can force down prices still more. As Mike says, 'I've seen some of them in action and the way they treat their suppliers is unbelievable.'

Greggs does not operate in that way. We want a keen price, of course, but we also want to treat our suppliers in the same decent way that we would expect them to treat us, and we want them to stay in business so that they can keep supplying us. They won't do that if we push their prices down so low that they stop making profits. This was Lesson Number Nine: Develop good long relationships with your suppliers.

Lesson 9: Develop good long relationships with your suppliers.

With his experience and these values I was confident that Mike would manage Greggs successfully and we decided that he should take over from me before Greggs went public. This was a huge step in the development of the main board, setting the scene for going public the following year and providing a structure that was to work well for almost twenty years without significant amendment. The change allowed us to say in the prospectus:

Ian Gregg, aged 44, joined the company in 1964, having qualified as a solicitor. He has been instrumental in taking Greggs from its origins to its present position and was Executive Chairman and Managing Director until 1st January 1984. Following Michael Darrington's appointment as Managing Director, Ian Gregg retains the role of Executive Chairman and is now responsible for overall strategy.

Michael Darrington, aged 42, joined the

company in August 1983. He is a chartered
accountant who has spent seventeen years with
United Biscuits (Holdings) plc initially in various
management roles and latterly as Managing
Director of the D S Crawford Bakery Division. On
1st January 1984, he was appointed Managing
Director of Greggs.

Mike was very different from me in many ways.
Where I was quiet and reserved, he was charming, out-
going and gregarious. He also liked to have fun – he
enjoyed his work and wanted everyone else to enjoy
theirs, provided that they worked hard as well; if there
was a night out from the office, he'd be there, making
sure everyone had a good time, getting some nice photos
for them, and so on. He was also a very good listener.

Mike had a remarkable understanding (and
retention) of figures and financial matters. I found such
areas difficult and trying so I focused more on general
principles. Mike didn't ignore these, but his financial
acumen made him more cautious than I was. He often
said that the worst reason for doing anything was
because the boss had told you to, and the best reason
was because you wanted to; he treated it as a defeat if
he had to tell someone to do something. He would much
rather have talked it through with them, even if it
delayed a decision, so that in the end they came to the
decision for themselves. That way they had ownership
of it and belief in it. You have to be very patient if you're
going to do that, and not everyone can work in that way,
but that was Mike's approach and I saw it pay dividends
over and over again.

Mike's appointment proved an excellent decision for

Greggs, marking the start of more than twenty years of continuous sales and profit growth (apart from a blip in 1991), and sheltering me from the pressures of day-to-day management of a fast-growing public company. However, at the outset it created problems for each of us and for others at Greggs. The arrangement was quite clear between us. I would look after strategy and Mike would manage the day-to-day business with all senior managers reporting direct to him. His title might have been managing director but his position was what we would now term chief executive, with one significant additional responsibility: he would also manage the City aspects of being a public company, dealing with institutional investors, financial press and public relations, brokers and merchant bankers, which was usually the role of the chairman. Malcolm Simpson was also very strong in this area and made a huge contribution to it. They had both shown aptitude and appetite for being involved in the City, and proved to be a formidable partnership. I struggled with some of the more technical aspects of this and was more interested in spending my time with people and products in the shops and bakeries. I never again went to London and the City on company or financial business.

The greatest danger Mike and I faced was that after a few months, when I had become bored with my new strategy role, I would start to interfere with daily executive decisions in the business. We had heard of this happening in other companies. It is not easy to stand back and allow decisions to be made (with which you may not entirely agree) in respect of what is essentially your life's work.

There were times when I was with managers in

shops or bakeries and badly wanted to resume greater involvement. I was able to resist the temptation, partly because I did not want to confuse or undermine Mike's position but also because I was relieved not to have the responsibility. Much as I would have liked to, I knew I couldn't have my cake and eat it!

I had never been particularly good at strategy, except on the hoof, and now I was no longer continually surrounded by people, products and all the decisions that needed to be made. Under my direction, Greggs had developed opportunistically rather than strategically, and the reality was that Mike and Malcolm were better at it than I was. Quite soon it came off my job description, was added to Mike and Malcolm's, and I acquired more active and appropriate responsibilities.

Our carefully laid plans encountered other problems. The opposition I had faced in making an outside appointment redirected itself into giving Mike a hard time. It was always going to be hard to follow in the footsteps of the founder of a successful business. People were bound to make comparisons, and some of the necessary changes would not be popular, in particular more formality and structure to equip Greggs to meet current requirements and proposed future growth. In addition, in a difficult market, with a new managing director, the City would watch particularly closely the progress of a newly quoted public company.

Everything was now in place for the company to go public, the only question being one of timing. Margaret Thatcher had come to power in 1979, following the 'Winter of Discontent' when numerous public-sector workers had staged strikes that threatened to bankrupt the UK economy. Against this background and in the middle of a worldwide recession, the Thatcher government sought to bring inflation under control by monetarist policies, lowering taxes, and launching a wave of privatizations and trade-union laws. It achieved a reduction in inflation from 22 per cent in 1980 to 10 per cent by the end of 1982 and five per cent in 1983, but at the cost of closing many inefficient factories, shipyards and coal pits, and sending unemployment soaring to three million, resulting in riots in Liverpool, London, Bristol and elsewhere.

Strikes fell to their lowest level since 1950, the economy began to recover in 1982 and by 1983, following a decade of extreme financial uncertainty, company profits had started to rise. This, with the victory in the Falklands in 1982, resulted in growing confidence that Britain could regard the anarchy of the 1970s as over and look forward to a period of stability. It also encouraged more companies to 'Go Public!' In 1983 Logica and APB floated, followed in 1984 by the Body Shop, Reuters, Iceland and BT, the latter initiating the media hype that accompanied the privatization programme.

It was against this background that Greggs decided to go public. There followed six months of regular meetings in London and an exhaustive inquiry into every aspect of Greggs, particularly its audited accounts, but also its properties, taxes and contractual liabilities. Meeting after meeting produced the prospectus, or offer for sale, which set out all the information the public might require before buying Greggs' shares.

Three memories of this process stand out in my mind. The first was the excellence of the professional team Greggs had from the north-east, in particular our company secretary, Neil Calvert, and Alan Wardropper, our auditor, who more than held their own with their London counterparts. Whether the issue was Greggs' depreciation policy, payment of corporation tax, actuarial pension contributions, or valuation of goodwill or freehold properties, I cannot recall an occasion when they lost an argument or had to make a concession. Greggs was fortunate to have their services over a long period. During the going-public period, they proved a formidable team, with Mike Darrington and Malcolm Simpson, who both excelled in the cut, thrust and parry of financial debate and strategy development.

My second recollection is that much of the preparation of schedules centred on the dining arrangements that each visit to London involved. Everything had to be fitted around the long, wine-soaked lunch, which we were required to attend with merchant bankers, stockbrokers, solicitors, institutions and potential major shareholders. Now such meetings are accompanied by nothing more luxurious than sandwiches, fruit and water, but back then it was very much full-on dining in old-fashioned style. Astonishingly, there were eighteen dining rooms at the Hambros' offices, all supported by the necessary kitchens, chefs, staff and sommeliers, which sounds over the top, unnecessary and pointless, except that a shrewd banker could learn something about his clients, their history and intentions, which might not have shown up in the company's accounts or in the more formal atmosphere of the boardroom. Greggs' representatives seemed to survive these alcoholic events without putting a foot in it, or maybe we just didn't remember!

My third recollection was the day when the bankers, stockbrokers, accountants and solicitors left the City to inspect the Greggs business. We selected Newcastle as the location, which was well beyond their normal horizons and necessitated catching a train before seven a.m., which they duly managed. We had invested much planning in the day: bakery and shop visits, solicitors' meetings, accountants' meetings and, of course, the venue where everyone should have lunch. Gosforth Park Hotel? Fisherman's Lodge? Private caterers in the boardroom? 'Of course not!' I said. 'They're coming to see and learn about the business and will sample sausage rolls, pies and sandwiches in the back of one of the shops.'

'You can't do that!' chorused the going-public team, but we did and it was a great success. Not only did they learn what a sausage roll and a stotty cake were, they actually liked them, and they referred to our products with what seemed genuine affection, encouraging us to think that Greggs might even successfully open shops in the City one day.

The production of the offer-for-sale document was an important undertaking and it was vital that every tiny detail was precisely correct, down to the last comma, full stop and capital letter. Responsibility for the production and accuracy of the document was assigned to Andrew Davison, who had recently become articled to Neil Calvert and took over as company secretary when Neil retired. Enormous security surrounded the production of the offer-for-sale document, but the printers were using a new computerized system that somehow managed to lose the entire thing on the Friday before D Day. A new proof had to be produced and Neil, Andrew and their colleague Andrew Harman had to spend the entire weekend checking it to

ensure that it contained all the changes and amend-
ments that had been so carefully agreed over the
previous months.

The great day, 27 April 1984, finally arrived, and at
ten a.m. 10,800,000 shares were offered for sale at 135p.
They were oversubscribed by a factor of ninety, and the
shares increased in value to 170p on the first day's
trading. The professional team, led by Hambros Bank,
had done an excellent job. Everything had turned out as
planned – in fact, better than we could have hoped for.
Of course, I was extremely proud that Greggs had completed the process so successfully, and to acclaim from
all quarters, but I also felt a pang of sadness that we
could never return to the size and culture I had enjoyed
over the previous twenty years, particularly in those
halcyon early days. I also suffered persistent nagging
doubts about the uncertainties that might lie ahead and
worried that events could now move out of our control.

The decision to go public had been extraordinarily
difficult, the pros and cons equally balanced. The
original decision had been marginal and tentative. Had
we been carried along by the process itself? The senior
team had been keen and it had provided an opportunity
for all employees to share in Greggs' growth. There was
no going back. The key was to make sure Greggs kept
increasing sales and profitability, while ensuring that
Greggs' values were maintained.

10

SHARING SUCCESS
Pudsey Bear

Greggs sold 650,000 bears as part of its fundraising campaign for Children in Need, which raised over £1 million in 2012

A key element of our values had been to share success (Lesson Number Ten) with employees and the community. Throughout the process of preparing the company for a public quotation, we had always been keen to ensure that employees should be able to participate in the opportunities it would offer. We had already prepared the ground to some extent, because in 1981 we had introduced a share-purchase scheme under which employees with at least two years' service were able to convert their profit-share entitlement into shares in Greggs. This enabled them to save tax on their profit share, provided they held the shares for seven years. It was an excellent scheme, which enabled employees to save and participate in the growth of Greggs, and provided them with a long-term incentive.

Lesson 10: Share success.

Later we introduced a savings-related share-option scheme by which employees with two years' service (and working twenty-five or more hours each week) were able to save money with a building society by a monthly deduction from their salary. Income tax was also saved on this deduction, which, accumulating over five or seven years, provided a useful sum to buy shares at the price (less a discount) ruling at the time the savings contract was started. A million shares were set aside for this purpose and the price frozen.

This was a win-win situation for employees. If the shares had not increased in value, they could simply take the money they had saved, which would include the tax saving and interest at more than 10 per cent. If the shares had increased in value, they could use the money saved to buy the shares at the price they had been five or seven years previously. It encouraged employees to save on a regular basis and gave them an additional interest in the business. When the savings contracts matured they could either continue to hold the shares as an investment or sell them to fund a special holiday or buy a house, car, caravan or some other major purchase.

All Greggs' staff had, and still have, the option of joining the company's share-buying scheme and many of them now do so because it is such an attractive option. It has been a considerable surprise to me that few other companies have followed our lead and established similar schemes. However, when the share-purchasing scheme was first introduced, some Greggs employees were deeply suspicious about it. 'We didn't even know what shares were back then,' one said to me, 'but when we saw how much money the ones who joined at the start had made, we soon got the hang of it!' The first share option was priced at £1.35 a share, and enough employees conquered their initial suspicion for the shares to be oversubscribed three times. Five years later, each one was worth ten times the initial price, and even if they had only bought 100 shares, they had made a profit of at least £1,000, which was a lot of money then.

Generally, the staff who joined the scheme have done very well from it. It has also given many people an opportunity they would otherwise never have had. Some still hold shares, as part of their retirement planning, while others have sold them. One baker from the Gosforth business, Geoff Armstrong, paid for the first proper holiday his family had ever had by selling some of his shares. Lillian Patterson, PA to the managing director of the Gosforth bakery, used her windfall to pay for a conservatory, and Lynn Matthews, Mike Darrington's PA, paid for her three daughters' weddings with the sale of some of her shares. Tony Vasconcellos took every opportunity to participate in Greggs' share-save schemes and used his initial involvement to help purchase his first house in 1984. The scheme has been a huge success and it's one of the things that I'm most proud of because it really has made a difference to the lives of many people who've worked for us over the years.

I also often encouraged employees to consider taking out a mortgage. Many had always lived in rented homes, whether from private landlords or the local council, and some were resistant to the idea of owning their homes. In the early days we made loans to one or two people to enable them to fund a deposit on a house, and I don't think any of those who bought a property have regretted doing so.

From a personal point of view, the successful flotation meant that in future I could avoid being put under the sort of intolerable pressure I had suffered in the late 1970s, and would now have the opportunity to pursue other interests that I had been unable to make time for. Even so, in retrospect, I did not fully appreciate the scale of the opportunity I was given by the combination of financial security, time of my own, and a managing director to run the company.

The lifting of the pressures came too late to save my marriage. Over the years I felt we had changed and we had drifted apart, growing more and more distant from each other, to the point where the breakdown had become inevitable for me. I had always seen marriage as one of the pillars of our communities and of society as a whole, and divorce was a breach of those values. But I decided there was no option other than for us to part. It was the saddest moment of my life, and explaining it to our daughters was torture. Edith and the girls remained in the family home, and I went to live at Tweed Cottage. I believed that those in positions of responsibility should set a good example and the sense of failure was overwhelming.

Even though we were now a public company, I saw no need for any dilution of Greggs' charitable and community work – in fact, quite the reverse. It was an opportunity to increase and build on those activities.

One of the most demanding but also most satisfying was our involvement in a 'fun run' to raise money for child cancer research and treatment. It was started by my brother Colin in 1982 when he was headmaster of Kings Junior School in Tynemouth. Christopher Peacock had joined the school aged eight. As a very young child he had been treated successfully for cancer. Successful treatment was rarer then than it is now. Colin had promised Christopher's parents that the junior school would raise money to donate to North of England Child Cancer Research (NECCR). The fun run was to be organized by staff and parents of Kings Junior School and Colin approached Greggs for sponsorship.

A few years earlier I had taken part in my first charity run, the Great North Run, a half marathon between Newcastle and Whitley Bay. I decided to run the race carrying a tray of stotty cakes on my head, partly to attract more sponsorship and also as publicity for Greggs. It poured with rain and my baker's whites and the stotty cakes became soggier and heavier with each weary mile. I was an easy target for Geordie humour from the spectators. 'I hope yer stotty kyek is fresher than ye.' I just made it in some three and a half hours. And my stunt attracted not a single jot of publicity. Nevertheless, with this experience in mind, we decided that we could put on a fun run to help NECCR. In discussion with Christopher's parents, Colin agreed that he would organize a five-mile family fun run in Gosforth Park in the hope of raising £10,000 towards research. I told him that was much too ambitious and, not for the first or last time, I proved to be completely wrong.

Through Greggs shops we opened the event to

anyone and everyone. It grew and grew and grew. Our sales office was taken over for the duration, and on the morning of the run, the training room became a production centre for hundreds of ham and pease pudding stotty cakes. We couldn't do it like that for long. Within a few years it had grown to 10,000 entrants, and had to be run with almost military precision and a huge army of volunteers.

The living room of Lynn Matthews was stacked with Greggs plastic trays, filled with race numbers, sponsorship forms and all the other paperwork that went with the event, and her family were roped in to help her sort them and keep on top of it all. On the morning of the race, the ground floor of the bakery was cleared and scores of volunteers came in to pack picnics for the contestants. It turned out to be a great social event, and to keep the kids happy while the race was taking place, we had some of our confectioners near the finishing line in Gosforth Park, with enough ingredients and equipment to allow the kids to ice some cakes to take home with them, which they loved, of course.

Colin and I completed the run. Lillian Patterson stood on the finishing line that year and for the next twenty-nine, handing out a commemorative medal to every contestant as they crossed the line. People who'd taken part in the run could drop off their sponsorship money, mainly in paper bags, at any Greggs shop, or with parents and staff at Kings School, Tynemouth; the area managers were picking up bags full of money from all over the place, putting them in plastic carriers, and bringing them back to the sales office at the Gosforth bakery. Lillian or Lynn would then transport them to Colin's home on their way home from work. He took the money to Kings Junior School where it was counted and banked. That first year the run made £48,000, to everyone's amazement and joy.

As the company expanded and its profitability increased, I felt some of the profits should be put back into the communities we served. I still wanted to do something to protect the environment, and it became increasingly frustrating that we had no defined strategy for charitable giving. As well as the growing number of miscellaneous requests we received, there were major and compelling appeals for causes and charities outside the UK. In 1984, amid all the focus on money that accompanied the company going public, the famine in Ethiopia provided a stark contrast. Horrendous pictures of starving children appeared in the press and on television. The effect of these images was widespread, profound and deeply moving.

The Live Aid concert, arranged by Bob Geldof and Midge Ure, was an historic recognition of our responsibility to help alleviate global famine, deprivation and disaster. My younger daughter Felicity was desperate for two tickets, which I eventually managed to get for her. She and a friend went to the concert and I listened to it in the car, happy that the event was taking place, that Felicity was there and that attention was being focused on this appalling situation. Thank you, Bob and Midge, and well done, but it isn't much better today.

As deserving and compelling as such appeals were, I felt, rightly or wrongly, that charity should begin at home and in 1987 I set up the Greggs Trust (now the Greggs Foundation), into which Greggs and I would pay money each year. However, this proved to be no more than evidence of good intentions. The Trust could not seek out projects and causes, it could not assess requests or monitor results and, like the Peebles Plan, seemed to be gathering dust in a drawer. We found ourselves deluged with appeals for funding, almost all of which had considerable merit, but I was so busy that I had no time to deal with them adequately

By now, I had fallen in love with the woman who was to become my second wife, Jane, who was one of the warmest and most caring people I had ever met. We made Tweed Cottage our home, extending and improving it. There was an old quarry in the gardens that we turned into a pond, and we also had a beautiful summerhouse, commissioned from a master cabinet-maker at terrifying expense, which became the focal point of several exhibitions we staged to promote local artists and craftsmen. We were also heavily involved with the local community, helping to raise money to restore the statue of William Wallace in the village. A few years later we moved to the Lowther Valley, near Ullswater in the Lake District, but still have many friends in the Scottish Borders.

One evening I arrived home from Greggs to Tweed Cottage with a carrier bag full of letters seeking charitable support and I asked Jane to look through them. Given her strong social conscience and caring nature, as well as her work in social care and her own experience as a single mother bringing up four children, I trusted her judgement and she seemed the ideal person to help. She read every single letter, many of them reducing her to tears. From this point on she came with me when I went into work at Greggs and borrowed my office to sort and answer all the appeals for help and to set up a system for dealing with them. Most appeals had to be refused, not through any lack of merit but through a lack of sufficient finance. Resources were increased both from the company, which was donating half a per cent of annual profits (a proportion now increased to a full one per cent) and from shareholders (I donated Greggs shares and my daughters donated a proportion of their share dividends).

Jane devised some rudimentary guidelines to help focus our grant-making and became involved with the Tyne and Wear Foundation, part of the Community Foundation movement that had crossed the Atlantic from America and had become a catalyst for developing the voluntary sector in the north-east. The charismatic CEO of the Foundation, George Hepburn, approached Greggs to make a contribution (which we made) and Jane subsequently joined their Board and in particular their grant-making group, learning much about the needs of the north-east in particular, and the organizing of grant-making in general.

She also went round the other Greggs regions, encouraging them to set up charity committees and introducing a payroll-giving scheme which, with tax concessions and Greggs matching donations, meant that their original donation more than doubled and employees could either request the charity they wished to support or let their charity committee decide. The regional committees were also awarded a lump sum from the Trust central funds according to their number of employees and the amount of fundraising they achieved within their community.

At the heart of these regional activities were people like Lillian Patterson from Newcastle, Charlotte Ferguson from Cumbria, and Tracy Lynch from the

Midlands and many, many more who give so much of their time. They are the unsung heroes of Greggs' community engagement.

Lillian Patterson joined Greggs in 1980 as a part-time holiday relief, but quickly graduated to become PA to the Gosforth managing director. She was soon orchestrating local charity initiatives, organizing all the social evenings including the huge annual staff dance and, as part of her paid employment at Greggs, Lillian became more and more involved in our charity work. She estimates that she was eventually devoting most of her working hours to the charity work in addition to a substantial part of her own time. She became treasurer for the Gosforth Charity Committee, which among many other things, helped to build St Oswald's Hospice in Gosforth. Lillian also made time to visit organizations that applied for donations from the Trust. One such visit was to a women's refuge, where she met some of the women and heard their stories. Afterwards she sat in her car and cried. Needless to say, the refuge became a beneficiary of the Trust.

As the Trust took on more and more projects, my daughter Felicity became involved, having just completed a diploma in Travel and Tourism in Edinburgh. With George Hepburn, we devised a long-term plan with five years' guaranteed funding from Greggs; we also organized a Greggs' charity conference. This was the first time that people from every division of the company had come together in the interest of its charitable activities and with the Managing Director and Chairman as delegates, with no more right to be heard than a shop assistant or baker. At first these events were held bi-annually in different divisions but now they are held every year and Jane and I are privileged to take part.

We were directing most of our energies towards social issues so the wildlife and conservation dreams I had long nurtured would have to wait, but it made more sense to invest in the communities where Greggs shops were flourishing and where many employees and customers lived. Now that the Greggs Trust had a strategy and clear objectives, family shareholders and the company could increase their donations so that the Trust could make a more meaningful contribution to ease local poverty and deprivation.

All this required considerable work and effort, in particular by Jane and Felicity, who worked both on behalf of the Community Foundation and the Greggs Trust. This close liaison was important, enabling the Trust to learn how to develop procedures for selecting projects and monitoring progress, and clarifying and refining the boundaries between the two organizations. Although a few larger grants were made, the Trust continued to focus mainly on alleviating personal hardship and small local projects which often struggled to secure funding.

Felicity's role at the Tyne and Wear Foundation included managing their hardship grants scheme (small grants to individuals in dire need) on behalf of other charitable organizations. These small grants were difficult to manage, which was why other charities were reluctant to become directly involved in this area. Because Felicity was so concerned that the scheme should not only continue but expand, the Greggs Trust agreed to take over this fund when she eventually left to move south with her fiancé.

There were lots of requests and they were all urgent, so decisions had to be made quickly. They were also emotionally draining, particularly if the money had run out and they had to be rejected. There was also the strategic issue that the grants were not tackling any underlying causes and only acting as temporary sticking plasters, but the people needing immediate financial help for essentials such as clothes, a bed, furniture, a cooker or food, were not interested in strategy. The amount available was small (usually up to £200 a time), but it made a huge difference to individuals who had suffered accidents, domestic abuse or a family break-up and often sheer bad luck. Today, more than £200,000 is donated annually from the Greggs Trust through a network of social workers and others with community links. A total of £2.2 million has been given over the past eighteen years, providing urgently needed help to more than 100,000 individuals in difficulties. Other charities in the north-east donate to this fund, taking advantage of the systems established by the Greggs Trust to ensure as little as possible is spent on administration.

The second area of small community grants provided vital funding, with minimum bureaucracy, to small local projects such as self-help groups, children's recreation areas and youth clubs. The Trust could help a local community develop a project and provide the first essential building block of a funding package that might help attract other funders. Each year the Trust also supported a number of major initiatives such as Sunderland Headlight, which funded a development worker to support people with mental health problems in Sunderland city centre, and the Trust tried to provide continuity of funding wherever possible, so that promising initiatives could flourish. It also supported causes that were difficult to fund elsewhere, such as the West End Refugee Service in Newcastle, and contributed to the core costs of charities that support disadvantaged communities, such as the Neighbourhood Advice Centre in Hebburn, an area badly affected by the closure of heavy industry along the river Tyne, with consequently high levels of unemployment.

We also became involved in supporting the People's Kitchen in Newcastle, founded by Alison Kay. Her son, who had advised Greggs on several senior appointments, was tragically killed in an air accident in 1985. That year Alison read in the local paper about a homeless person whose body had been found in bushes on some waste land. She was so saddened by the thought that any man or woman should have to die alone in that way that, although she was already in her seventies, she began to organize regular weekly events at which the homeless in Newcastle could expect to find food and companionship. Alison became their hero and friend. The gatherings that developed under the arches of the railway bridge in Newcastle became legendary, as did her love for those who came, whatever their background and whatever the reason for homelessness. Her attitude was 'There but for the grace . . .'

Alison received regular support from Greggs, largely through the good offices of Maurice Alderson, who worked in various positions at the bakery in Gosforth, including despatch and hygiene. Maurice characterized the best aspects of traditional working-class values. He was the union representative and became mayor of North Tyneside. He did not enjoy the best of health but he always found the time to make sure Alison had rolls to go with the soup she served and whatever else he could legitimately find to help her menu planning. Like Alison, the only question he asked of those who came to the People's Kitchen was 'How can I help?'

At first, the Trust's work was focused mainly on the north-east but it steadily spread to every region where we operated, with money distributed through regional charity committees, which also organized untold good deeds, volunteers, donations of cakes and products, assistance with raffles, and general help to communities. As it got busier and busier, the Trust also took on a full-time administrator Jenny Wagstaff and a part-time professional adviser Terence Finlay. My daughters Fiona and Felicity also became trustees and some years later, two more trustees were recruited from the independent charitable sector.

Apart from the major funding the company provided to the Trust, it also made increasingly significant contributions to local communities. The Breakfast Clubs provide free breakfasts to many schools in the most socially deprived areas. Greggs' support for them began after Mike Darrington went on a Business in the Community visit in 1999: he and other business heads were taken round various projects to make them aware of needs. The projects included the Breakfast Club in West Walker Primary School, Newcastle, set up by Norma Redfern, the school's head teacher, who was always looking for ways to improve the lives and attainments of the children and their parents. The Breakfast Club was designed to ensure that any child could have a decent breakfast. In some cases, the meals they had at school might be the only proper food they had all day.

Mike Darrington was bowled over by what he saw at

West Walker and immediately said to Norma that Greggs would sponsor it for at least two years – in 2013, we still sponsor them. He went back to the office extolling the virtues of Norma's Breakfast Club – 'I've just seen the most fantastic opportunity to help disadvantaged youngsters in their formative years, and we're going to do something about it.' Lynn Matthews and Richard Hutton, who became the finance director in 2006, were very involved at the initial stage, while Norma helped and encouraged us.

Breakfast Clubs have grown steadily in both numbers and influence and are a key part of Greggs' contribution to local communities. Any profits or royalties in respect of this book, earned by the company or author, will be donated towards opening new Breakfast Clubs.

11

IVORY TOWER AND PASTY TAX

Pasty

Greggs makes several types of pasty, most of which are oblong shaped. This major break from tradition came about for two reasons: an oblong shape is more convenient to eat and it does not involve the waste of pastry incurred when cutting out circles of pastry

Although the recession had ended in 1982, unemployment continued to rise and was over three million by 1984. The miners' strike which started in March of that year continued for more than twelve months, badly affecting the north of England where Greggs' businesses were located. Tensions caused by the Thatcher reforms were high throughout the country and reached boiling point in July 1985 with the Brixton riots.

The Thatcher government evidently did not feel

that the miners' strike, political uncertainty, high unemployment and social unrest were a sufficient test for our new managing director, and in March 1984, Chancellor Nigel Lawson introduced an amendment to extend VAT to all hot food, and specifically included pies and pasties. Via the National Association of Master Bakers, Greggs argued vehemently that pies and pasties that had been freshly baked and not kept hot in a heated cabinet should continue to be zero-rated. Hot food served in cafés and restaurants, or through other outlets, had long been liable for VAT, but bakery products were exempt. Greggs accepted that soup, tea and coffee, bacon, sausage and any other products kept hot so that they could be sold hot in our shops were liable to VAT, but freshly baked products were sold to the customer at the temperature they happened to be, which might be hot, warm or cool, depending on supply and demand. Much debate took place about the impracticality of deciding whether a savoury was hot or not. Were Greggs expected to record the temperature of every pie and pasty sold?

A four-year battle took place. Each of Greggs' businesses received numerous visits from local tax inspectors, and large files of correspondence, legal opinion, argument and counter-argument built up. Eventually the issue was decided through legal process right up to the Court of Appeal. It focused on Pimbletts, a small pie business in Liverpool. Citing Chancellor Nigel Lawson's answer to a question in the House of Commons that bread and pies 'which are sold warm because they have to be freshly baked, and not to enable them to be consumed while hot, are outside the scope of the standard rate of VAT announced in the budget', the

Court of Appeal ruled in our favour and Greggs heaved a long sigh of relief.

Our carefully laid plan that I should maintain a low profile after Mike had taken the reins of the company was blown out of the water when, in February 1984, I was chosen as the first North-east Businessman of the Year. The event was sponsored by the *Newcastle Journal*, which ensured that the award received maximum possible publicity in the region. As if that was not enough, Mike had to deal with the domestic upheaval of moving house and relocating his family, including a spell living in temporary rented accommodation. It is not surprising that his first year was difficult and challenging. In business, as in politics, a week can be a long time and a year an eternity.

Nonetheless, whatever the problems we faced both of us remained firm in our resolve to make it work. I supported Mike as much as I could, and gradually his strength and ability came through, with his obvious enjoyment of driving the business. Others soon came to learn that he had the same passion for the excellence of the product that we'd always had, and the same commitment to the values at the heart of Greggs. They also recognized that, if we were to consolidate and move forward with sound systems and structures, his management and business expertise were invaluable, and when it came to financial management, accounting and budgeting, he was both numerate and astute. He was more cautious and prudent than I had been, particularly in respect to budgeting. I had been happy to fail gloriously in the pursuit of ultra-challenging budgets while Mike tended to shape them in the light of more realistic, if still stretching, aspirations.

In practice, he and Malcolm Simpson developed a sensitive and remarkably accurate budgeting process over the years, allowing each business to develop its own plans, but introducing an adjustment at group level referred to as 'conservatism', which reflected what they considered to be a realistic outcome. This allowed local ambition and ownership to continue, but ensured that the overall group budget was not too ambitious.

Over the months, we learned a lot about each other. The most important thing I discovered about Mike was that evolution, not revolution, would be his approach to major decisions and strategies. He believed in changing things gradually. He took longer to reach decisions than I had, whether about structure, major projects, products or people; I had always been eager to move forward as quickly as possible. So was Mike, but not before he had checked it from every angle first and, if possible, trialled it in part of the business. Our structure at that time of four separate autonomous businesses lent itself to this process. An idea could be trialled in one business and possibly compared with a different idea in another and, in the case of new or changed products, these could be tested in a small group of shops, then extended to a larger group, before being rolled out over the whole of that business. From time to time this evolutionary approach stretched the patience of our more impetuous senior managers, but it was a strategy that paid great dividends, and achieved steady and consistent growth.

I felt I was a valuable sounding board for Mike, particularly in his early days with the company. He felt able to discuss with me any major or minor issue, decision or direction that he was considering. There was complete trust between us from the beginning, and that remained true throughout our working life together. We remained very conscious of the risk of my interfering and getting directly involved in executive decisions, and in those early days, before he had established his credibility in the business, Mike was naturally concerned about it. I would not have been surprised if he had wanted to keep me away from too much direct contact with the bakeries, shops and people, but he knew how much I missed this direct involvement, so he encouraged me to spend time in the businesses, with the people and tasting the products. This meant I was happier, they were pleased to see me, and Mike trusted me not to get involved in discussing or commenting upon the decisions he made. I justified his trust. Managers soon learned that my visits were largely designed to keep me up to date with the business at shop-floor level, and that I would not be drawn into executive decisions, which I always referred back to Mike. Being up to date with what was happening on the ground also made me a better sounding board for him.

This was not enough to keep me occupied, though. I needed something to replace my strategic role, preferably something that required me to be out and about in the business, and we decided that I would be the best person to send into any new business that Greggs acquired. This was work I would enjoy and could do well, and we did not have long to wait before I could be tested in this role.

We had already announced in our share-offer prospectus that we were hoping to expand into the midlands or the south of England. At the time, we had already started tentative negotiations with Braggs Bakers in Birmingham. When Mike and I looked at the

Braggs shops, we could see how busy they were and that there was virtually no competition. The products were good too, and we soon realized that it would be a useful acquisition.

Charles Bragg had started the business in 1931 and expanded it steadily in the Birmingham area around his bakery at Alum Rock Road. His sons, Michael and John, had taken over from their father in 1965 and continued to expand the business until it had twenty shops and a substantial wholesale business, in particular with Sainsbury's in the midlands.

Michael was concerned that the rise of the supermarkets would lead to the demise of small bakery shops and had assigned his wife Meredith to the task of developing the wholesale business. Some years before, Michael's training at Borough Polytechnic in London's Elephant and Castle had been punctuated by sailing boats across the Atlantic and Pacific to Australia. This was in the early 1950s, before the world had been shrunk by jets, modern travel, package holidays and the Internet. At that time it had been a remarkable thing for a twenty-year-old to embark upon. He met Meredith in Australia, they fell in love and he sailed back with her. Somehow he had managed to settle down to running the business, though he and Meredith remained great sailors whenever the opportunity arose.

With his brother John, Michael had worked hard for thirty years to prepare the company for the challenges of the twenty-first century. They had tried many initiatives – extending and improving the product range, installing shop ovens to bake-off savouries, developing sandwiches and takeaway, refitting shops in a new livery – but although the business had made some progress, nothing delivered the quantum improvement they were seeking, or the level of profitability that would have allowed them to compete with the supermarkets or even rival other bakery businesses, such as Greggs or Birds of Derby.

This worried Michael, his main concerns being how the business would survive in the future and what would happen to the staff with whom he had worked for so many years. His three children all had successful careers elsewhere and did not want to come into the business. By 1984, John had retired, and Michael was already at an advanced stage of negotiation with three new senior managers. This strengthening of the management team was Michael's latest and most significant attempt to secure the future of the business and provide it with long-term management succession. He believed the new structure would provide that, but he could not be sure. Greggs could offer that additional element of certainty – or so we argued in our long negotiations with him. Michael, eventually, accepted this. We completed negotiations in 1984 and bought 90 per cent of the business for £810,000 with options in place to acquire the remaining 10 per cent.

This was the situation that Greggs inherited in Birmingham and I was charged with helping to integrate Braggs into Greggs, the easiest job I have ever had to do. I did not have to worry about the rest of Greggs. I could go to Birmingham for two or three days a week and work with Michael on introducing things that would make a difference to the company and bring Braggs into line with Greggs' methods and values.

The shops were well located in a tight cluster around the bakery, the products were excellent – at least as good as in the other Greggs' businesses – and the employees were loyal and enthusiastic. The bakery and equipment were old, but well maintained, and Michael and Meredith were liked and respected throughout the business. It required just a few changes, which I could implement with the confidence of knowing they had worked elsewhere. The shops were given mini refits to bring them into line with the Greggs specification but retained the Braggs name, which carried an excellent reputation for quality. We gave more prominence to bake-off and sandwiches, and less to cooked meats and delicatessen. We introduced more aggressive pricing and special offers, and brought in profit-sharing and share options. Within twelve months, the local team had gained the necessary confidence to develop the business and open a series of new shops, for which there were huge opportunities in the greater Birmingham area.

It was a pleasure to see the Greggs formula work so well and so quickly, and I enjoyed my time with Michael, Meredith and their management team. The three new managers – Horace Bennett, Steve Emery and Ian Pegg – were kept on after the takeover, made major contributions to the Braggs' business, and developed successful careers within Greggs. I was really sorry when my involvement came to an end and concerned about what might replace it, but I need not have worried: Mike Darrington and Malcolm Simpson were already in the process of making another acquisition, this time in South Wales.

The Merretts' business in Cardiff, part of Allied Bakeries, was looking to dispose of its shops, which did not fit well with the wholesale business, supermarkets and major retailers that dominated Allied Bakeries. The twenty-six shops had suffered from neglect and lack of investment and were no longer profitable. In 1985 Greggs acquired them for £775,000.

Mike and Malcolm spent a lot of time on potential and actual acquisitions, and Mike took a particularly hard-nosed approach on price. Nothing could be overlooked: the deal had to offer good value to Greggs and, unless he was completely satisfied on all counts, he was prepared to see deals go away. Mountstevens, a family business with a large bakery and shops in Bristol, would have fitted well into Greggs, but the deal came to nothing because Mike refused to pay more than he considered appropriate. In the end the company went broke.

We made Taylors of Cannock, in the west Midlands, a good offer, because it would have been a good fit with Braggs, but were told, 'We're not interested in selling.' However, they weren't making any money. The earlier generations who'd set up the business had bought a lot of freeholds and Taylors was now surviving by selling them. They also went broke.

Similarly lengthy negotiations had taken place over the Braggs business and at one stage had been broken off for several months because of a failure to get anywhere near what Mike believed was the right price. The gap was eventually bridged, but only after Braggs had satisfied certain conditions, and the expectations of both sides had been conditioned by a period of attrition. The negotiations for Merretts shops had also taken several months and involved some bruising exchanges with the accountants from Allied Bakeries. In the end, the fact that no other companies were looking for loss-making or marginally profitable chains of retail shops strengthened Greggs' position.

The Merretts deal was only for the shops, not the bakery. As Greggs had no bakery in South Wales, and Birmingham was too far away and, in any event, did not have enough spare capacity, the best short-term option was a supply contract with the Merretts bakery until we had established our own production facilities. This was not ideal, since products made for the wholesale market are not always suitable for retail shops, and if there were breakdowns or supply problems, Tesco and other major supermarkets would understandably be given priority over Greggs. The pressure was on for the property department and the local agents to find a suitable site for a new Greggs bakery in South Wales, and they duly did so by locating an existing building on a large industrial estate on the outskirts of Cardiff near the river Taff. The Treforest Industrial Estate was being revitalized and redeveloped by the Welsh Development Agency, which was a great help to Greggs, securing the site quickly and providing grants towards refurbishing the building, which offered good-quality production capacity at great value for money. The building has since been extended and remains the production and distribution centre for 170 shops in Wales and the south-west.

The Merretts acquisition proved a much more difficult proposition than Braggs, where Greggs had inherited an experienced management team and all the sound traditions of a family business. In the main, the product range was designed for long life and supply to the supermarkets. The shops were generally run-down and a bakery had to be developed from scratch, but there were pluses too. The shop staff were great and, led by inherited area managers Jenny Pelosi and Pat Jenkins, all responded to the challenges we set them.

In 1986 the new bakery started production under the management of Steve Tune, who had joined from Sayers of Liverpool. A programme of shop refits began, under the new trading name of Greggs of Treforest, and we made considerable progress. We were continually looking for special local products that would draw attention to our presence and attract new customers. Welsh cakes – similar to a griddle scone – seemed a possibility and we put on a competition for the best recipe; it was won by Mrs Williams of Pontypridd and resulted in a substantial increase in sales.

Not all local products proved equally attractive, as far as I was concerned. I had heard of laver bread and was told it was made from seaweed, rich in protein and vitamins and sometimes described as 'Welshman's caviar'. I searched bakers' shops and supermarkets without finding any, becoming more convinced with each abortive search that laver bread had been dropped from the Welsh menu, just as the stotty cake had been on Tyneside, and that it offered huge revival potential . . . if only I could find some. I eventually tracked it down on a breakfast menu, served with bacon and eggs, in a greasy-spoon café. I eagerly ordered it and sat there in a fever of anticipation until my plate arrived. To say that I was disappointed would be a considerable under-statement. Gelatinous and smelling like a dirty fishing harbour on a hot day, laver bread ranks among my most disappointing gastronomic experiences.

Even with all the improvements we introduced to

■ WELSH CAKES ■

8oz/220g self-raising flour
2oz/55g cold butter, cut into small pieces
3oz/85g caster sugar
2oz/55g currants

½ tsp mixed spice (optional)
1 egg, beaten
1 tbsp milk
butter to grease pan

1   In a large mixing bowl, combine the flour and butter, and rub the butter into the flour until the mixture resembles breadcrumbs. Add the sugar, dried fruit, spice if you are using it, and then the beaten egg. Mix to combine and tip onto a floured surface. Knead gently to form a ball, using a splash of milk if needed.

2   Roll out the dough until it is ⅖in/1cm thick and cut into rounds with a 3in/8cm cutter.

3   Grease a griddle or heavy-bottomed frying pan with butter and wipe the excess away. Place over a direct heat, and when hot place the Welsh cakes on the griddle or pan. Cook for about 2–3 minutes each side, turning once. Each side needs to be caramel brown before turning.

4   Remove from the pan and dust with caster sugar. Eat with butter while still warm.

Merretts, the transformation in profitability did not happen as quickly as we had forecast. Thankfully, because the other five businesses were all progressing well, this did not have the impact that under-performance in Glasgow and Manchester had inflicted during the 1970s, but it was not until Steve Smith, one of John Thomas's protégés from Hagenbachs, took over several years later that the South Wales business really moved forward. Steve was young, ambitious, thorough, and had been extremely successful in his position as sales director of the Thurston business in Yorkshire. He knew how to drive sales and, as part of the small senior management team, had picked up enough knowledge of production and accounting to make him confident that he was ready for a general management position.

It is interesting to reflect on whether Braggs, at a total cost of around £1 million, or Merretts, at £775,000, provided better value for money. Merretts had more shops (twenty-six versus twenty) and gave us the opportunity of building a bakery and appointing a management team that matched Greggs' aspirations for Wales and the south-west. Braggs was a soundly managed business with a bakery, excellent products and a good reputation. It was lower risk, more easily integrated into Greggs, moved into profitability more quickly and delivered better value for money. However, both acquisitions provided cost-effective entry into major new geographical regions and provided platforms for significant contributions to growth and profitability over the next twenty-five years.

By 1986, despite the disappointing profit progress in the Welsh business, growth across the whole of Greggs was excellent. Mike Darrington was now in his third year and well established throughout the company, the industry and the City. The business had moved forward and become stronger; we had negotiated two acquisitions and the Greggs formula was working in both, to particularly good effect in the case of Braggs.

12

THANKS TO THE EARL
Egg mayo

Greggs shops make 2 million sandwiches every day. A gastronomic moment not to be rushed, whether they form part of a leisurely family picnic or a short well-earned break at the office, or sustenance on a day's walking or fishing

With Braggs and Merretts (now Greggs of Treforest) both inducted into the Greggs' way of doing things, I found that there was not enough to occupy the four days a week I was contracted to work for the company. I had already enrolled in an Open University arts foundation course in which I could start to explore art, architecture, music, literature, religion and philosophy. This required about twelve hours a week of my time, which nicely filled in the free day I had created. I was enjoying doing it, receiving high grades for my assignments, and expected this pattern of four days' work and one day's culture to last for many years to come. So, what to fill those four days with? Answer: sandwiches.

Greggs had been slow to move seriously into the sandwich business. In the early seventies when that market was starting to take off, I had been reluctant to follow suit in case it detracted from Greggs' strong lunchtime savoury business. By the late seventies sandwiches were being sold in all Greggs' shops, but they were still overshadowed by the savouries. Each of the six businesses had developed its own sandwich range and recipes without any major resource or direction from the centre and, although our sandwich sales were growing, it appeared that some of our competitors were selling more.

We decided to appoint Jane Milton as our sandwich development manager. She was from Scotland, in her twenties and passionate about food, and I was charged to work with her and produce a plan for the business. We were to review the market, the range Greggs offered, recipes, specifications, costings, production methods and marketing strategies. This was a big and interesting challenge, which lasted for the best part of a year, during which we ate our way through countless sandwiches, looked at production equipment, trialled storage and display systems, considered (and quickly dismissed) central production and looked at the implications for shop layout.

Eventually we produced a full report on the exercise and on how Greggs should move forward. Mike Darrington had thought that, as well as keeping me usefully engaged, the founder's stamp on the project would give it a better chance of achieving uniformity across the business, but that wasn't to be. Official copies of the sandwich report soon found their way to the back of shelves or into drawers to gather dust alongside the Peebles Plan. However, the exercise had moved sandwiches up the agenda in each business. All six had had some involvement in the process and they set about applying their interpretation of what they had learned. Most, like Steve Smith at Thurston's, revamped their entire range and enjoyed significantly increased sales as a result.

After those slow, uncertain beginnings, for a period of almost twenty years, from the mid-eighties to the mid-noughties, sandwiches were at the heart of Greggs' growth and increases in profitability. Little had the Earl of Sandwich known, when he accidentally invented the sandwich so that he could spend more time working, what an opportunity he was creating for Greggs!

Whether the earl ate his sandwich so that he could spend longer on his admiralty and political business or at the gaming tables, it is unlikely he gave it proper attention. It would have been, as it still is today, a gobbled, unappreciated 'put-off' to the next proper meal. What a missed opportunity! A sandwich can be a gastronomic moment not to be rushed, whether part of a leisurely family picnic, a short break at the office, or sustenance on a day's walking or fishing.

My fishing and writing hero Chris Yates takes cake with him to guarantee a memorable day, regardless of whether the fish are biting. Salmon fishers take a bottle of good malt whisky. I take a sandwich. Egg mayonnaise is my favourite – one fresh egg boiled for about seven minutes, the yolk just firm but not dry, coarsely chopped with a little creamy mayonnaise, fresh, soft bread. Perfect, with a cup of tea, while you're waiting for a kingfisher. Even more delicious, if you're making it at home or the office, after boiling the egg don't chill it and enjoy the filling slightly warm.

Until the mid-eighties, Greggs' business had been developing and expanding in the context of a declining market. Bread and confectionery sales contracted steadily during this period. Although the consumption of brown and wholemeal bread has remained relatively steady, at around 150 grams per person per week, the weekly consumption of all bread had fallen from 1,752 grams per head in 1945, to 1,080 in 1970 and 882 in 1980. The decline has continued: the figure for 2009 was 590 and bread now accounts for only three per cent of household food expenditure, compared to eight per cent in 1945.

Unsurprisingly, the number of independent bakers' shops has shown a similar decline. In recent years, some commentators have attributed this decline to

Greggs' successful expansion, but I don't believe this is the case. The trend had begun long before Greggs started to expand and is primarily due to three factors: the decline in overall bread (and confectionery) consumption, the huge expansion of the supermarkets, and the failure of many independent bakers to adapt to the changes in market and consumer requirements. Those businesses that did adapt – Birds of Derby, Greenhalghs in Lancashire and many others in different parts of the country – have flourished, as have a number of small artisan bakeries focusing on producing premium-quality fresh bread and confectionery. The latter businesses are enjoying a healthy revival, the desire for real bread touching the same chords as the revival of real ale. In fact, there are many parallels between the two industries, from the destruction of quality and individuality through automation from 1960 onwards, to the current rejection of mass-produced products and the search for individual, local, flavoursome alternatives. Both industries love yeast, which helps them to make best use of their favourite and most profitable ingredients: air and water!

There were various factors behind the decline in bread consumption, some of them own-goals for the industry, but the growth of the convenient sliced and wrapped loaf was at the heart of it. During the 1930s in America, it enjoyed a meteoric rise to form 80 per cent of all bread sales, but in Britain this phenomenon occurred much later. For economic reasons, slicing and wrapping was banned during the Second World War and did not resume until 1950.

In 1961 the Chorleywood process introduced

high-speed mixing of dough and removed the need for the lengthy bulk fermentation that imparts so much flavour and texture to bread. It dramatically shortened production time, with a loaf being produced from scratch, mixed, baked, sliced and wrapped ready for despatch, in little more than three hours. In addition to the traditional flour, water, yeast and salt, the Chorleywood process required the addition of ascorbic acid, emulsifiers and enzymes to increase the softness of the bread and extend its shelf life.

In large plant bakeries, the dough was easier to handle and the process allowed more (cheaper) home-grown wheat and a greater quantity of water to be used. Within fifteen years, 75 per cent of the bread sold in the UK was made in this way and most of it was sliced and wrapped. Mass production and focus on profit margin, driven very much by the supermarkets using sliced bread as a loss leader, resulted in poorer quality. In addition, product ranges were rationalized and reduced, limiting choice, and the industry was slow to promote the excellent nutritional value of good bread, allowing articles about its harmful effects on health and obesity to run unchallenged. People were becoming more health conscious, eating more fruit and vegetables. Standards of living were rising, and meat and fish became more affordable. People travelled abroad and tasted food from other countries, and if they didn't, they could see it on television. Our former staple diet of bread and potatoes was seriously challenged, but the bread industry did not respond to that for almost a quarter of a century.

In addition to a whole-market decline, the share enjoyed by bakery shops also dwindled, as the super-

markets focused on bread and other daily fresh purchases to attract more customers more often into
their stores. They did this using both quality and
price, producing good-quality fresh bread and confectionery from in-store bakeries and cutting prices,
particularly of the standard sliced loaf, to cost or below.
This was possible on a tiny part of their product range
if it brought in customers who then purchased other
foods, including an increasing proportion of higher
margin non-food items. In the late seventies, Greggs
had tried to compete in the sliced-bread price war, but
had gradually withdrawn. Mike Darrington was
adamant that Greggs should not become a 'busy fool',
and should focus on freshness, quality and convenience,
which were all important criteria for developing a
sandwich business.

Against this background, the year-on-year growth
in the sandwich business from the mid-1980s onwards
was hugely important to Greggs. It is not easy to
see where all these consumers appeared – and kept
appearing – from, but it seems to have been from a
variety of sources. The number of people sitting down to
lunches in canteens, restaurants and pubs decreased
steadily under several pressures. Some companies
introduced policies forbidding alcohol at lunchtime, and
for an increasing number of people, a large evening
meal was becoming the norm. Two big meals a day
was excessive and unhealthy. Work pressures were
increasing, and there wasn't time to sit down for a full
meal at lunchtime: it became much easier to grab a
sandwich, which was better value and, with a bottle of
water or fruit juice, quick, nourishing and healthy.
Rising living standards and time pressures also meant

that many people did not have a chance to make up a sandwich box during the morning rush when there were so many other things to do, including getting the kids to school.

These were some of the factors that drove the market forward, encouraging the sandwich producers and retailers to put more resources into developing new and better products. New entrants to the market included the supermarkets (both in the large stores and in their mini versions) and major chains such as Marks & Spencer, Boots and WHSmith, resulting in more and better sandwiches under the customers' noses wherever they went. This virtuous circle, an apparently un-stoppable merry-go-round of growth, continued for more than twenty years.

Greggs was ideally placed to participate in this growth. We could produce special bread and rolls fresh every day in our expanding number of strategically placed bakeries, close to the major conurbations where our shops were located. This provided an immediate advantage over our competitors of freshness, extended even further by making the sandwiches from scratch in each shop every day, and not just once but several times, in small batches, to guarantee peak freshness. Our shops were conveniently located in shopping centres and on high streets, close to where people worked. The continued support of our ever-growing number of customers is the only seal of approval we need, though it was gratifying to see our success recognized by our peers when, in 2012, Greggs was chosen as Sandwich Retailer of the Year by the British Sandwich Association at its annual award ceremony, 'The Sammies'.

So, thanks again to the earl, for creating this golden opportunity for Greggs and providing me with an interesting project that helped to move forward sandwich development in Greggs and, for a while, kept me out of my ivory tower.

13

BUILDING THE FUTURE
Oval bite

In the late 1980s Greggs developed several special large rolls such as the Oval Bite and the Whopper. The oval bite was developed in Glasgow, is made with a variety of fillings and is Greggs' bestselling sandwich

During the ten-year period from 1984 to 1994, Greggs' profit had increased six-fold from around £2 million to £12 million; the share price also increased by approximately 600 per cent. Greggs was now fully established as a reliable, successful, professionally managed public company with excellent growth potential. This was achieved by a continuing high level of expenditure on shops and bakeries, prudent acquisitions, strengthening of the management team, and the encouragement of an ethos of ownership and mutual responsibility among our employees. Mike Darrington was very much at the helm throughout this period and, with the sandwich project completed and my own essential involvement in the company reduced to non-executive chairman, I was eager to find more hands-on activities to interest me.

At that point, just at the right moment and completely out of the blue, I received a proposal that could not have been better tailored to my interests if I'd come up with it myself. I had been a keen angler for as long as I could remember and, for the past fifteen years, particularly interested in salmon fishing on the river Tweed. I kept pestering the Tweed commissioners, who managed the river, asking them why they were doing certain things and not others. I was keenly interested in all aspects of conservation and frequently argued with their responses.

Eventually their chairman, Bill Thompson, asked me to go and see him in his offices in Edinburgh. His approach was straightforward: 'If you think you know so ****ing much about it and have so many ideas, why don't you take over from me?' To a non-establishment figure in a region that contained more dukes and earls per square mile than practically anywhere else, I was taken aback. Could this be an opportunity to engage in a second career, which might build on my childhood passion for nature? Even though my education and career had provided no opportunity to nurture or expand it, my passion had never diminished, but to take it on would mean giving up, at least for the time being, my study of the arts, which I was enjoying.

I was still living at Tweed Cottage, near Melrose in the Scottish Borders, right next to the river. Bill told me that the position was voluntary and, he claimed, not too onerous, requiring no more than the day a week I had made free. It took only a few moments' thought before I had decided to go for it, and embarked on an adventure that has lasted twenty-five years and still continues. That position and those that followed were, as Bill had promised, voluntary and unpaid, but they definitely exceeded a day a week! From that moment on, about half of my working week and energies were given over to the conservation of rivers and the countryside, which meant that, even though my enthusiasm for, and commitment to, the success of Greggs remained undiminished, the company would no longer have my services for the planned four days per week.

That might have been impossible had Mike Darrington not settled down so well in his role but, as it was, a reduction in my input would merely provide more room for Mike and others within the company to develop. As long as I was available as a sounding board, visited each of the businesses to reinforce personal interest and maintain the family connection, and chaired board meetings, Mike was happy and enjoyed driving the business. There was still plenty for him to do.

In 1989 Greggs acquired five shops under the name of Flour Power in Edinburgh, with a small bakery that supplied the scones, morning goods, cream cakes and other products where freshness was critical. We already had shops in Edinburgh, which had been supplied from the Glasgow bakery but would now benefit from this extra freshness. Once Greggs had a local production facility there, we were able to exploit many other local trading positions in and around Edinburgh. This business had its own management team, providing a development opportunity for up-and-coming managers. Six years later we built a small new bakery.

In addition to expanding retail bakery shops, we wanted to widen Greggs' activities into other areas, including wholesale food manufacturing. We made several approaches to the Jolly Baker, a cake and pastry wholesaler with a strong jam-tart business. We also had serious negotiations with a supplier of salads to major retailers, and talks with a wholesale frozen-gâteaux manufacturer reached an advanced stage.

The owner had obtained a series of large government grants to build and equip the factory. The gâteaux were delicious and it was a very modern and efficient plant, so it would have been a good purchase at the right price: we could have taken the gâteaux, chilled them and sold them fresh in our shops. However, it was a new company, the owner was a flamboyant, strong-minded and erratic entrepreneur, a loose cannon who would have been very difficult to manage, and there was a sizeable question mark over the company's finances.

We were almost at the final hurdle in our negotiations to take over the business when a serious disagreement led to the termination of discussions. Not without some relief, Mike set off for his annual holiday. A week later he was sitting on a balcony in the South of France with a gin and tonic in his hand, reflecting on how much more difficult life might have been had the acquisition proceeded, when the telephone rang. Malcolm Simpson was at the other end of the line, proudly reporting that he and the Greggs advisers had now gained concessions on the outstanding points and rescued the deal.

After a few moments' thought, abandoning his

normal democratic and consultative approach, Mike thanked Malcolm for his efforts, but said, 'I'm sitting in the sunshine, enjoying my gin and tonic, and the thought of having to manage that business and deal with that man is putting me right off. We've had a lucky let-off. The answer is definitely no.' It is a good example of Lesson Number Six in practice.

Whether by good luck or good management, none of the potential deals had come to fruition. They would all have required a significant investment of resources, and without them, Greggs was able to keep its powder dry for the moment, which came soon afterwards, when a major opportunity presented itself. Mike and Malcolm revelled in the excitement that such negotiations provided, but the determining factor was always Mike's insistence on value for money and a good return. It was also important that any exciting new opportunities did not deprive the existing business of its steady and substantial requirement for capital. On average, we were opening fifty new shops a year at an annual cost of £5 million. A similar amount was being spent on extending, upgrading and refurbishing existing shops, and there were always new vehicles, computers and other miscellaneous requirements to fund. Total capital expenditure during this period averaged more than £20 million per year between 1984 and 1994; much more in later years.

The high level of capital expenditure was largely due to Greggs being both a manufacturer, needing to invest in modern bakeries and production equipment, and a retailer, requiring constant investment to keep shop premises modern and attractive. We had started primarily as a bakery business but over the years had increasingly become a retail concern, with manufacturing facilities to support it.

This became apparent in the bakeries, where more and more space was given to the storage of sandwich ingredients and drinks, and to despatch areas, but although the manufacturing area was reduced, it was still considered essential to Greggs. Other takeaway sandwich and coffee-shop businesses, such as Subway, Pret A Manger, McDonald's and Starbucks, function without central manufacturing premises and have to buy important parts of their product range, particularly bread, rolls and cakes, from suppliers who are often located long distances from the point of sale, possibly compromising both cost and freshness. Greggs' bakery heritage gave us a real and important marketing advantage, enabling us to set our own high standards for quality and freshness. This delivered benefits across all product ranges but was particularly relevant to the sandwich business in supplying our shops with fresh, high-quality bespoke bread and rolls.

The Scottish business, under Ken Middleton, brought in Peter Rossi as sales director in 1988. Peter was of Italian extraction, thoughtful, enthusiastic and with a twinkle in his eye. He knew the food market and Glasgow well, having successfully managed the family pizza business. Under Ken and Peter, Scotland started to make real strides forward by developing new sandwich products, giving Greggs a major boost in this important market. Until now our sandwiches had been largely in wedge format, made from sliced bread, with some standard-sized bread rolls. All this was changed with the introduction of the 'Big Softie', a large, soft roll that achieved huge sales from day one. It was followed in Newcastle and the north-east by the 'Whopper', a very large roll that we continued to produce after surviving a legal challenge from Burger King, which claimed it had copyright in the name. The products were individual and focused on the Greggs' bakery heritage. We were able to produce bespoke products, fresh each day for our sandwiches, setting us apart from our competitors, who were more reliant on the standard sliced loaf made the day before in a distant wholesale bakery.

The most notable example of our competitive edge was the 'Oval Bite', introduced in Scotland under Alison Lawson, the local sandwich development manager. That roll, filled with chargrilled chicken and salad in a honey and mustard mayonnaise, was a real game-changer. It was almost 50 per cent more expensive than the average sandwich at that time and its introduction was famously challenged by the now retail director, Raymond Reynolds: 'It's fifty per cent more expensive than any of our existing sandwiches,' he said. 'Our customers will never buy that.'

Alison was energetic and confident and wasn't going to be deflected. 'It's full of fresh chargrilled chicken, a delicious honey and mustard mayonnaise, in a super-large new roll. It's different and worth every penny!'

Raymond reluctantly agreed a limited trial. At eleven a.m. on the launch day, Alison called Raymond: 'The trial shops have all sold out,' she said. 'What did I tell you?' Fresh supplies were produced and it kept on selling at treble the rate of the previous best-seller. A sandwich star had been born! Today Greggs sells an average of 290,000 Oval Bites per week, with a variety of toppings and fillings.

In the midst of all this activity and development, concern continued about how Greggs could develop more uniformity and similarity between the businesses and improve quality, while at the same time preserving the essential elements of ownership and autonomy that were such powerful motivators. While managing all the change that had been taking place, Mike Darrington was also building a structure that would allow Greggs to develop and expand. The management board was the key to this. Each of the six Greggs' businesses operated as an autonomous division with its own management structure, product range and profit-sharing; Braggs in the midlands and Thurston's in Yorkshire were still trading under their old names. Somehow they needed to be managed as part of a cohesive whole. Accounting systems were standard and consistent throughout the company, as were (with the odd historical exception) pay rates and conditions. Items of major capital expenditure had to be approved at the centre, which provided some checks and balances, but there were many areas, in particular product range, product development and pricing, where the local divisional managing directors could head off in their own directions. In other key areas, such as shop-fitting, there were manuals but they were looked upon as advisory rather than mandatory.

The combination of freedom and strong independent local management nurtured the ethos of ownership, commitment and hard work that had been at the heart of Greggs' growth, but unless we could establish a touch on the tiller that was strong enough to secure sufficient consistency, it might also prove a recipe for un-manageable chaos. One way of avoiding this was to spend plenty of time with senior managers, both at the centre and out in the businesses, discussing plans and priorities, always being available to help with a decision and generally trying to nudge people in the preferred direction. Despite the administrative and other pressures of an expanding public company, Mike Darrington liked that close personal contact and always made time for it, but he needed more, and the management board was the mechanism he chose.

When the business had been smaller, just two or three divisions, I had appointed the senior managers at the centre and the divisional managing directors to the main board. This became unwieldy as the business grew, the number of senior managers increased and the local managing directors had local priorities, which might be more important to them than the general priorities of the whole company.

The board (known as the main board in Greggs to distinguish it from the management board) played a vital, behind-the-scenes role, approving major decisions, revenue budgets and capital expenditure. From time to time measures were taken to strengthen this important function. In 1992 Sonia Elkin was appointed. Sonia had been Confederation of British Industry (CBI) Director for the regions and smaller firms in which capacity she had met Mike Darrington on several occasions. He recommended that she join the board, on which she served for the next ten years with great enthusiasm and feistiness. Following her retirement she became Chairman of the Trustees of the Management Pension Scheme. She made a major contribution, not least helping to steer the Pension Fund through a period in which many pension funds experienced great problems.

From 1968–1995 the secretarial functions of the

main board were carried out by Neil Calvert. At every stage, in particular in the going public process, Neil provided impeccable service to the board and there was great concern about his retirement and how to replace his skills and experience. We need not have worried. He had trained his understudy well and Andrew Davison seamlessly filled the role and navigated the company without fault for the next fifteen years through whatever legal and corporate governance problems it faced. Tragically Neil died from cancer after a year of retirement.

The main board directors were expected to think strategically on behalf of the whole company and took the really big decisions or ratified them. The management board had no legal status and focused more on operational matters, going into subjects and issues in detail, finding workable solutions, then advising the main board. The management board kept everyone moving in the same direction and, even though at that stage we were still operating under different names, if you went to a Thurston's or a Braggs, you could see it was very similar to Greggs, with similar shop design, colours and layouts, similar products and value-for-money offers.

Developing the importance of the management board was significant for a number of reasons. It provided a meaningful role and status for the growing number of senior managers now that a main board appointment was no longer a possibility and, most importantly, it helped to bring some uniformity and consistency to the company by involving senior managers in decisions and, in a sense, conditioning them.

Meetings of the management board were held

regularly (about every six weeks) and often lasted for more than a day. They covered every major decision and issue the company faced: expansion strategy, management structure, product range, wage increases, shop design – the list was endless. Management board meetings were not always popular, on account of the often long and turgid debates that took place, frequently involving quite arcane detail, taxing the patience of some. If the subject under review was technical, it might also leave those without the relevant expertise twiddling their thumbs while their fellows debated the fine detail. On one such occasion Ken Middleton, never lost for a sarcastic observation, had noted that one member had not opened his mouth since he sat down two hours previously: 'I don't think So-and-so should even be in this meeting,' he said. 'He's just using up badly needed oxygen.'

The one thing that most senior managers would have been keen to learn about (not unnaturally) was overall company profitability, but that was not on the agenda because of the stock exchange rules on confidentiality. Local management knew the profitability of their own business but not of the whole company. No doubt some might have had an idea of how other local businesses were trading but, even if they had all compared notes, their calculations would not have taken into account costs and provisions at the centre, of which only Mike Darrington and Malcolm Simpson were aware. Unpopular as they might sometimes have been, those meetings played a key role in the management of Greggs for more than twenty years.

In 1989, with three other executives, Horace Bennett, Neill Hastie and Brian Wildblood, Mike

Darrington set off on a grand tour of Europe including France, Holland, Spain and Italy, visiting the very best bakeries and associated retail businesses with a view to ascertaining the main elements that made them excellent. The two key areas in which European companies invested heavily were training and product development. To make progress in these areas, Mike decided that Greggs needed a Centre of Excellence, based in the midlands, to which our staff could be sent to learn how to make the very best products. We identified a potential site and plans were drawn up, but Mike was never able to win sufficient support for it. The managing directors of the Greggs businesses saw it as a threat to their autonomy, and Malcolm Simpson was not convinced of the return that would be achieved.

Mike and Malcolm were great friends and allies and a formidably effective negotiating team, but they were also very determined characters and had some ferocious arguments, during which the walls of the boardroom would shake and employees passing by would duck and run for cover. Mike always used to say that Malcolm was one of those people you had to punch on the nose before he realized you were serious, but after they'd expressed their opinions loudly and forcefully, there was never any residual bad blood between them. They'd shake hands and be laughing and joking again by the time they emerged from the boardroom. One management board member who witnessed some ferocious exchanges, commented, 'I always feel really good when Mike and Malcolm are arguing, because when the lions are fighting, the Christians live longer!'

Although the Centre of Excellence was never built, testimony to Mike's democratic management style,

Mike won agreement and support for new management appointments and, eventually a Technical Centre at the Central Savouries Unit at Balliol Park, Newcastle, both of which delivered most of the benefits that would have come from the Centre of Excellence.

In 1991 Mike developed an ambitious ten-year plan for the business, forecasting that by the year 2000, the number of shops would have increased from 500 to 1,000, and profit from £7 million to £25 million. The plan set out where this growth would come from, including diversifying into another associated area, such as catering or wholesaling of bakery products, the training and development required, plus improvements in information systems. It clarified the need for additional senior managers and a harmonization process to achieve more consistency between the different Greggs businesses, and set the scene for Greggs' expansion and growth in the nineties. Most important, it also identified the process that would ensure Greggs' values were reinforced as the company grew larger.

In the early nineties we started to arrange meetings for sales managers to co-ordinate sales initiatives and began using TV advertisements, featuring some of our sandwiches and savouries. The adverts were created by Robson Brown and Partners, a local Newcastle advertising agent. Twenty years earlier, when Alan Brown had set up his business, Greggs had been his first customer and, to help the cash flow of his new business, we paid in advance for some point-of-sale materials. Now it was a major regional player and produced some great campaigns and TV commercials for Greggs that made people laugh and boosted sales. Most memorable of these was the board meeting with executives around the table, immaculate and serious, until there was a very loud rumble. Cue embarrassed glances, chandeliers breaking up, pictures falling off the wall and the most attractive executive standing up and rushing – 'I've got to get to Greggs' – into a Greggs shop for a cheese and onion pasty, with a voiceover from Paddy McGuinness before he became mega-famous.

The period from 1984 to 1994 laid the foundations for Greggs' future growth. The original four businesses expanded steadily. Geographical expansion took place into the midlands, Wales and Edinburgh, production capacity increased, several senior managers were appointed and profitability and investment went up year on year. It was appropriate that, towards the end of this period, we moved our head office from the modest house we had previously occupied in Lambton Road, Jesmond, to a more suitable property, Fernwood House, in nearby Clayton Road, a Victorian mansion on three floors and surrounded by extensive gardens; it remains the company head office to this day. Originally built for an admiral, the house had previously been used for a variety of purposes, including the maternity home where, by a strange coincidence, my brother Colin, sister Gay and I were all born.

The new building was significantly larger and more expensive than the old one, but still modest relative to the size of the company. Whatever the increase in costs, our policy remained that these had to be met from within the head-office charge of 1.25 per cent of turnover levied on each individual business to cover all costs at the centre, including salaries. This was extremely low compared to head-office charges in most other companies, reflecting Greggs' devolved structure and a desire throughout the business that head-office operations should be kept in check. There were regular battles over the percentage, with local businesses trying to drive it down and head office trying to push it up, but it stubbornly (and healthily) remained at around 1.25 per cent for more than twenty years.

14

EUPHRATES
Scone

The purchase of Bakers Oven doubled at a stroke our number of shops to over 900. A key feature of these shops was their in-store bakeries, which produced fresh bread, scones and cream cakes

In January 1993 David Woodward, the CEO of Associated British Foods (ABF), the owners of the chain of Bakers Oven shops, rang Mike Darrington and asked to meet for a chat. Initially the conversation was about various loss-making shops that we had and they had, and he hinted that if we closed ours and they closed theirs, both sides would be winners. Mike wouldn't consider that. David's next approach was to say, 'Well, you know our shops in [he named an area] aren't doing particularly well for us. If you wanted to make an offer for those, we might be willing to talk about it.' Mike made noncommittal noises and a few minutes later, David said, 'In fact, if you wanted to make an offer for all the Bakers Oven shops, we might be willing to discuss it.'

That simple query provoked months of often frenzied calculations and negotiations, some soul-searching too. At first glance it was a tempting prospect. They had over 400 shops, almost as many as we had at the time. They were a good fit with us geographically: many of their shops were located in areas where Greggs' coverage was weak or missing – the east midlands, Greater London, south-east England, in market towns and smaller conurbations some distance from the major cities around which Greggs shops were concentrated. If we bought them, we'd also have one less big competitor to worry about.

So, at Mike's direction, we started to look into it, slowly and methodically, sending people to all the sites to assess them, which was no small undertaking, but essential if we were really to understand their business and what we would be taking on. We were already well used to assessing potential sites in terms of what their catchment was and what their turnover might be, so this was just more of that process but on a very much bigger scale. By the end of it, we had a pretty good idea of what we would do with the sites if a deal went ahead, which ones we'd dispense with, which we'd keep and so on.

There were compelling arguments as to why we should go ahead. ABF were offering us the chance to almost double our number of outlets, from 502 to at least 900 at a relatively modest cost. Mike was confident that acquiring Bakers Oven would not result in any dent in Greggs' profit performance in the short term, and in the long term would provide a basis for full geographical coverage of England, Wales and Scotland, and solid future profit growth.

Bakers Oven would also offer an opportunity for Greggs to learn more about catering and in-store baking, and we were fortunate to secure a consultancy agreement with Harry Guest, the catering guru who had been the architect of ABF's catering strategy and operations. He was a great tutor with a wealth of experience and wisdom to draw from. For me his wisest utterance was 'Beware the effect of accounting conventions on middle management', by which he meant 'Don't worship the idol of profit margin at the expense of sales volume.' He had seen ABF seriously damage its bakery and catering interests because middle management had become obsessed with achieving their recommended targets for material and wage costs, which they could only do by increasing prices. That had put off customers, reduced sales and eroded profitability. It was one of the prime reasons that ABF was now presiding over a loss-making Bakers Oven division.

Nonetheless, this was a huge decision for Greggs. It was certainly not the evolution that Mike Darrington had promised, and I was far from enthusiastic about it. Greggs was doing well and did not need to take risks of this magnitude; the memory of the last time we had attempted to double our size at a stroke and the resulting traumas of Manchester were burned into my psyche. However persuasive the strategic and financial arguments put forward, my subconscious prevented me from being convinced.

I was able to counter with strong arguments (at least, I considered them as such) as to why Greggs should not go ahead. Bakers Oven was making a loss – £1.64 million in the year to September 1993 – in spite of significant investment in new shops, shop refits, the closure of 132 loss-making shops in the two years to September 1993 and a further seventy-two during 1994. This had significantly reduced the loss of more than £5 million in the year ending September 1991, but this improvement might only turn out to be short term. Loss in morale and excessive price increases meant that sales volume was haemorrhaging badly. Increasing that volume was the only platform for a viable business in the future and there was no indication that this was happening in 1993/4. There was every possibility that the business would continue to decline and eventually close, leaving the field clear for Greggs.

Bakers Oven prices were also about 20 per cent more expensive than Greggs' and, with the exception of some of the bread, scones and cream cakes made in-store, were neither competitive in the market nor value for money. The catering units were small, and often squeezed into spaces not really large enough to accommodate them, in addition to in-store baking, sandwich-making and the traditional bakery shop. In spite of the presence of ovens in many shops, savoury sales were very low, with pies and pasties often spending long spells in heated counters, which did nothing for their flavour. The ethos and values of the business were completely at odds with our own. Bakers Oven had been centrally controlled, had lost many of its good managers in the rationalization process and morale had suffered. Unless Greggs could reverse these trends and rapidly resolve these issues, there was a risk that the downturn in Bakers Oven would continue and damage the excellent performance Greggs had achieved over the ten years since it had become a public company in 1984.

During the prolonged, top-secret negotiations, code-named 'Euphrates', that took place, I was able to indulge the luxury of sticking to this negative position. Mike Darrington was keen, though absolutely determined that the price would not only properly reflect the risks but be well covered by the value of assets. I maintained my position, compelling him to convince me of the wisdom of proceeding, which he eventually did, as I'd suspected he would!

The negotiations were spread over seventeen months. As time went by, they started to push us for a decision, which is always a good sign when you're negotiating: if the other side is showing a sense of urgency, it's always easier to win concessions. By the end of 1993, we were ready to say, 'Yes, we're genuinely interested and committed to negotiate with you, but you now need to open your books to us so that we can assess the figures.' We began to go through the accounts in minute detail, assessing what the rents and rates were, whether the shops were freehold or leasehold, the profitability of the business, its cost structure and the trends in its trade. It was not just a question of how the business was trading then, but how it had been performing over the previous few years. Was it on an up- or a down-curve? Which parts of it were performing well and which badly?

As we studied the figures, Mike's belief in the opportunity grew progressively stronger. We would be able to re-energize and motivate the Bakers Oven managers and staff quickly, and they would respond well to local rather than central decision-making. Management would also be encouraged by freezing or even reducing prices, which would check the haemorrhaging of volume that had been occurring, and there were considerable cost savings to be made. From examining the cost structure, we could immediately see that the losses they were making were in great part because of the way they did their purchasing. A lot of it was in-house with transfer pricing – buying materials from another part of the ABF business – and we knew that the market price was well below what Bakers Oven was paying. We could also see what they were being charged for their central IT services: Bakers Oven was bearing a substantial proportion of the costs of a major computer centre that was about £1 million a year more than we would be charging, using our more nimble technology. We had been at the forefront of developing mini computers, which ideally suited a decentralized business. Without doing anything else to the business, we could transform the bottom line just by making those changes. There were lots of other issues to resolve but that was a very encouraging basis on which to begin serious negotiations.

While the negotiations proceeded, a strategy and grand plan was being drawn up, so that Greggs could hit the ground running if the acquisition went ahead. The plan was to retain the Bakers Oven brand. It would be a separate business with its own head-office staff. It would retain rather fewer than half of the 424 shops: those with catering, or in-store bakeries, or located in more rural areas away from the major conurbations where most Greggs' shops traded. About thirty shops would be closed because of overlap with Greggs' units or lease expiry. The other 200 would, over a period of time, either go into a new division, which would be supplied by the newly acquired bakery in Twickenham, or be absorbed into the Greggs businesses in Glasgow, Newcastle, Yorkshire, Lancashire, the west midlands, South Wales and North London. All this would be phased over the following two years.

As the protracted negotiations continued, there were some increasingly tough exchanges between Malcolm Simpson and Mike Darrington and the ABF team led by Harry Bailey. Mike was, as usual, determined to achieve the best possible deal for Greggs with minimum risk, and he was aware that the ABF team probably had nowhere else to go. After lengthy talks they reached a point in June 1994 where the two sides were not far apart on a figure, but Mike then said, 'OK, but we now need to have the most up-to-date figures to see how you've been trading in the last few months while we've been negotiating.'

When those figures were produced, they were quite alarming, showing a steep drop in sales. When Mike and Malcolm arrived for what was expected to be the final meeting, Mike had decided to ask for a substantial reduction in the price negotiated to reflect the loss of core sales volumes that had taken place. ABF were probably expecting us to sign that day, but instead Mike said, 'Unless there's a substantial renegotiation of the price, to reflect the worsening of your trading position, we can't go ahead.'

Harry and the ABF team were willing to discuss a concession to reflect this but, they said, it would not be a substantial one. Mike and Malcolm were not prepared to talk about anything other than a substantial reduction and within five minutes they had left the meeting to catch a very early train back to Newcastle.

They still knew that there were big advantages to Greggs in doing a deal and they wanted to do it, but not at any price.

Two years earlier, Greggs' senior management had taken part in a negotiating-skills seminar in Wetheral, near Carlisle, led by Durham Business School, and Mike knew that, in the mantra of the Business School, 'Whoever picks up the phone first has lost.' The aborted meeting had taken place on Friday morning and the rest of Friday, all day Saturday and all day Sunday, Mike's phone did not ring. Neither did he make any attempt to contact Harry at ABF. Monday also passed without a call and the tension at Greggs was unbearable. Mike and Malcolm met briefly before going home that day and agreed to review the situation the following morning. At about eight p.m. on that Monday evening, Mike's home phone rang and Harry said, 'Mike, we need to talk.'

The next morning Mike went to London, and met Harry at two that afternoon. This time the two men met one-to-one to thrash out a deal, without any advisers present. Negotiations proceeded very slowly. Mike whittled away at the price all day, eventually achieving a total reduction of about £5 million, and sealing a very good deal for Greggs, procured without the cost of merchant bankers. However, it was also a good deal for ABF, securing a future for a relatively small part of their business that must have seemed an unsatisfactory and disproportionate drain on resources for a long time. This was a nice clean exit for them.

Although the headline purchase price was £18.95 million, with the benefit of a £6 million cash inflow from the ABF shops, plus working capital and other factors, the net cost was nearer to £12 million, which was financed from Greggs' cash and credit reserves. Greggs had purchased only the assets we required from ABF, not the whole company. In addition to the shops (seventy-eight of which were freehold or long-leasehold, and 346 short-leasehold), we acquired two major bakeries, one in Twickenham, and Carricks in Newcastle, which supplied most of the Bakers Oven shops; 170 shops included seated catering and 169 in-store baking facilities.

Greggs now had two distinct brands: Greggs (with the Braggs and Thurston's variations) and the Bakers Oven. Each was to be distinct and separate and have its own management structure. Bakers Oven was to have higher prices and quality (difficult for a Greggs' person to accept), with an in-store bakery and/or seated catering facilities. The shops would look very different from Greggs, aiming to appeal more to higher socio-economic groups.

The presence of in-store bakeries in the Bakers Oven shops was a key difference between the two brands and one we were determined to maintain and develop. The ability to have available a constant supply of warm bread and rolls, with their appetizing aroma, would be evident to Bakers Oven customers and help to justify the higher price structure. The availability of fresh-baked scones, pastries and dairy cream cakes reinforced this and also provided an important part of the menu in the cafés located alongside the in-store bakeries.

It sometimes took people who'd been working under a different system a while to adjust to the Greggs way of doing things. Under ABF, Bakers Oven managers had

■ SCONES ■

8oz/220g self-raising flour
½ tsp salt
2oz/55g cold butter, cut into small
   pieces

2oz/55g sultanas or currants
1oz/25g caster sugar
5fl oz/150ml cold milk, plus extra
   for glazing

1   Preheat the oven to 220°C/425°F/Gas 7. Lightly grease a baking sheet.

2   Sift the flour and salt into a mixing bowl and rub in the butter until the mixture resembles breadcrumbs.

3   Add the sultanas, sugar and then milk, mixing with your hands to get a soft dough.

4   Turn the dough onto a floured work surface and knead very lightly. Pat out to a round ¾in/2cm thick. Using a 2½in/6cm cutter, stamp out rounds and transfer them to the baking sheet. Lightly knead together the cuttings and stamp out more scones to use up the dough.

5   Brush the tops of the scones with a little milk, and bake in the preheated oven for 12–15 minutes until well risen and golden.

6   Cool on a wire rack and serve with butter and good strawberry jam and maybe some clotted or whipped cream.

been used to a 'command and control' regime, with senior management issuing the orders, leaving little room for initiative further down the management pyramid; they now had to adapt to the Greggs system where, within guidelines laid down from the centre, the regional managing directors were given great freedom of action to run the business, while managers and employees down the line had more autonomy and responsibility for their own decisions, rather than being told what to do. But most welcomed the Greggs' approach: 'Speak to people as you would wish to be spoken to yourself.' That pretty much sums it up and, no matter how large the company grows, we still show our respect for our employees and customers in everything we do. One or two former Bakers Oven employees have told me since that they were baffled by how relaxed, laid-back and friendly Greggs management seemed to be, compared to how they'd worked before. Most people who joined us came to understand and appreciate our values and discovered that it was not only a better and happier way to run a company, but also more profitable.

We set up the Bakers Oven business with three divisions: north, midlands and south-east. We established the new Greggs' division at Twickenham and the other businesses took on various numbers of Bakers Oven shops. The bakery at Twickenham provided production facilities to supply shops to the south and west of London, with Greggs' existing bakery at Enfield supplying the north and east. The Carricks bakery in Newcastle had savoury production facilities, including cryogenic freezing, and produced savouries for all Bakers Oven shops and Three Cooks (Rank Hovis McDougall).

The bakery manager at Carricks was John Bailey, who had joined our Gosforth bakery as a confectioner in 1968, and had been promoted to bakery manager in 1973. Several years later he had left to join Carricks for what he'd thought was a better job, a lone swimmer against the tide of managers from ABF to Greggs! At Gosforth I had given him a hard time on some of our early-morning walkabouts. I had developed a sixth sense for uncovering anything that was not quite as it should be, whether some frozen pies out of proper rotation at the back of the deep freeze, pastry cuttings left in the fridge that should have been used up in the first mix-in that morning, bread or cakes that were not up to standard. I suppose I was a bit obsessive, looking in every corner and feeling inside trays that were too high to peer into. When I made my first visit to the Carricks bakery after the takeover, John saw an opportunity to get revenge for the early-morning ribbings he had received all those years ago. I was starting a cold and feeling 'sub par', or I would have noticed that he was unusually well wrapped up. Carricks had several large freezers and John kept me in each for as long as he could, showing me the latest technology and how well ordered everything was. By the time I realized his mischievous intent, it was too late. I was shivering so much my teeth were chattering and my slight cold was a streamer, verging on pneumonia.

We ran the Carricks bakery for another four years, but in 1998 savoury production was transferred to Balliol and soon after that Carricks was closed. There had been at least two hundred people working there, almost half of whom were offered jobs elsewhere in the company, but the 108 redundancies that resulted were by far the largest in Greggs' history. In line with our company values, they were handled over a long period and with as much sensitivity as possible. We offered assistance to those we had to let go in finding suitable employment. John Bailey returned to the Gosforth bakery where he carried out a variety of roles until his retirement in September 2012, when he received a lifetime award for services to the industry at the annual Baking Industry Awards.

Even the cleverest accountant would find it difficult to attribute the exact profit that Bakers Oven contributed to Greggs. Overall our profits grew strongly over the years following the acquisition and at a faster rate than beforehand. A major contribution to this growth came from the transfer of Bakers Oven shops to the existing Greggs divisions. The addition of significant numbers of new shops to an established business and cost base can bring big marginal or additional profitability. The Bakers Oven business also moved into profit, though not at the level that had been budgeted.

If Mike Darrington's desire to acquire Bakers Oven did not comply with his evolution strategy, his development of Bakers Oven did. There were those in Greggs who would have favoured an early merger of the two brands, but significant differences remained. Greggs did not have the same commitment to, and experience of, instore production and seated catering, which were key to the viability of the larger, more expensive Bakers Oven units, and managing them would have taken up an undue proportion of Greggs' management time and effort.

There were regular debates within Greggs about the desirability of continuing with the two brands as, over the years, the differences between them, particularly the initial 20 per cent price differential, were progressively eroded. Some of this was the result of the drive to make Bakers Oven competitive and stop the loss of sales volume. The keen competition that existed between the two brands (which could only be loosely regulated due to the autonomy of the local managing directors) kept pushing the Bakers Oven management into closing the price gap in an attempt to achieve sales levels nearer to Greggs', while Greggs continually strove to improve quality and add value, which tended to nudge prices upwards. This made good sense as Greggs tried to improve its offer to attract and keep the increasing number of more affluent customers on high streets and town centres, in particular many of its new sandwich and takeaway customers.

Moreover, both Greggs' and Bakers Oven managements were always keen to copy any runaway success the other enjoyed. Bakers Oven wanted to match Greggs' savoury bake-off success and increasingly these savouries came from the same bakery; if Greggs' new Oval Bite sandwich with chargrilled chicken, or the doughnut filled with vanilla custard and topped with caramel fondant were winners, it wasn't long before something similar was featured along the street in Bakers Oven and vice versa.

In the dozen years following the acquisition, Greggs' profit trebled, which was a compelling argument against any radical changes, but the underlying reason for the two-brand strategy was that it achieved better coverage of high streets, town and shopping centres, and focusing on in-store bakeries and seated catering would help to achieve greater market share by satisfying more upmarket customers. This strategy required there to be significant and discernible differences between the two brands, but over the years the differences became eroded and it became less justifiable to maintain two separate brands.

15

LONDON
Coffee

It is reckoned that the British consume over 511 million cups of coffee per week. Coffee is particularly important in London and the south-east, which were different and difficult markets for Greggs to enter

Even before the Bakers Oven acquisition, Greggs had already begun expanding into London. A metropolitan area population estimated at between twelve and fourteen million and a further five million in the remainder of the south-east, meant that London and the south-east was always a target area for our long-term expansion, but after we had gone public in 1984, there were other, geographically closer, conurbations where we could pick off the low-hanging fruit first: the midlands in 1984, Wales and the south-west in 1985. At the same time, we were building up our knowledge and understanding of London, studying the retail bakery businesses there, investigating suitable trading locations and product range, and assessing the particular problems that London would pose for Greggs. There were several, and they were serious enough to make us doubt that the Greggs formula would work there at all.

First and foremost, the socio-economic profile of the London area, and particularly central London, was very different from the traditional working-class regions where Greggs' business had been established. London's population contained a greater proportion of the higher socio-economic groups, who ate less bread and cake and, in particular, fewer pies and sausage rolls. How would Greggs be able to overcome this? The merchant bankers and professional advisers who had visited Newcastle in 1984 before Greggs went public had loved the products but that was hardly broad-based scientific market research! London also contained a very different ethnic mix, some sections of which had little or no bakery heritage.

Even achieving similar sales levels per shop in London as elsewhere would not yield a satisfactory level of profitability: we needed to achieve higher sales levels just to cover the increased costs we would face. Rents and rates in most of the Greater London area were significantly higher. Transport costs would also be greater because traffic congestion made van journeys from bakery to shop slower and therefore more expensive. Most products would have to be delivered during the night or they would never get to the shops at all, and deliveries could only be made within narrow time slots because of regulations about noise. Wages were higher, people had to travel further to work, and there were more job opportunities, creating less stability. Would Greggs be able to recruit and retain the excellent local and friendly shop staff, who were such a feature of our shops elsewhere?

These difficulties were daunting, but similar businesses seemed to be prospering despite them. Percy Ingles had a bakery near Enfield and thirty shops in East London and Essex. Their product range and quality, particularly their crusty bread, were excellent, and sales volumes appeared from the outside to be similar to Greggs, but their price structure was higher and we wanted to maintain the same pricing as the rest of our UK business. Although Percy Ingles would have made an excellent platform for our expansion into London, the company was not for sale, but a smaller business was. In 1986 we made our first small step into London by buying Geary's from its owners, the flour millers, G. Garratt & Sons, for £350,000.

Geary's was a loss-making company, with a modest bakery in Enfield and twenty shops, but it provided a foothold where we could test the Greggs formula and find out more about the London market. We enlisted help from other Greggs' businesses to achieve the necessary turnaround in its fortunes: Laurie Rotin and Julie Harrison came from Gosforth and Horace Bennett from Braggs in the midlands. We began a programme to refit the better shops and made improvements to the product range. Multi-product price promotions featured strongly and sales levels started to improve, but after the experience in Glasgow and Manchester, we were not expecting any short-term miracles.

The purchase of Geary's brought with it a major and unexpected benefit: Greggs entered into a flour-supply agreement with G. Garratt & Sons. This provided Mike and the Greggs management with a much better understanding of the cost structure of the flour and milling industry, which helped us to negotiate better prices and agreements with our other flour suppliers. For example, millers had traditionally charged higher prices for wholemeal and brown flours, even though they retained a higher proportion of the grain and required less work and refining. This should, therefore, have made them cheaper, and they became so for Greggs in future.

The next year, 1987, Greggs bought a 2.6-acre car park in Enfield on which to build a new bakery when sales levels warranted it, and which would ultimately be able to service North and East London. Traffic congestion and distances made it impractical for any bakery to service all the shops in London from a single site and we had projected that Greggs would eventually need at least two bakeries, and began looking for a suitable existing bakery or development site to cover the south and west of the capital.

For the next four years, Horace and his management team gradually improved the shops, products and standards of Geary's business, with assistance from other Greggs' businesses. This involved capital expenditure on shops and bakery improvements, with additional revenue costs, mainly in the form of management, but in spite of improving shop sales and bakery efficiencies, the business continued to trade at a loss of around £250,000 per year during this period. There was little brand awareness of Greggs in the south-east and it was proving difficult to find enough customers to establish sufficient volume of savoury sales. It was chicken and egg: without the numbers of customers, there could not be a steady supply of fresh-baked products throughout the day.

Mike Darrington considered such a loss an acceptable price to pay for a ticket into the London market. Horace and his team thought otherwise and strove for that elusive profit, which would reward all their efforts and had seemed quite possible at the start of the nineties. In 1991, in order to generate some extra volume, we bought a bankrupt bakery and twelve shops, close to Enfield and trading under the name of Hibberds. We had wanted the company for its shops – with the existing Enfield bakery and the development site we had bought there, we had all the present and future baking capacity we needed in that part of London – and sold the Hibberds' bakery site at once, donating all the equipment to bakeries in Romania. Group production director Neill Hastie and Peter Spence, Enfield engineering manager, headed up this excellent project to provide a little help for a country undergoing huge problems, with encouragement from Enfield managing director Horace Bennett, who even raised extra funds by collecting sponsorship money for shaving off his moustache.

We then made Greggs' task in the capital even more daunting by simultaneously opening up in South London. In 1991 Graham Randell rejoined Greggs to develop this business, opening shops that were still supplied from the old Geary's bakery at Enfield, since the new bakery there had not yet been built. David Parker came down to help with this development but it was a struggle in South London with large management costs in relation to the size of the business, disappointing savoury sales and constant difficulties in recruiting and retaining good staff.

All the things we had worried about in relation to London were coming to pass. In addition, there was fierce competition from other retailers for suitable sites, resulting in us having to agree higher than anticipated rentals. Transporting the products across London was also proving difficult. All this increased the London loss to over £500,000 in 1991, when the South London shops were made part of the Enfield business, due to the difficulty of building them quickly enough into a stand-alone business.

The Enfield team worked valiantly to reduce the loss, with regular and invaluable support and encouragement from Mike Darrington and Personnel Director, Ian Edgeworth. In 1992, they halved the loss and then turned it into a small profit of £100,000 in 1993 and 1994, a huge and welcome achievement. At this stage the business had fifty shops and the bakery site was working at above optimum production levels with the aid of Portakabins and mobile fridge/freezer containers. The pressures and inconvenience this created were more than compensated for by the exhilaration of that profit breakthrough. After labouring under the cloud of loss for eight long years, the Enfield team could now look forward to increasing that profit to the levels achieved elsewhere in Greggs . . . or could they?

Now that the London business was making progress, Mike Darrington felt that the moment had arrived to develop the new bakery at Enfield. It opened in 1994 at a cost of £9 million. The resultant increase in operating expenditure, with the disruption created by the new building and the Bakers Oven acquisition, sent the business back into a loss of more than £500,000 in 1995. Commissioning and running-in a large new bakery is a major test for any management team. On top of this, the Enfield management had to cope with integrating those Bakers Oven shops in North London that were considered more appropriate to the Greggs brand. The additional volume did, however, help Enfield to break even in 1996 and 1997, before moving into steady and very satisfactory profit growth from 1998, thirteen years after entering the London market.

They did this despite losing the shops in South London, which, from 1994, became attached to the recently acquired bakery in Twickenham and, together with eighty-nine of the Bakers Oven shops, formed a new division, Greggs of Twickenham. Andrew Savage was appointed managing director. He was tall, athletic and, though a little reserved, very competitive with a sharp intellect. He had joined Greggs two years earlier and now faced an important and extremely difficult assignment. The bakery was old, the production equipment antiquated, and the transport fleet not fit to supply and deliver a substantial part of the product range to almost five hundred Bakers Oven units in the south and midlands. Morale in both shops and bakery was low, with some staff feeling Greggs had cheated them of their redundancy. Standards were generally poor, and every day a series of equipment failures and vehicle breakdowns resulted in products arriving late or not at all.

The key management appointment was a sales manager, who could improve standards in the shops and drive sales forward. Trevor Ferrigno had joined the Gosforth business in 1994 from Allied Bakeries. He quickly came to the conclusion that, as we were unable to secure the same employee stability in London as elsewhere, Greggs needed to modify and simplify its shop processes. He reduced the product range, simplified the sandwich range, introduced round pricing (5p and 0p endings) and bought in some ready-prepared sandwich fillings to make the processes easier. Trevor's new approach was an important part of the process of learning to cope in the London market.

Our core strategy remained to improve products, develop confidence, rebrand the Bakers Oven shops as Greggs as quickly as possible, and focus on growing sandwich and savoury sales, using bumper promotions and special price reductions. The really difficult problem Greggs of Twickenham faced, though, was finding the right price model. The Bakers Oven prices the company had inherited did not represent value, given the product quality, and were too high if we wanted to grow the business to the volumes Greggs required. Our prices were 20 per cent lower, but to reduce to that level seemed like financial suicide. Volume sales would have needed to increase by 30 to 40 per cent to maintain profitability, which was most unlikely to have been achieved, even if we could have produced the extra amount, which we could not.

We experimented with a more modest price reduction of around five per cent across the board, but this did little to lift volumes, and experiments with larger price cuts in other small groups of shops were no more successful. It was apparent that customers in the south-east needed more than price reductions to convince them of Greggs' merits. Just as in Glasgow and Manchester, we had to settle in for the long haul, and it took nearly five years to reach break-even point, and eight years of price stagnation, product quality improvements, lifting of standards and morale, and continuous investment in the shops and bakery before Greggs of Twickenham began to make a reasonable profit. It had been another gruelling marathon for Greggs management.

In addition to turning round that business, Andrew Savage had also been given the task of developing a Greggs sandwich-bar unit with a limited product range. We had noted the success of Pret A Manger and other takeaway operators, and this seemed a more suitable model for the City and central London, with their high rents and focus on takeaway lunch snacks rather than take-home bread and cakes. Andrew developed special sandwich takeaway units, sourced from the Twickenham bakery, and looked at possible business acquisitions. In particular Greggs came close to acquiring Benjys, which had thirty shops in central London, and had been taken over by a management company with venture-capital backing. This failed and the subsequent restructuring resulted in terminal failure.

Greggs could so easily have had its fingers burned in the feverish and frenzied scramble that swept through the high streets of large cities (particularly London) during the nineties. Sandwich bars like Pret A Manger and EAT, coffee bars like Starbucks, Costa and Caffè Nero, and a welter of mobile phone shops, were jostling and competing for pitch, racking up rents to unsustainable levels. A good example of this fever was the $83 million Starbucks paid in 1998 for the sixty London outlets of the Seattle Coffee Company, which, ironically in the circumstances, had been developed in London by two Americans after they'd seen the phenomenal growth of Starbucks in America. This bonanza for them encouraged other entrepreneurs to open coffee shops in the hope of making their fortune. Competition for shop sites was further intensified by the supermarket chains. The proliferation of supermarkets on high streets, town-edge and out-of-town locations had resulted in planning restrictions for this type of development, and in order to maintain growth and compete with local fresh-food suppliers, the major supermarket operators had embarked on a rapid expansion plan of smaller-format convenience stores, like Tesco Express and Sainsbury's Local.

It was frustrating to see those coffee shops, sandwich bars and convenience stores taking so many of the shops Greggs wanted but felt were unaffordable at the rents that were now being charged. However, we always looked to the long term, and when the inevitable financial crash and recession finally arrived, we were relieved not to have to carry the burden of excessively high rentals, or the debt we might have incurred by having to fit out the units to the expensive standards required for such premium locations.

By 2002 we had two separate profitable businesses in the Greater London area, Greggs of Enfield in the north and east and Greggs of Twickenham in the south and west, but the need for a cohesive presence in London, a single PR and advertising strategy, unified products and prices, making the best use of resources and optimizing distribution meant that we should merge the two businesses. Another pressure bearing down on this decision was the need to keep pace with our vision of reaching a sales level of £1 billion by 2008. In 2002 this target looked as if it would be a stretch, but if we were to achieve it, the biggest opportunity for new shops and extra sales was in the south-east.

Merging the two businesses was another major step towards a more central approach, in conflict with all the forces of local autonomy and ownership that had served Greggs so well in the past. It also required a very different management structure, and managing a business of more than two hundred shops was a massive learning curve. This was more than twice the size of the normal Greggs business, and came on top of our most ambitious shop-opening programme. The business also badly needed better production facilities, and many of the shops, particularly the old Bakers Oven branches, which had received a quick facelift and mini refit, were now looking tired and dated in an increasingly competitive market. These pressures, with the changes that resulted from merging the two London businesses, demoralized some managers, who moved on, creating gaps in the management structure that were difficult to fill.

Not surprisingly profits dropped and plateaued for the next few years, but we were learning invaluable lessons about how to manage centrally, and about the management structures and processes required to run a larger business in the very different market of the south-east. One important issue was how Greggs might take a share in the market for coffee, which had developed so rapidly during the nineties. Like sandwiches in the eighties, from small beginnings the market expanded year on year as more and more coffee shops appeared on the high street and the citizens of London showed an insatiable thirst for real coffee, whether latte, cappuccino, espresso, long black or one of many other modern manifestations. The coffee converts were also willing to pay a high price, around two pounds, for a cup. Greggs customers spent a similar amount when they visited our shops, but two pounds bought several items, not just a coffee. Given the relatively low cost of the ingredients involved, two pounds seemed expensive and we found we were able to offer coffee at around half this price, still using the best-quality beans and the highest-specification equipment, which was more in line with our value-for-money approach.

16

VISION AND VALUES
Simnel cake

*Our values – how we all aspire to behave. We will be
enthusiastic in all that we do, open, honest and
appreciative, treating everyone with fairness,
consideration and respect*

During the nineties it had become fashionable for
companies to have a mission statement providing inspiration to management and a reference point for
planning, strategy and major decisions. This process
had already begun at Greggs in 1991 as part of the Ten-
year Plan. By 1995, Greggs had enjoyed twelve years of
steady growth in profitability, had started to make
progress in the key London and south-east market and
had doubled the number of its retail shops with the
Bakers Oven acquisition. This period of uninterrupted
progress was a huge achievement for Mike Darrington

and his management team. They would have been justified in looking upon it as an opportunity for consolidation, but taking a breather was not in their nature. They were excited about what had been achieved and wanted to accelerate the rate of expansion.

However, they needed a mission statement to guide them in the way forward. 'Visioning' may have been a new concept in the UK, but Mike had learned about the concept twenty years earlier at Harvard. Visions are the first step in the long-term planning process. Mission statements guide the day-to-day operations while visions provide a sense of direction, the means to the future. It was a process that appealed to him and fitted well with Greggs' strategies of involvement, ownership, enthusiasm and search for excellence, so he began a major visioning exercise, based on building a successful business for the benefit of employees, customers and shareholders, and involving consultation and participation at all levels over several years. By 1998 the process was sufficiently developed for Greggs to publish and communicate its mission statement throughout the business, and to feature it in the Annual Report.

Our group conference in May 1998 brought together at least a hundred senior managers from all parts of the business to discuss our mission, vision and values. Under the theme 'Simply Towards Excellence', it set a clear agenda for Greggs' continued growth and development over the next ten years. In 2000, as part of this process, Mike Darrington and Alan Dick, the managing director of the midlands business, went on the Service Excellence Tour (organized by the Manchester Business School), a one-week study tour of ten companies in the USA with outstanding reputations for service, excellence and quality. Such was their enthusiasm for what they saw that they decided the entire management board should share a similar experience. The trip was planned for late September 2001, but because of the terrible events of 11 September, it was postponed for a year. When the trip took place a year later, the fourteen managers were split between two planes on all flights.

The experience had a major and lasting effect on the entire management board, but two businesses in particular had a profound impact. The first was South West Airlines and 'fun' was probably the one word that summed up a business that had won a whole raft of awards for being the best US airline for punctuality, baggage handling and customer satisfaction. The fun culture (allied with hard work) rubbed off on its customers, led to great teamwork and resulted in outstanding efficiencies. Mike also picked up a useful tip from their head of recruitment and development – 'Recruit for attitudes and train for skills' – which he went on to use, and often quoted. For example, when recruiting pilots, South West Airlines often did not select the very best candidates, who might be too self-centred and not good team players, resulting in poorer efficiency and safety. Instead they picked those just below that level, who were still very good.

The second landmark business was Stew Leonard's. This supermarket was cited in *The Guinness Book of Records* as having the highest sales per square foot of any food store in the world. Its passion for customer service was etched into a six-ton rock at the store's entrance: 'Rule 1 – The customer is always right! Rule 2 – If the customer is ever wrong, re-read Rule 1! Signed, Stew Leonard.' The staff were sent to Disney to learn how to entertain their customers, and the over-riding belief was that attitude leads to teamwork, which leads to excellence and hence to success. In 2000, they had only three stores, but each one turned over around $100 million a year. Mike was also impressed with the attitudes imbued in Ritz Carlton staff, whose mantra was 'We are ladies and gentlemen looking after ladies and gentlemen': they were expected to treat hotel guests in the same way they would visitors to their own home, not subservient and grovelling, but warm and welcoming. Greggs' managers also made visits to some of the best companies in Europe and Japan.

What underpinned the Greggs vision, and was probably even more important in the longer term, were the Greggs values. It was vitally important to find some way of incorporating the principles and values on which Greggs had been founded, and which everyone was keen to nurture, into the future. At the outset, these had been fundamental and simple: provide products that are delicious and good value for money; treat people fairly. In the early days of the business there was no need to develop this simple message into anything more elaborate – it hardly needed saying at all – but as the business grew in size and complexity, faced different issues and entrusted decision-making to an increasing number of managers and employees, it became necessary to develop the simple but important message into something that was woven into the fabric of the business, and which everyone understood and was committed to. Mike Darrington had felt comfortable with Greggs' values and fully appreciated their importance. He had come from a larger company, United Biscuits, where values had been considered of the utmost importance, and he had been greatly influenced by its chairman, Sir Hector Laing, who stated, 'We are prepared to change everything except our values.'

Our vision and values were regularly debated at all levels in the business and we made huge efforts to communicate them. By 2002 they were considered important enough to appear on the front cover of the Annual Report:

Mission Vision and Values

OUR BUSINESS

Greggs plc is the UK's leading retailer specializing in sandwiches, savouries and other bakery-related products, with a particular focus on takeaway food and catering. We continue to show significant growth and now have over 1,200 retail outlets trading under the Greggs and Bakers Oven brands.

OUR VISION AND PURPOSE

Our vision is to be Europe's finest bakery-related retailer. Our purpose is the growth and development of a thriving business, operating with integrity for *the benefit and enjoyment of our people, customers and shareholders alike*.

OUR STRATEGY

Our people will be enabled within overall guidance from the centre to work towards the successful attainment of world-class standards. To achieve this, the focus will be on:

A great place to work. We will place major emphasis on promoting a culture that encourages personal development, leadership qualities and creativity.

Enjoyable experience. We will deliver customer satisfaction by offering great-tasting food at unbeatable value to the highest standards of food safety. This will be achieved from shops that provide friendly and efficient service in attractive surroundings.

Business excellence. Our people will seek continuous improvement in their areas of responsibility, enabling them to make a real and lasting contribution to the other objectives of the company.

Challenging targets. We will strive to achieve a turnover of £1 billion by 2010 through continued core growth and acquisition of new units taking us to over 1,700 shops.

Caring for the community. Our emphasis on social responsibility will encourage even greater involvement in local charity activities and social projects and a strengthened focus on protecting the environment.

OUR VALUES

As a people-focused business we aim to be enthusiastic and supportive in all that we do, open, honest and appreciative, and to treat everyone with fairness, consideration and respect.

Personnel Director Ian Edgeworth was a great upholder of Greggs' values. He reinforced the message at every possible opportunity, via briefings, staff magazines, notice boards and posters in the canteen, and they became, and still remain, an important part of the induction process for new employees. Ian had joined the business in 1982, taking over from Ken Middleton when he had become managing director of the Scottish business. As Greggs grew, Ian kept in close contact with people at all levels of the business. He had a brilliant sense of humour and really cared about what people thought and felt. Greggs relied heavily on him to ensure that it adhered to its values about people.

Ian made sure that employee surveys were regularly carried out by independent consultants to establish how well Greggs was measuring up to its values and aspirations. At major management conferences they were revisited, reinforced and, if thought necessary, refined and improved. At the biannual management conference in 2003, the values aspiration had been distilled to:

> Our values – how we all aspire to behave. We will be enthusiastic and supportive in all that we do, open, honest and appreciative, treating everyone with fairness, consideration and respect.

This was allied with the following culture statement:

> We are achievers working hard together in a friendly and informal way where everyone matters.

Tragically, just as he was about to embark on a well-deserved retirement, Ian died of cancer at the age of sixty-three. He had retained his wicked sense of humour to the end, surprising the overflowing congregation at the crematorium in Newcastle with Judy Collins's 'Send In The Clowns' for the entry of the coffin, and Arthur Brown's 'I Am The God Of Hell Fire' for its final descent.

The development of Greggs' values gave rise to a number of interesting and important debates, in particular whether the interests of the shareholders came before those of the customers and employees, which they generally did in public companies. In fact, a feature of the nineties and the noughties was the extent to which, in other companies, the short-term interests of shareholders were increasingly given priority over those of customers and employees, not to mention other important stakeholders, such as the community and suppliers. This unfortunate trend had started in the 1980s as Mrs Thatcher rolled back the excessive power of the trade unions, ushering in an era of short-term self-interest, which, in my opinion at least, has made the capitalist model of doing business, as practised today, unsustainable.

It was difficult for those with a City background in the Greggs boardroom to accept that the interests of shareholders should not take precedence over those of employees and customers, but they could not hold out against the ethos and values on which Greggs had been founded. Some were concerned about what the City would make of it. The City was surprised, but Greggs was not blacklisted and our shareholders did very, very well.

No one at any level in the company was able to act in contravention of the values. On a number of famous and frequently referred-to occasions, even Mike Darrington found himself being shown a yellow card for behaving too autocratically or not listening properly. Mike had been particularly passionate about developing the Centre of Excellence in the midlands and had tried to push it through a management board meeting. He was prevented by Malcolm Simpson, who showed him a yellow card because neither he nor some of the managing directors had been adequately consulted or felt convinced of the benefits.

The values also found expression in other ways. Greggs usually steers clear of direct political engagement. However, one exception to this rule was when the government, first under Mrs Thatcher and then under John Major, sought to deregulate Sunday trading. Greggs' main concern was the impact this would have on staff, many of whom already worked on Saturdays. Sunday was an important day in the family week, offering staff the opportunity to escape normal daily pressures; very few wanted this to change.

If Sunday trading was deregulated, Greggs would have no choice but to open. In many shopping centres the lease required tenants to open if the shopping centre was open. Moreover, Greggs could not afford to lose customers to competitors by remaining closed when they were open. Also, it was generally believed that Sunday trading would increase costs at a faster rate than turnover, and that large supermarkets and hypermarkets would be better placed to absorb this increased expenditure.

The prospect of Sunday trading would be another pressure on profits, but our main opposition was the impact it would have on the quality of life of our staff and their families. Greggs gave substantial financial and moral support to the Keep Sunday Special Campaign – a broad coalition of retailers, trade unions, religious and community groups, whose peace and quiet on Sundays was threatened in various ways. The campaign, led by Michael Schluter, who went on to found the Relationships Foundation, fought a David and Goliath battle, delaying Sunday trading for several years and ensuring valuable limitations were put in place. In 1994 MPs at Westminster decided by the narrowest of margins (eighteen out of 600 votes cast) to allow shops to open for six hours on a Sunday.

Another example of Greggs' values at work is the lack of pressure on staff to move from one business to another. Some staff have moved to advance their careers or for other reasons, but there is no expectation, as there is in some companies, that they should move to a vacancy arising in another location; there is never a presumption that personal and family considerations should be sacrificed to meet the needs of the company.

In 2009 we faced a decision about whether to replace the ageing bakery in Penrith, which no longer met modern standards. In future, the bread, rolls and other products for the shops in Cumbria were to be supplied from the new bakery in Newcastle. The most cost-effective way of producing the confectionery then being made in Cumbria would have been to build an extension to another bakery nearer the centre of the UK, perhaps in Birmingham. However, the closure of the bakery in Penrith would have involved major redundancies and would have been a serious blow to the largely rural local economy. There were few alternative sources of employment, other than tourism, and most of the jobs in that industry were seasonal and often part-time. After careful consideration of all the relevant issues, the board opted not to close down the Penrith bakery altogether but instead to replace it with a state-of-the-art confectionery bakery, to produce specialist confectionery for all our shops throughout the UK. Greggs had passed one of the most demanding tests of its values by looking after the interests of its employees, in recognition of the important, sometimes vital, role it plays in local communities.

It meant, too, that Greggs retained the great confectionery skills base that had been developed since the Cumbria business started in 1890, which ensures that longer shelf-life confectionery, such as caramel shortcake, chocolate brownies, muesli slice, biscuits, gingerbread men and seasonal novelties, are made to the highest standards for all Greggs shops. It also means that specialist products, such as Simnel cake, which would be too complex to produce at each bakery, is available at Easter in every Greggs shop.

17

THE GOLDEN YEARS
Chutney

*Total quality management helped. Scotland became the powerhouse
of the business in both profit and innovation*

The second period of Mike Darrington's reign, from 1995
to 2008, achieved remarkable growth, with profits more
than trebling from below £15 million to £50 million.
Given the size of the company, this was an even greater
achievement than the six-fold increase in the previous
ten years. It was the most exciting and dynamic period
in Greggs' history as the management team grappled
with the challenges created by the increasing size and
complexity of the business.

In the years following the Bakers Oven acquisition,
just over two hundred of the shops were absorbed into
the Greggs' businesses and the other 200 were forged
into three separate Bakers Oven operating divisions;

major initiatives were launched to increase shop sales to levels nearer Greggs'. The company's main focus had inevitably been on realizing all the benefits that the acquisition offered but this did not prevent the pursuit of other acquisitions.

By 1995 Greggs had bought thirteen shop units in the midlands from Pork Farms, a subsidiary of Northern Foods, to be absorbed into Braggs and Bakers Oven. Shortly afterwards, we acquired Olivers, which had twenty-one units, mainly in Scotland, with a strong bias towards hot bread and catering. It appeared that Mike Darrington's ambitions knew no bounds when he followed up these purchases with another tilt at Sayers of Liverpool.

Sayers was a long-established bakery business, which United Biscuits had bought from the Sayers family in the 1970s. It had a large (and old) bakery in Liverpool, with around 150 retail outlets in Merseyside and the west side of Manchester. Sayers also had substantial delicatessen and catering sales with a strong meat and pie business. Mike Darrington had managed the business from 1978 to 1983 on behalf of United Biscuits, so it was understandable that he should be drawn to it. Soon after Mike joined Greggs in 1983 he made an approach about Sayers to Sir Hector Laing, his previous boss, but was summarily dismissed. Now Mike was back with a second bid but, however strong the emotional ties he felt to the company, he would not offer any more than he thought it was worth and he was unable to agree a price.

Three Cooks, part of Rank Hovis McDougall, owned by the Hanson conglomerate, also approached us. Mike and Malcolm went down to Putney, in London, for the main negotiation. They offered £10 million. The lead RHM negotiator simply couldn't believe we had made such a low offer and basically threw Mike and Malcolm out. Mike heard afterwards that they'd been looking for £30 million – a ridiculous sum. Like Taylors and Mountsteven, Three Cooks effectively went broke, so RHM lost the £10 million we would have paid for the company, in addition to all the trading losses they incurred. It was a shame because we'd offered a fair price for the business, and we could have made it work.

In 1996, Mike and Malcolm agreed a £3.3 million deal to buy Birkett's, another well-established family business with 600 staff, a bakery in Penrith, and fifty-seven shops in Cumbria, north Lancashire and the Scottish Borders. This purchase was right on my doorstep and blew an enormous hole in my plans to fade quietly and anonymously into the Cumbrian countryside. I was now living in a farmhouse near Ullswater, just a few miles from Penrith, from which I carried out the same sort of induction for Birkett's as I had for Braggs and Merretts.

The acquisition also brought full circle two random and interesting threads. Thirty years previously, when I was trying to make a baker of myself, I'd travelled to Birkett's, following the Roman Wall along the A69 from Newcastle to Penrith, eagerly looking for help with recipes, production processes, shop-window displays, and anything else I could glean that might be of benefit to Greggs. I returned with my mind and my briefcase full of recipes for steak mince pies, meringues, Scotch Demerara shortbread, biscuits and ginger snaps. There was production equipment that we might one day afford, new products and processes, and my head swam as I tried to prune the endless list of must-dos and must-haves into something that might be manageable and affordable. I became good friends with Nicky Birkett, who was kind, amiable, devoted to his family and of generous proportions – very much the archetypal baker – and we exchanged ideas on a regular basis over the next thirty years.

Birkett's had been established in 1890 and had an excellent reputation for quality. It seemed appropriate that, if it was sold, Greggs should be the purchaser. The business closely matched our aspirations in the north-west and fitted well with our values. Nicky Birkett retired at the time of the acquisition but Chris Malpas, the production director at the Penrith bakery whom I had first met thirty years earlier, stayed on. A keen sportsman, well respected by his employees and the whole bakery industry for his technical knowledge and commitment, Chris continued to do a great job over the next sixteen years. In 2013 he received a lifetime achievement award from Greggs for his services to the company and to the industry.

Birkett's bakers had skills levels that matched or even exceeded those of Greggs' and at the time of the takeover, 80 per cent of Birkett's production was still hand-made by those skilled, apprentice-trained bakery staff. The older employees still have the same skills today but they are much less used as a result of mechanization.

Birkett's employees had one other thing in common with Greggs': a fondness for pranks and practical jokes. For years, apprentices at Penrith had been initiated by being picked up and dropped into a barrel of flour and, says one, 'You never wanted to be there on your birth-day – malt extract was an awful thing to get off!' Even the bakery owner could be the victim of a prank, although the most celebrated incident was entirely unintentional. Nicky Birkett always had a huge turkey at Christmas. It was bought early and kept in one of the big freezers at the bakery until it was needed. One year, Chris Malpas took Nicky's twenty-five-pound turkey out of the freezer to defrost, but left it on the tailgate of one of the delivery trucks while he went back inside to get something. When he came back out, he was just in time to see the truck turning out of the factory gates, still with the turkey sitting on the tailgate.

Chris sprinted to his battered, second-hand Austin A40 and roared off in pursuit with his heart in his mouth. If it came off the tailgate, travelling at thirty or forty miles an hour, a twenty-five-pound frozen turkey could have knocked down a bus queue like a row of skittles and easily killed someone. Chris breathed a sigh of relief as the truck cleared Penrith and began to accelerate up the hill towards Carlisle. He was still flashing trying to get the driver's attention when the truck took a sharp bend and the turkey flew off. It went over the fence and down the hill like a bouncing bomb, even clearing a stream before it eventually came to rest against a dry-stone wall.

Chris pulled to the side of the road and clambered down the muddy field to collect the turkey, then took it back to the bakery to rinse off the mud and gravel. When he delivered it, Nicky stared at Chris's mud-stained trousers and said, 'Did you come cross-country, Chris?' He had to confess what had happened, but Nicky saw the funny side and he and his family still ate the turkey that Christmas, pronouncing it full of flavour, deliciously tender and mercifully gravel-free.

The other thread to Birkett's business was Pettigrew's Jam and Chutney. Around 1990 I had been asked by a friend of one of my daughters to look at the Pettigrew business, which he was interested in investing in. It was located above a shop in Kelso, in a ramshackle four-level tenement. I watched Mrs Pettigrew stirring the lemon curd with a huge wooden paddle, the air heavy with butter and the sharp tang of lemon, mingling with the scents of other fruits and spices emanating from the boxes and cartons scattered randomly over the four floors, amid packaging and bottles. Eventually, and by some miracle that would have defied any formal analysis, it all ended up as delicious jams and chutneys in shining jars with frilly tops.

Some years later Birkett's bought Pettigrew's, to sell the jams and chutneys in their shops and to use the jam in the bakery, and now Pettigrew's was part of Greggs and we were not sure what to do with it. Selling jars of jam and chutney didn't feature much in our retail strategy. The production premises were a potential liability and needed replacing, and the business was located in the Scottish Borders, far away from any other Greggs company. However, Greggs' values also applied to companies that had only just joined us and we were well aware that a decision to close down Pettigrew's would have a severe impact on the economy of the area. We needed more than sentiment and fellow-feeling, though, to justify capital expenditure on something that was not part of our core business.

The Pettigrew's staff were not dismayed by that prospect. They were proud of their products and the

■ CHUTNEY ■

(You can use any available vegetables for this, e.g. peppers, swede, tomatoes, etc.)

2 onions, finely chopped
8oz/220g carrots, diced
2 courgettes
1 small cauliflower
8oz/220g runner beans
6 garlic cloves
2 Bramley apples, unpeeled and finely chopped

8oz/220g sultanas (or currants or dates)
10oz/285g brown sugar
1 tsp salt
15fl oz/425ml malt vinegar
2 tsp mustard seeds
2 tsp allspice
1 tsp cayenne pepper

1   Mix together all of the ingredients in a large, heavy saucepan, and bring to the boil, stirring continuously.

2   Reduce the heat to a very gentle simmer and cook for around 2 hours, stirring regularly until the liquid has evaporated and the mixture is thick.

3   Seal in sterilized jars, and store for a couple of months before eating.

business they had built up and, with help and guidance from Chris Malpas, they put forward a plan for a new production unit on one level to make special chutneys for Greggs' sandwiches. The plan was adopted and has proved to be a remarkable success. Pettigrew's now makes all the chutneys, pickles and pizza toppings for Greggs, which accounts for 65 per cent of its total production. They help to give our sandwiches another special advantage over our competitors. In addition to fresh, locally made bread and rolls, Greggs has added its own custom-made pickles, such as fresh vegetable pickle (replacing Branston): it contains five freshly diced vegetables (turnip, onions, carrots, courgettes and cauliflower), with tomatoes, apples and dates, plus herbs and spices. Chutneys and special sauces are also specially developed to enhance the flavour of particular sandwiches. For example, Pettigrew's makes a delicious mango chutney (mangoes, golden sultanas, ginger, garlic, mustard, coriander and cayenne) for Greggs' mango chicken sandwiches, and Cossack tomato sauce to spice up the hot bacon rolls for breakfast.

While I was enjoying myself on my doorstep inducting Birkett's, the management team was looking further afield. With our network of shops now covering most of Britain, we were keen to expand into Europe. After careful consideration and market research, we chose Belgium and Flanders on the basis that English is widely spoken and the people are cosmopolitan in taste, compared to other European nations. Takeaway food – or food on the go (FOTG) as it is increasingly known – was only just beginning to emerge there and it seemed we had an opportunity to be the number-one player in that market. When we announced our plans, the newspaper headlines that greeted us included 'Greggs Croissants The Channel'.

Our first shops opened in Leuven and Antwerp in 2003. The offer was true to Greggs' traditions, with bakery, sandwiches and savouries featuring strongly alongside some local specialities, such as continental pastries; our sausage rolls, exported all the way from Newcastle, ready to bake in the shops, sold well. We recruited an excellent local management team and all our staff there had a great work ethic, operating with very high standards of customer service and with great passion for quality. Baking in the shop throughout the day was something that came very naturally to them and we found that we were able to translate our values and culture to a new territory. They loved working for Greggs and became a valued part of the company.

Between 2003 and 2006 the business grew to ten shops, five in Flanders and five in Brussels. We were well liked by our customers and sales grew steadily, but several underlying problems persisted. Although sandwiches sold well, we never enjoyed UK levels with the savouries business, our long-range supply chain and management were complicated and expensive, and the cost of employment was much higher than in the UK – at the time, National Insurance contributions from the employer in the UK were 11 per cent, compared to 40 per cent in Belgium. We also realized that the Greggs format would need some adjustment to cater for the continental café culture. We were making an annual loss of around £200,000 per year in Belgium, which had been considered a not unreasonable price to pay for entry into Europe.

The real key to profit growth throughout this period

was not expansion into new areas as much as the steady progress made in each of the established Greggs businesses. Gosforth enjoyed a long and settled period under Graham Randell, who had moved from the south-east. He had a relaxed and participative style, which suited that part of the business, and he was increasingly assisted by Gillian Long, who succeeded him when he retired in 2009.

Families also continued to feature in the Gosforth business. I had first met Michael Harrison in 1976 when he joined us as a cleaner, with long hair and a silver earring, an unusual sight then, to me at least. On breaks he sat apart from his workmates and studied for his GCEs. He steadily worked his way through various positions in the bakery, eventually becoming personnel director until his retirement in 2010. He married Pauline Seymour, who was a shop manager in Newcastle for twenty-five years. And there was Stephen Raine, who joined the company in 1968 when he was barely fifteen, was promoted to various management positions, and eventually became night-shift manager. Stephen's brother, Dixon, worked for thirty-five years in the confectionery department, and his daughter, Lianne Bellshaw, was in retail management. These families and the long service of their members and other staff continued to provide an important element of stability to the Gosforth business.

Glasgow gradually became the powerhouse of the company, both in terms of profit generation and innovation. Its progress seemed unstoppable. New shops in that business invariably exceeded budget, new products (particularly new sandwiches) achieved huge volumes and many, such as the Oval Bite, became the benchmark for the whole company. In 1996 it passed the 100-shop mark with a new opening in Govan, performed by Mary Doll (Elaine C. Smith), the long-suffering television 'wife' of Rab C. Nesbitt. Fifteen years later Govan won Shop of the Year for the best all-round performance out of Greggs' 1,600 shops.

The manager eventually responsible for designing and shop-fitting around 150 shops in Glasgow was Donald Brown, who worked for the Glasgow business from 1986 until 2009. He remained a great example of the spirit and commitment that existed throughout this part of the business, despite the rotten cards he was dealt. His first wife died of cancer, his sister's two adult children were killed in a car crash, and he became increasingly incapacitated from 2008 with motor-neurone disease. His second wife, Pat, nursed him through two years of this cruel illness and they received regular support from his Greggs colleagues, who took him in his wheelchair for visits to new shops until just before he died in December 2010. When I saw him a few weeks before he died, I was amazed at his positive approach and his continuing interest in all that happened at Greggs. He showed no bitterness, just appreciation of the part he had played in the business and of the continuing support of his colleagues.

A key factor in the continuous improvement of the Glasgow business was Total Quality Management (TQM). Based on the belief that the quality of our products and the need to equal or even exceed our customers' expectations was the responsibility of every-one – not just production-line workers, but management, sales people, clerical staff and outside suppliers as well – TQM was a type of quality circle that brought together all our employees to solve problems in their areas of the business. Everyone from the managing director to the last operative in the bakery had responsibility for our high standards. Once more, our principle was that we were all in it together.

TQM originated in America. Its adoption in the Glasgow business arose from an incident in the savoury department. While the bakery manager was on holiday Ken Middleton thought he would take advantage of his absence to make some 'improvements'! He told the pie maker to make the pie lids thinner. When the pies were baked the next day the filling burst out and they had to be scrapped. In the investigation that followed the pie baker said 'I could have told you that would have happened.' 'Then why didn't you say?' 'Because you never asked'.

Over a period of years, many areas of the Scottish business went through TQM. In virtually every instance it was possible to find improvements, whether reducing costs, improving quality or making the job more enjoyable for employees. Scotch pie production was always a difficult area and provided an excellent example of how effective TQM could be. The curing (drying out) of the shells (pastry cases for the pies) took up large areas of the bakery and huge numbers of racks and baking sheets. The machinery that made the shells was old-fashioned and labour intensive. Despatching the shells and filling separately, so that they were put together just before baking in the shops to retain the crispness of the shell, was a complex process. Improvements were only made when the people involved in the processes were given the resources they said they needed to achieve them.

TQM involved the whole management team, who moved on from using its principles for specific projects to visioning and five-year business planning. TQM was at the heart of the success of the Glasgow business, helping to develop the management team into a confident and cohesive group and providing a lead in many areas for other parts of Greggs to follow. At the annual Glasgow staff dance, the haggis and whisky were piped into the ballroom, along with the sirloins of beef. The wine flowed and the assembled company raised the roof with the Tina Turner anthem 'Simply The Best' in a display of corporate pride and confidence that rivalled that at Gosforth fifteen years earlier.

The business in Glasgow even found its way into the Edinburgh Festival with 'Seven Bridies for Seven Brothers', a comedy about life in a Greggs shop. Mr Gregg's Scottish voice boomed from the back shop instructing his shop assistants on how to sell more and chastising them for over-baking the rolls. It was very successful, went on tour and later greatly amused several audiences of Greggs employees.

In 2003 when Ken Middleton was due to retire, there was great concern about whether his successor would be able to maintain, let alone improve, performance but Raymond Reynolds did continue to improve profits until he was appointed retail director for the whole UK, a new appointment that became a key part of the centralized structure. His successor, Alan Greenshield, built the first of the new generation of bakeries in 2007, at a cost of £16 million.

In Yorkshire, Brian Wildblood had retired in 1997, to be replaced by Peter Rossi, previously sales director in Scotland. True to his Yorkshire roots, Brian had achieved results by keeping investment low and costs tightly controlled. Peter's style was conscientious, participative and caring to a fault, and he set about using what had worked well in Scotland, from the large sandwich rolls to the TQM approach, which had brought so many improvements. He developed a strong management team, increased investment significantly, completing large £3-million extensions to the bakery and offices in 2005, and developed the shop-opening programme by expanding into new areas, such as Humberside. As is often the case, it took longer than expected for the efforts and changes in strategy to bring about the budgeted improvements, but the Yorkshire team was pursuing sound long-term strategies and they received regular support from Mike Darrington, who was particularly good at helping managers through difficult times until the anticipated improvements began to materialize.

I tried to visit each of the businesses officially once a year, but if I was in the area for other reasons, I popped into shops incognito. On one occasion I was helping to lay out my stepson's garden in a suburb of Leeds. During a break, I went with my wife Jane to the local Greggs to buy some rolls for bacon sandwiches. I was scruffy, in old clothes and covered with mud and cement. The bake-off rolls were, I thought, over-baked so I suggested we buy the bagged rolls, but they weren't as soft as I thought they should have been, so we bought a loaf instead. As Jane paid the bill, the shop manager whispered to her, with a knowing smile, 'You'd do better to leave him at home next time!'

In Lancashire this period started with a major tragedy when Les German died from a heart attack in

1995. Another recruit from Allied Bakeries, he had succeeded Stephen Greenfield as managing director in 1988. He was cheerful, confident and a born salesman, who was greatly admired throughout the business as much for his flamboyant tastes (he was never happier than on his motorbike in leathers, or racing Renault cars) as the new levels to which he pushed the business. He was affectionately known as 'Del Boy', which tells its own story. His place was taken by Ian Pegg, who moved up from the midlands to Manchester and, with a steady hand, steered the business towards building our second new-generation bakery, completed in 2009 at a cost of £16 million.

In the midlands, Mike Darrington chose to replace Ian Pegg from outside. There were no obvious candidates within the company, and it was an opportunity to strengthen the senior management team. Alan Dick, a Scot and proud of it, brought to Greggs a great level of talent and experience that quickly earned him respect throughout the company. He had previously been general manager of European manufacturing in the McVities part of United Biscuits, where Mike had worked with him and formed a high opinion of his ability. Over the next thirteen years Alan made a big contribution to Greggs in the midlands and to the company generally, expanding the shops in the region from fifty to 150, developing the bakery that went on to produce for 250 shops, and realizing the potential of this key region by opening shops in Coventry, Nottingham and Wolverhampton, as well as the traditional Birmingham area.

In 1993 Steve Smith was promoted from his position of sales director of the Yorkshire business to become managing director for Wales and the south-west. Under his management, the business quickly moved into substantial profit, and from 1995 passed swiftly through the £1-million, £2-million and £3-million barriers, becoming a major contributor to company profits and expanding successfully into the shopping centres across the Severn. David Marsh, who had been sales director in the midlands, succeeded Steve and, in 2008, developed a £4.5-million extension to the bakery at Treforest, enabling Greggs to expand further into the south-west.

During this period of remarkable growth, each of the managing directors of the still independent and autonomous divisions was becoming more experienced, more confident and less likely to follow the official line if they thought they had a better plan, while Mike Darrington's span of control – the number of directors and managers reporting directly to him – was constantly extended by the addition of new businesses and more functional directors at head office, leaving him less time to manage each of them. At one stage this span reached fifteen, double what is recommended in the textbooks. We had made efforts to reduce his workload in 1993 when David Parker was appointed to the main board with a view to taking over some of Mike's operational responsibilities. By 1995 David was responsible for most of the divisions, but in 1998 he died tragically at the age of fifty-one after a long and courageous battle with cancer.

Much discussion then took place, and we sought advice as to the best management structure to suit Greggs' business. Should we look for a replacement for David Parker? Should Greggs move away from local autonomy to a more centralized business? Eventually we decided to reduce Mike's span of control by creating a regional structure. The north-east, Cumbria and Scotland were managed first by Ken Middleton and later by Raymond Reynolds; the Lancashire and Yorkshire businesses were overseen by Peter Rossi; Alan Dick was given responsibility for the midlands, Wales and the south-west; Andrew Savage took on the whole of London, with Bakers Oven retaining a separate management unit.

This worked well, giving the senior managing directors more responsibility and an opportunity to show their further potential. They could also spend more time on helping and developing the local managing directors, who were now under their control. Although it was something of a compromise, this structure continued to deliver excellent profit and growth for Greggs for a further eight years.

It is difficult to do justice in a few paragraphs to the developments of this period and the individuals who managed the separate Greggs businesses. Whatever the problems with structure, span of control and achieving greater consistency across the UK, the collective progress and profit improvement were remarkable. The managing directors were becoming more successful and confident, and were transferring the most successful ideas from other Greggs' businesses to their own. The company was awash with new ideas, new products, new shop designs and formats with more takeaway emphasis, the pursuit of new non-standard locations, such as hospitals, garages, airports and industrial estates, and new bakeries, extensions and equipment. Driving all this was a powerful element of competition between the businesses, each one striving to move up the league table of profitability. At every opportunity the mantra of the vision and values was repeated.

18

BECOMING A NATIONAL UNIFIED BUSINESS

Sausage roll

Greggs make 2.5 million sausage rolls every week. If laid end to end, they could stretch from Land's End to John O'Groats in six weeks and around the world in three years

In 1984, when Greggs had become a public company, it consisted of four separate autonomous business divisions. The businesses in the north-east and north-west of England and in Scotland at least shared the name Greggs. The one in Yorkshire traded as Thurston's. All shared common accounting practices, and the English businesses all had the same wage rates and conditions, but there were major variations between them in terms of product range, product quality, management style, production processes and profitability.

Today Greggs is a unified single brand, with the same offer to customers across the UK in respect of 80 per cent of its product range, with 20 per cent of local products peculiar to each region. The changes that brought this about took place over twenty-five years, in accordance with Mike Darrington's over-riding principle of evolution not revolution; the tension between the need for consistency and the autonomy of local management was at the core of Greggs' development.

Throughout this period management board meetings made a major contribution. We had already seen how they helped to achieve some consensus and cohesion rather than further diversity and separation, and to aid this process towards consistency we made a number of senior appointments to strengthen management at the centre. These were tough positions. The holders had to achieve progress and change, not through any line authority, but purely by persuasion.

In the early nineties we made three new appointments. David Sillars joined as group production director and brought a new level of expertise and standard-setting within the bakeries. His experience in food factories, which had made products to the highest specification for national multiples, such as Marks & Spencer, was invaluable to Greggs. He and Neill Hastie were able to build new bakeries and bakery extensions to the highest modern standards. They introduced more formal quality-control methods, including regular microbiological and bacterial testing on savoury products and sandwiches, carried out by independent laboratories rather than done in-house, which increased product quality and security across the business.

We also appointed a marketing director, Tony

Barcroft from Procter & Gamble. This was the poisoned chalice in Greggs, his job being to persuade the powerful divisional managing directors – he could not issue orders to them – as to what they should be selling in their businesses, on which parts of the product range they should be focusing and how they should be pricing.

Alan Honeyman's appointment as group purchasing director also brought major benefits to Greggs. Local management resented the loss of freedom and independence with regard to where they bought their ingredients and raw materials, but using the same sources for flour, meat, eggs, cheese, fruit and other raw materials across the businesses removed another reason for differences between Greggs' businesses and products. If it was difficult to see or quantify the benefit of such changes in the product, there was no mistaking the financial advantage that a sharp full-time manager could achieve with bulk purchasing and forward contracts on behalf of the whole business. Although these changes were significant and part of the evolving process towards a more unified Greggs, the product ranges of the various businesses remained stubbornly different.

1995 offered a chance to make progress on unifying the range. The Glasgow bakery had reached capacity and Ken Middleton was keen to add a major extension. Pie and savoury production was a major part of the Scottish business, which was doing extremely well, so there was a very strong case for building an extension. However, space and automated equipment were becoming increasingly expensive, and we were concerned at the prospect of having to develop another modern savoury-production unit when we already had an excellent facility in Newcastle. Could we really afford to repeat it in Glasgow, then Yorkshire, Manchester, the midlands and so on? Or should we be thinking of one central facility, which, in the long term, could produce the whole, or a very large part, of Greggs' pie and savoury business, which would, of course, continue to be baked-off locally on site?

The suggestion was viewed as heresy, slaughtering a very sacred cow, and I was, at best, ambivalent about an idea that struck at the very foundation on which Greggs had been developed and at a key part of our product range. I could accept that one state-of-the-art savoury-production unit would produce even better quality products at a lower cost than a series of smaller, less sophisticated units spread across the country. A central facility would also attract the best possible management and expertise, but the big question was whether the businesses receiving centrally produced products would feel as passionate about them as the ones they produced themselves, had lived with and developed over the years. And what would the customers think? There would, inevitably, be changes in what they were used to. Whatever general undertakings were made about the quality and consistency of centrally produced savouries, people had been piling into the shops for years and in increasing numbers to buy locally produced products. My view was: if it ain't bust, don't fix it.

If Mike Darrington felt that a cause he was championing was sufficiently important, he could order its implementation across the whole business, but he rarely did so, preferring to coax and persuade local managements one by one, a slower but effective way of moving things forward. He now brought all of his considerable powers of persuasion to bear. For once, he had a job on his hands to convince me of the wisdom of his plan. Malcolm Simpson was firmly in favour, having developed the thinking behind it and discussed the financial implications with him. The next key person to get on side was Ken Middleton, because unless the Scottish management was enthusiastic it was a non-starter. A long courtship took place, mainly with Scotland but also with the other Greggs' businesses. It was important that they were all properly involved, because if the system was tried and worked well in Scotland, it could be their turn next.

The financial arguments were persuasive: Mike was not prepared to proceed with a new savoury-production unit in Scotland that would significantly increase the cost base of the business: if savouries could be bought in from another source, at a good price, and the Scottish management could expand the business, using the production space previously devoted to savouries to develop new products, without increasing costs.

Ken Middleton and the Scottish management eventually decided to support the project in the belief that they would receive the products they wanted, when they wanted them, at an advantageous price. I also agreed to go along with it and the board approved the decision. Scotland's bridies and sausage rolls would now be made by Geordies in Newcastle but Scotch pie production would remain in the Glasgow bakery: moving that would have been a step too far.

The central savoury facility, developed in 1997 at Balliol Park, north of Newcastle, at a cost of £10 million, was a massive investment and a considerable risk for

Greggs. It was opened by Her Royal Highness the Princess Royal who, a woman after my own heart, upbraided the local management for the fancy food laid on for her lunch: 'I came to open a pie factory and I would like to have sausage rolls and pasties for lunch – please!' And then – bless you, ma'am – she ordered a batch of each for her daughter's party in Edinburgh the following week. Greggs by appointment!

Mike still wasn't going to force any of our other regional businesses to accept savouries from the central unit, rather than making their own, but at the same time, he made it clear that he thought it was the way forward, that all sectors of our business would see gains in terms of improved quality and reduced costs and, given that, he was not going to authorize any further capital expenditure on savoury production in the regional bakeries. Faced with the realization that their own equipment would become increasingly outmoded and unreliable if they stuck to producing savouries locally, the regional bakeries slowly fell into line and began obtaining their savouries from the central unit.

The Glasgow management team was the first to bite the bullet and reluctantly agreed that savouries were better from the central unit and, after some teething problems, the deliveries improved. A sacred cow, or divisional dragon of the most ferocious kind, had been slain. Without exception, savoury sales grew whenever a business changed from producing its own to receiving them from the central facility: the quality and consistency were better, and their costs were reduced as well.

Three years later, in 2000, a Technical Centre was attached to the central savoury facility, salvaging at least part of Mike's ambitions for a Centre of Excellence.

Here we developed new products and improved existing ones, established standard recipes for the whole company, set up and trained tasting panels and established a range of quality tests. Paul Birchall was appointed manager and, with a small technical team and Andy Phillips, the hugely enthusiastic head chef, the Technical Centre has played a major role in improving standards, developing better and more consistent products and providing a great experience for Greggs' staff and visitors who go there.

We achieved further consistency with shop-design projects, led by Ken Middleton but involving senior managers and shop-fitting teams throughout the business. Initial design had been functional: racks for bulk storage, very basic display counters, cumbersome ovens, with noisy bells, linoleum flooring (often worn through in parts) and harsh fluorescent tube lighting. These features had largely been developed in local shopping centres and small towns – but was this image suitable for the more fashionable areas and city centres into which we were increasingly expanding?

We chose Crabtree Hall to smarten up Greggs' public face. They introduced the quattro dots that appear on our fascia and vans, and went on to propose brighter lights, curved glass counters, solid wood back-fittings, mirrors, glossy price and promotional materials, and a greater focus on takeaway, removing 'the Bakers' from the fascia.

In trials of the new look, sales increased, but not enough to justify the very considerable additional expenditure. There were also major concerns that the changes would make Greggs appear too expensive and 'posh'. Above all, our shops had to be classless. A war of attrition took place between the lofty aspirations of professional retail-design consultants and the combined forces of Greggs' grass-root origins, the objective of classlessness and the accountants who needed to see a reasonable return for additional expenditure.

The main battle took place in a warehouse in Byker, in the east of Newcastle, where a new standard shop was constructed. It never saw a customer but every detail and specification was thrashed out and written up. This vital effort to achieve the impact, but at affordable cost, was led by Chris Smailes, group shop-fitting manager, supported by representatives from each business. The result was a major step towards the development of the Greggs brand across the UK.

In 1998 the Birkett's, Braggs and Thurston's shops and businesses were changed to the Greggs livery: more heresy and another sacred cow slain. The decision was taken largely because they were now expanding into areas where the Braggs and Thurston's name was unknown, but once more the decision to change wasn't imposed by Mike. Even though he wanted to do it, he also wanted the Braggs and Thurston's staff to be the instigators of the move: he knew that if he tried to impose it upon them, it would lead to resentment and friction. So he waited, and eventually the Braggs' and Thurston's managements came to him, saying, 'Why can't we be branded as Greggs? We're missing out on the value of the branding, the reputation for quality and the TV advertising you're doing.' The change in branding did no harm to the business, quite the opposite in fact, because the majority of people affected were pleased and proud to be more closely linked with what was becoming a major national brand.

The shop-fitting manuals were not mandatory and

some local management teams retained a few variations close to their hearts, but a Greggs shop was now instantly recognizable right across the country. At a later stage we introduced warmer browns, oranges and creams, instead of the original blue, to be more consistent with wheat, flour, bread, baking and Greggs' bakery heritage, but still without putting 'the Bakers' back on the fascia.

Unification of the different businesses had had a setback in 1994 with the acquisition of the Bakers Oven shops. A significant part of this business was absorbed within Greggs, particularly in London and the south-east, but the rest remained under the Bakers Oven brand. In 1998 a major new central distribution depot was developed at Kettering in the east midlands to source the requirements of Bakers Oven and some of the Greggs shops in the midlands and further south. An increasing proportion of Greggs' business was now in takeaway. The sandwich fillings required, with miscellaneous drinks and snacks, could now be handled more efficiently in a bespoke modern warehouse than the despatch department of a traditional bakery, as could the large volumes of frozen savouries from central production. This was a major and controversial step for Greggs, but once more, after some initial hiccups, it worked, thanks in no small part to the persistence of purchasing director, Alan Honeyman.

TV advertising, too, made it necessary for the autonomous businesses to work together and offer consistent responses to particular promotions, and a series of memorable adverts helped to build the Greggs name: 'Great taste, great value'. 'Are your taste buds bored?' asked James Bolam, in his Geordie accent. 'What about a real posh stotty cake to revive them?' or a 'delicious doughnut or Whopper'. High-kicking dancing girls appeared in the background, to show the 'feel-good factor' as a sausage roll was bitten into – the great taste of Greggs.

We had a series of debates, over the years, about central projects that came to nothing, like state-of-the-art facilities to produce frozen dough, baguettes, Danish pastries and even sandwiches for the whole company, but if the subject of central sandwich production was flirted with only fleetingly, the question of sandwich fillings was seriously debated and tested. Initially, all the salad ingredients were prepared in each shop, as were the egg mayonnaise, tuna and cheese fillings. This was labour-intensive, wasteful of space and could lead to quality and consistency variations. We realized that this part of the sandwich did not need to be prepared on the premises, but could be done more efficiently and hygienically in an air-conditioned bespoke building, which was developed as part of the Manchester bakery.

From about 1995, there were regular discussions of the two main issues preventing Greggs from projecting one unified national brand: the separate Bakers Oven brand and the inability to achieve standard specifications for the main products across the UK. A doughnut or a chicken sandwich should have been the same from a Greggs' shop in Glasgow, Newcastle, Birmingham and London, but it wasn't. Some argued that Bakers Oven shops should be changed quickly to Greggs, but Mike Darrington wanted to preserve the pride of the Bakers Oven management in their brand, their higher price structure and their in-store and catering functions. However, over the next ten years, the differences between the two brands, particularly products and pricing, became so eroded and blurred that the change to Greggs was inevitable, and eventually took place in 2008.

Over the same ten-year period the move towards standard products was so slow as to be almost imperceptible. In 1995 Mike Darrington had set up a Greggs brand team, mainly made up of managing directors and chaired by one, charged with finding ways of working together, bringing extra consistency and standardizing the Greggs offer. This brought some progress, but not enough, so we formed an operating board of senior head-office managers to help the centralization process and provide a single, common offer. Once again progress was limited. People were resistant to the idea of centralization, mainly because they took pride in their locally made products. The sense of ownership and passion for the business that Mike had done so much to foster made managers reluctant to give up their part in the decision-making process, but the company had increased to a size that could not be effectively managed by a decentralized structure.

As late as 2000, in a plea for simplicity and efficiency, Malcolm Simpson pointed out that Greggs still sold fourteen different versions of sausage roll. They were brought before senior management in what became known as the 'parade of the sausage rolls'. The benefits of standard high-specification savouries were reinforced all the time, as sales of sausage rolls and pasties increased whenever businesses replaced their own with centrally produced savouries. A standard doughnut recipe and specification was adopted by all bakeries and resulted in improvements in volume and profitability, but other progress was unacceptably slow. Hours and hours of management meetings were spent in agreeing programmes of product standardization, followed some time afterwards by post-mortems into the reasons for failure to meet the programme and the setting of a new one.

By the middle of the noughties, progress in achieving consistency across the product range had seriously stalled. Equally, if not more, damaging was our difficulty in reacting quickly enough across the UK to new products, price fluctuations, promotions and trends. The retail market was changing at a faster pace than ever before. National multiples and supermarkets were driving forward with new sandwiches, new bakery products and new promotions. Competition, particularly in the sandwich and coffee-shop market, was still growing, with brands such as Subway, Costa and Starbucks expanding fast. Agreeing new initiatives in response to this across all Greggs' businesses was a laborious process and, even worse, agreements weren't always consistently and efficiently acted upon, being delayed in some quarters and changed in others. We were losing opportunities, which affected volume sales and profits.

In 2006 other factors were impinging on the bottom line, in particular a huge increase in energy costs and a reduction in interest from using cash reserves to buy back shares. Mike Darrington, abandoning his usual democratic approach, spearheaded a major campaign to strengthen the Greggs brand image and to introduce a series of trials to develop new ideas in Greggs' shops, but it was not enough to prevent us recording a reduction in annual profits in 2006.

In addition to the trials, Mike had also asked the operating board to carry out a major review of why the company was not performing as well as it had and to recommend changes. The main recommendation was that the management of the business should be centralized, which Mike accepted, even though it ran contrary to everything that had made the business successful to that point.

Whether Greggs was slow and should have made more fundamental changes earlier, is an interesting question, but warts and all, the decentralized structure had continued to produce excellent results until that point. Mike worked with the senior management to shape the proposals, which were approved by the main board and announced late in 2006. This was unquestionably the biggest change we had ever undertaken. The key people in the development of Greggs had been the managing directors of the local businesses. The posts of local managing directors and the businesses they controlled now ceased to exist. The bakeries were separated from the shops to create a central supply chain, managed by Nigel Oldham, who had joined Greggs in 1999 to be responsible for production facilities, including the central savoury unit.

Each group of shops was managed by a general manager (instead of a managing director), who reported to the retail director, Raymond Reynolds, supported by a central marketing team. At the same time a number of financial and administrative roles were moved from the local businesses to a central finance function.

Change on this scale is never easy, but we had little choice if we wanted to continue to develop. Not only was the old devolved structure groaning under the pressure, but most of the main players, particularly the managing directors, were approaching retirement. The decision could not be postponed any longer.

19

GREGGS TODAY

Steak bake

More than 650,000 people are friends of Greggs on Facebook, the armed forces amongst them. When asked what they missed most from home, they put Greggs at the top of their list

As we began the twenty-first century, with Mike Darrington, Malcolm Simpson and myself all approaching retirement, the Greggs board needed to consider management succession. Considerable discussion and planning took place to spread the changes over a reasonable period to allow people and the business to adjust. We needed a board with experience appropriate to the size of the company and which complied with the requirement for independent non-executive directors, who ceased to be considered independent after ten years' service. In 2001 my brother Colin retired from the board, albeit with considerable reluctance. He wanted to stay on but realized that changes were required.

Finding a suitable chairman to replace me was critically important. The board was determined that, in addition to all the other skills and experience required, my successor should embrace the ethos and values that had governed the management of the business at all levels, and show a genuine desire to make Greggs a good place to work and a contributor to the communities in which it operated. This was no easy task and the first two attempts via recruitment consultants produced no one we were happy with.

On the third attempt, with the help of Ffion Hague, who was a highly regarded director of headhunters Hanson Green, we finally secured a candidate who met our criteria: we appointed Derek Netherton as chairman designate at the start of 2002. Derek had spent his career in investment banking, retiring in 1996 as joint head of corporate finance at J. Henry Schroder, and he was also an NED in other companies, including Next. He took over from me as chairman later that year, though I was asked to stay on as an NED, which I did for a further five years.

Derek brought a wealth of business and commercial experience to bear on any board decisions. This, with his training as an actuary and his keenness to listen to and take into account the views of others, provided confidence in major decisions. Most important, he also saw the need to develop and strengthen the board and soon recruited several NEDs with the experience he felt would be required to meet the future needs of a larger and more complex business. I greatly enjoyed working with him, understanding the changes he wanted to bring about (not to mention hearing about his exploits as a breeder of rare pigs!), and seeing the experience and intellectual breadth of some of the talented people he brought on to the main board.

In 2004 Bob Bennett, who had been group financial director at Northern Rock, joined, followed by Julie Baddeley in 2005, and Sir Ian Gibson in 2006. This was a huge influx of talent and experience. Bob Bennett was highly regarded and used to dealing with all the financial requirements of a public company and the stock exchange. Julie Baddeley had been head of technology and human resources at Woolwich plc, with several non-executive positions. Sir Ian Gibson was a charismatic man, who could really inspire and motivate groups of managers. He had previously had an out-standing career in the motor industry, putting Nissan on the map in England. It was fascinating to observe the contributions these new appointments made, partly as a result of their previous experience but also on account of their natural acuity. This was what Greggs needed for the future.

In 2006 Malcolm Simpson retired as financial director, thirty-five years after joining the company. He had guided Greggs through the rigours of securing a quotation on the stock exchange in 1984, carried out the governance required of a public company during the twenty-plus years that followed without putting a foot wrong, but his greatest contribution was the part he played in the strategic development and expansion after 1984, when I began to play a less active role. Malcolm was replaced by Richard Hutton, who had worked as his understudy for eight years and been identified as his successor three years previously. Since then he had increasingly attended main board meetings and been coached both by Malcolm and Bob Bennett.

Richard was an excellent candidate. He was well-respected throughout the business, had shown a high level of financial expertise, was able to contribute to solving broader business and strategic issues and was a strong supporter of the company values through his active involvement in the Charitable Trust and the Breakfast Clubs. The change was seamless.

Raymond Reynolds also joined the board. He had started as an area sales manager in Glasgow, gone on to manage the satellite bakery in Edinburgh before successfully managing the Scottish business following Ken Middleton's retirement. In his own quiet and determined way he absorbed whatever extra responsibility was given him and he was now retail director for the whole business.

The big decision now facing the board was the appointment of a successor to Mike Darrington. Several senior Greggs' managers were assessed and the external consultants were impressed with them all, which confirmed my own high opinion of their ability and commitment. In my other interests outside Greggs I had met senior managers and directors of other companies; none had held a candle to any of those senior Greggs managers.

In 1983, when Mike was appointed, I had not felt that any internal candidates had the necessary experience and ability to take the company forward, but now I felt there were suitable contenders, and I confess that I was initially disappointed when Derek Netherton informed me that the board's decision was to go for an outside appointment. They had found an exceptional and very experienced candidate who would make a major contribution to Greggs' future development and, most important, aspired to the values that had always been at the core of our development.

In retrospect I concede that Derek and the board made the right decision. Ken McMeikan was chosen for his leadership qualities and values. His father was a Scots Guardsman and by the age of eight Ken had travelled from his hometown of Stranraer in Scotland to live in London, Edinburgh, Munster in Germany, Farnborough in Hampshire and back to Stranraer. At school he was a very keen sportsman, representing Scotland boys clubs in an under 14 football world cup. Ken believes his competitive drive in business possibly came from sport where he also learned the need for great people, motivation and commitment. He came from a working-class family with loving parents who made sure their three children were raised with deeply-rooted values about the importance of working hard and treating people with respect. She was a huge influence on him and passionate about race and sex equality, the importance of treating everyone as equals and the need to stick up for those less fortunate. She was also a great baker. Ken's favourite treat was warm, freshly-buttered Scotch pancakes straight from the frying pan, which his mother often made in the shape of each child's initial. These were his earliest recollections of baking which began a life-long love of food.

Ken joined the Royal Navy in 1981 at the age of 16 and served for five years, going to the Falklands twice, once during the Falklands war. He went on to spend the next five years with the retailer Sears and then joined Tesco in 1990 where he spent 14 years in a variety of roles, starting as a training manager in London, responsible for the development of 8,000 people. He was promoted to management development manager where he first began working on strategy with Sir Terry Leahy and Philip Clarke, the current Tesco CEO. After two years in this role and a variety of retail shop management positions, he became retail director in Scotland, then in Hertfordshire and Essex, Tesco's 'jewel in the crown' where the company started, as Greggs did in the north-east. In 2005 he was appointed CEO of Tesco Japan. Shortly afterwards he was asked by Justin King to turn around Sainsbury's fortunes. After three years as their retail director this was successfully achieved and the company has gone from strength to strength.

Ken proved to be not just a safe pair of hands to steer Greggs through the most difficult trading conditions for more than half a century, but a man with the experience and business ability to develop new strategies and a more central structure to take Greggs forward. He also had a passionate commitment to the values we promoted about people and the community. Soon after he joined us, he stated that 'A company or individual that is doing well has a disproportionate responsibility to help those that are less fortunate within their communities.' He embraced the concept of Greggs values and the importance of its charitable activities. He joined together the Greggs Trust and community work of the company within the Greggs Foundation, putting it 'front and centre' of everything that Greggs did.

Mike Darrington's reign as group managing director of Greggs had come to an end. It had lasted twenty-four years, providing the leadership and stability that had enabled the company to grow from a modest regional business to a well-recognized national brand, and the net profit to increase from £1.5 million to more than £50 million in his last year. That performance is, by any standards, remarkable and much of the credit for this must go to Mike himself for his total and unswerving commitment, his work ethic (usually first to arrive in the morning and last to leave in the evening), his financial acumen, his passion for making products taste good, his determination to stick to the long-term goal, whatever the short-term problems or distractions, and his ability to leaven all this with a sense of fun and, whenever possible, a good party – after which he would still be the first into work the next morning. Yet he would also be the first to acknowledge that it was a team effort: at every level of the business, Greggs was driven forward by great people who had been attracted to the company by its success, its values and the challenges created by devolved responsibility.

Mike was awarded a richly deserved knighthood for his services to industry and the community in the north-east in the New Year's Honours List of 2004, and since then he has been awarded honorary doctorates by the universities of Northumbria and Sunderland. In spite of the increasing levels of corporate governance and personality changes, he still loved the job and the company, and left Greggs in robust good health, though facing very challenging trading conditions with the recession beginning to bite and world commodity prices rising fast. He stayed for a further year as an NED, to help with the transition, and continued as a trustee of the company pension scheme.

When Ken McMeikan joined Greggs in June 2008, the process of change to a central management structure was already well under way. The new structure, described as a 'national unified business', was not a fully centralized model but was more readily accepted by people as a move forward in that process. A significant degree of control over product range, price and promotions was still left with the former managing directors, now general managers, and their teams, but with more influence and decision-making starting to come from the centre.

Ken considered that the business needed a still more centralized structure and that, for a variety of reasons, the pace of change had to be increased. First, competition was growing at an ever faster pace and was expected to escalate in the years ahead. Greggs had to compete with national and global companies of significant scale, such as Subway, the American franchised sandwich business with 1,400 shops in the UK; coffee chains, such as Starbucks, with more than seven hundred shops in the UK, and the fast-growing Costa; and supermarkets, which were not only expanding with out-of-town sites and hypermarkets, but increasingly moving into convenience shops located on high streets and in neighbourhoods where Greggs and other local bakers had established themselves over many decades. Tesco led the move into convenience shops, with its Tesco Express and Metro formats, and Sainsbury's with its Local shops. Morrisons entered the market in 2012 with the launch of their own convenience shops (M'Local) and Waitrose with Little Waitrose.

Second, Greggs needed the ability to make faster decisions at a national level if it was to compete with national brands. The general managers' limited control over product range, pricing and promotions slowed and fragmented management decisions. This needed to be replaced by a more powerful central trading and marketing function.

Third, Greggs needed to unlock the benefits and financial savings that would come from more centralized control, harmonizing recipes for national products, enabling ingredients to be purchased in bigger volumes and at a better price, and agreeing one design and layout for all new shops and refits, which would reduce the cost of new equipment and fit-out expenses.

In the light of these pressures, Greggs made several major changes. Marketing was separated from retail, and customer contact was centralized, so that customers would have a consistent point of contact and their views on what they liked or disliked about Greggs and what they thought of competitors could easily be gathered. We created a customer and marketing team to look at the latest ways of communicating with the UK consumer through Facebook, Twitter and apps, as well as conventional TV, radio and press advertising. Today the company has more than 650,000 Facebook fans and growing!

Decisions about range, promotions and pricing were moved from the general managers to newly appointed category (bread, cake, savoury, sandwich) managers, reporting to the trading directors. The purchasing teams, who buy Greggs materials and ingredients, were brought together with the category teams. The role of general manager was changed to head of retail, concentrating on running the shops, with the accelerated new shop-opening programme and refitting of existing premises. We brought the property and shop-development teams together to create a central function that would enable the company to refit shops at double the level it had historically achieved. The new role of communications manager was introduced, alongside a dedicated corporate and social responsibility manager, both reporting to the company secretary, to ensure that, as Greggs continued to grow, the vital roles of communication and social responsibility were given even greater prominence and focus.

This was a considerable change and a challenge, and that it was achieved without apparent damage to the business and profitability was a great reflection on management and staff throughout Greggs. Some might have felt the loss of challenge, satisfaction, regional identity and their ability to innovate that local autonomy had given them, but others gained in responsibility, and almost all came to acknowledge the strength and benefits of a much more robust national brand and image. Under the new structure, there were still ample challenges for everyone in achieving the required standards and moving forward their part of the business.

Greggs has always been a complex business, and management has continuously searched for ways of making it simpler. Under Ken McMeikan, a number of other decisions were made to help achieve this. The 160 remaining Bakers Oven shops were rebranded as Greggs so that there was only one brand to manage. Also it was clear that the business in Belgium, after six years' trading, was unlikely to make a reasonable profit without a steep increase in investment or a major acquisition. With the full co-operation of the team in Belgium, we decided to cut our losses and sold the shops as a going concern to a local operator, who also took on the staff, securing their future employment in line with Greggs' values.

With a fully centralized management structure to

drive the business forward, Ken set out his strategic goals for the company. In October 2009, at a time when many companies were thinking about reducing investment and conserving cash to ride out the storm of the recession, he announced a bold and challenging five-year plan: 'Delivering Growth'.

It called for:

- double the rate of shop openings to around seventy per year, leading to a 40 per cent growth from 1,400 to more than 2,000 shops, and double the number of refits from around sixty a year to 120
- more new shops to be opened in non-traditional locations, shifting some of the emphasis from our traditional high streets to locations where customers are at work, leisure or travel
- increased investment in improving production facilities
- the removal of all artificial colours, flavours and hydrogenated vegetable oil from Greggs' food, with a reduction in salt and fat content, nutritional information to be made more easily accessible to Greggs' customers
- a move into the breakfast market, with new breakfast ranges, earlier opening hours and the installation of freshly ground coffee machines in all shops
- a move into the bake-at-home market, with the introduction of new ranges in the future and also wholesaling through Iceland's 750 shops across the UK

All of these decisions were being taken and implemented against the background of the financial débâcle of 2008 and the subsequent recession, which had huge implications for Greggs. Profits grow very well when sales volumes are increasing, but if sales volumes drop, the pressure on profits becomes significant. Greggs is a vertically integrated business, acting both as a manufacturer and a retailer of bakery products, resulting in a high level of fixed overheads, which in turn makes profitability very sensitive to sales volumes.

During the recession, volumes suffered throughout the food sector and not just at Greggs. At the same time, the rising cost of ingredients, energy and transport put further pressures on profit margins, creating a very tough challenge. In this climate of economic hardship and volume decline, there was constant debate about how much of these increases could be passed on to the customer. Inevitably prices had to go up, but Greggs chose to absorb some of the cost, passing on only part of it to customers in order to preserve our great reputation for value.

Customers were suffering from a nasty cocktail of higher fuel costs, higher energy costs and higher food costs, combined with pay increases below the rate of inflation. The only way for them to cope with this was to spend less, by buying less or reducing their shopping frequency. This has contributed to a 10 per cent reduction in footfall on high streets since 2008.

Record shop openings – sixty-eight in 2010, eighty-four in 2011 and more than one hundred in 2012 – have added much-needed volume to the bakeries. Without it, the Greggs team would have found life even tougher, and it has enabled Greggs to maintain its profits at more than £50 million per year during the most difficult and extended trading period in living memory.

By the end of 2012 the UK economy was in double dip recession. It was always going to be a tough year even before the government announced in the budget of 21 March 2012 that it was going to introduce VAT on pies and pasties. Back in 1984, a previous Conservative government had tried to do this. Greggs, along with the National Association of Master Bakers, had successfully argued that pies and pasties, which had been freshly baked and not kept hot in a heated cabinet, should continue to be zero-rated. Since then, such savouries in bakery shops had not been subject to VAT unless they were kept hot, and at Greggs, savouries are neither kept hot nor advertised as hot: they are sold at the temperature they happen to be when the customer asks for them.

There had been no warning that the government would once more try to impose VAT on hot savouries, or any prior consultation. We faced a nightmare scenario if it went ahead with the proposal. Greggs' shops are very busy, with staff making sandwiches, baking off savouries and trying to serve customers with products that are as fresh as possible, as quickly as possible. How could they cope with separating hot savouries (liable to VAT) from cold (zero-rated)? Would they have to check the temperature of every sausage roll, pie and pasty, and even if they could, what was to be the determining temperature? Ambient (what was proposed) would vary between summer and winter and between Aberdeen and London. It would have been impossible to manage and the price increases required would have been very damaging at any time, particularly so in the current recession.

Our one consolation was that the government had at least agreed to a consultation period on what the press quickly branded the 'pasty tax'. Ken McMeikan and his team made the most of this opportunity. They lobbied MPs and, with support from Mike Hollins, of the National Association of Master Bakers, and Mark Muncey, of the Cornish Pasty Association, set about engaging the public in supporting an industry-wide petition. More than three hundred thousand signatures were gathered at Greggs' shops, and in total, half a million were collected from all bakers' shops, helped by media campaigns in the *Sun*, the *Journal* in Newcastle, the *Western Morning News* in Devon and Cornwall, and the *British Baker* magazine.

More than four hundred bakers, with banners, pies and pasties, came together in the rain at the head of a march to deliver the petition to Downing Street, showing, as Ken said on the day, 'resolute determination to explain to the government why they needed to change their plans to apply VAT to savouries'.

Two MPs – Stephen Gilbert (Liberal Democrat) and George Eustice (Conservative) – became particularly vocal in supporting the bakery industry's argument and cross-party support, including the Labour leader Ed Miliband, was quickly established. Ken appeared on *Newsnight* to argue our case and gave a very good account of the issues, although the headlines the next day were all about him criticizing the government for being out-of-touch. In fact, this related to a point Jeremy Paxman, not Ken, wanted to make! Ken's real thrust was that the Treasury was in danger of forcing savoury prices up by 20 per cent at a time when life was already tough enough for ordinary people. It would have meant people buying fewer savouries, many bakery shops closing and jobs being lost in the industry at a moment when we needed more shops to open to bolster flagging high streets and create more jobs to combat rising unemployment.

Further presentations were made to the Treasury. Greggs' managers and customers were encouraged to write to their local MP and explain their opposition to the tax, and their concerns about rising costs, job losses and shop closures. The *Sun* campaign continued, with fantastic support from Steve Hawkes, the City business editor, which kept the public profile high. At one point it made the front page of the *Sun* and several other national newspapers and was being reported as far afield as Australia and the United States.

On 28 May 2012 when, unexpectedly, the news broke that the government had backed down, the relief was incredible. This was a remarkable achievement by everyone concerned and a great victory for common sense. The government is also to be applauded for honouring its commitment to hold a consultation period and having the courage and wisdom to adopt a better proposal that is right for the UK consumer, the bakery industry and also for itself, removing anomalies and still raising millions of pounds in revenue.

It had been an unwelcome distraction for senior management at a time when everyone's undivided attention was needed to steer the business through a most testing period. It is to Derek Netherton and his board's credit that the company has continued to invest heavily in new improved production facilities and better-fitted shops. They have opted to take the long-term view, rather than hold back investment until the economic position improves. Derek and his board have also continued to uphold the Greggs values even when their application might have had an adverse impact on short-term profitability. The best example of this was the decision made in 2009 to invest in the new confectionery baker at Penrith, rather than build one further south in a more central location.

The management team had done a great job in these circumstances to maintain profitability, and Greggs is fortunate to have low borrowings and a strong cash flow. These, with substantial recent investment, should ensure that the company will continue to provide security and opportunity for employees while delivering good-value products to an increasing number of customers and a good return for investors.

At a dinner to celebrate Mike's retirement in 2009, I had said to Ken that, of the three of us, he faced the greatest challenge of all. Not only was he having to lead the company through massive change as the business became more centrally run, he had to manage it through a savage financial crisis caused by the banks and the consequent global recession. I was not aware at that time that the recession beginning in 2008 would continue for four years and still have no end in sight. It was a great disappointment that, having steered us through what we hope will prove to have been the worst of it, Ken announced in December 2012 that he would be stepping down as CEO of Greggs to take over at the catering wholesalers Brakes Group, a decision based partly on his desire to be nearer to his five children, all based in London. Everyone was surprised. Ken had seemed to fit so well into the Greggs culture and ethos. He had done so much to develop the central management structure and proved himself able to manage the most difficult situations, in particular the economic crisis and the pasty tax, and he had worked so hard to develop the Greggs image as a national brand. He has left large shoes to fill, but Greggs' success does not rest on the contribution of any individual.

Also in 2013 Derek Netherton will be retiring, following more than ten years' service as chairman. It is never easy to follow in the founder's footsteps, but Derek's wisdom, experience, willingness to listen and adherence to the core values made the transition seamless. He managed successfully the change of CEO from Mike Darrington to Ken McMeikan, and helped to steer Greggs through the turbulent economic times following 2008, at the same time maintaining increasing levels of investment.

Probably Derek's main contribution has been his strengthening of the main board. Since my retirement in 2007 he has made several NED appointments: Roger Whiteside, chief executive of Punch Taverns, in 2008; Iain Ferguson, formerly chief executive of Tate & Lyle, in 2009; and Ian Durant in 2011. With such a strong board, it was not necessary to look outside for a successor to Derek. Ian Durant will take over after the AGM in May 2013. Aged fifty-three, with experience in the financial, retail, hotel and transport sectors, he is currently chairman of Capital & Counties Properties plc, and an NED of Green King plc and Home Retail Group plc. He admires the Greggs values and has been on the board long enough to understand the changes that have taken place and the issues the company faces – but not so long as to preclude a fresh approach.

The strength and depth of the board that Derek

developed was further highlighted by the appointment of Ken's successor, Roger Whiteside. His five years' experience with the board gave him a good understanding of the issues faced and future plans, enabling him to hit the ground running. His experience with Marks & Spencer, Ocado and more recently as CEO of Punch Taverns, made him a good candidate to take on this challenging role. At Marks & Spencer over twenty years Roger filled a variety of roles – as a buyer, working with suppliers, developing their sandwich business and specializing in fresh foods. He worked as personal assistant to Sir Richard Greenbury before being promoted to head of the food business, where he was responsible for developing the first stores in the Simply Food chain. Greggs offers him the exciting opportunity to become involved again in the retailing of fresh food.

The economic problems faced by the UK and our massive burden of debt means that we are not likely to enjoy growth for some time; spending cuts and job losses in the public sector will be felt for years as the private sector struggles to create sufficient new jobs to offset the losses. This rebalancing will be painful and the high street is unlikely to recover quickly, although I still feel optimistic about its future in the longer term. There are now indications that rental levels are falling and landlords beginning to accept that the upward-only rent reviews they have enjoyed for decades are now a thing of the past.

Before the recession, the vacancy rate on high streets was five per cent; today it has risen to 15 per cent, with nearly one in three shops in some towns sitting empty. It will take time to rebuild and, in the meantime, fewer people will be attracted to high streets.

Greggs has been responding to this by opening more of its new shops (nearly 30 per cent in 2012) in sites such as motorway service stations, airports and retail parks to provide a more balanced portfolio of trading locations.

The company is also looking at new shop formats that will enable it to achieve better coverage of retail locations and maximize the potential of any particular site. The new Greggs Moment Coffee Shop on Northumberland Street, Newcastle, for example, offers us the opportunity to compete with Starbucks, Costa and other operators in this large and growing market. Moment shops will offer a greater range of foods than the normal coffee shop and, though recognizable as Greggs, will be quite different, able to trade close to existing shops without creating competition because they appeal to a different market: shoppers and others wanting to sit down to enjoy a treat.

Greggs the Bakery is another new format on trial, offering a significantly different product range from the normal Greggs shop. These units will do more in-store baking, including a range of bread and rolls, and offer sandwiches made to order. The initial trial in Gosforth High Street, just north of Newcastle, and several other refits have been well received by customers and resulted in significant sales increases. Between four hundred and five hundred Greggs shops should ultimately benefit from conversion to the Bakery.

These new formats, with an estimated five hundred to six hundred potential new outlets in the UK, provide opportunity for growth over the next ten years, which will be supported by further improvements to bakeries and production capacities. The investment in new shops, refits and bakeries demonstrates to staff our belief and confidence in the longer-term future, and shareholders should benefit from a more efficient, modern business. Communities will also benefit from the creation of jobs at a time when a generation of youngsters is at risk of being robbed of a meaningful career. Last but not least, more customers will have access to Greggs shops and products, which will benefit from this investment in terms of quality and value.

EPILOGUE
Toast

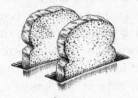

Our work in the community is worth around £2.5 million every year. Breakfast Clubs are an important part of this

It is always difficult to know whether early childhood recollections are directly remembered or the result of other people recalling events and repeating the stories. I suspect my memories of evacuation to Longframlington in mid-Northumberland from 1941 to 1943 fall into the latter category: the beautiful country lanes, blue butterflies, picking fresh vegetables in the cottage garden (maybe that was where my lifelong passion for growing vegetables came from), and inviting in a platoon of soldiers for a 'tup of tea', which Mum generously provided from her limited rations. All this was often recalled with great fondness and a liberal supply of photographs. What a strange contrast it evokes – the simple scene of idyllic bliss in the midst of all that death, destruction and awful uncertainty about the future. But perhaps adults could still enjoy the immediate on a day-at-a-time basis, and that was all a child was aware of.

Back in Newcastle in 1944 (I can only assume it was the pressure of running the business in Dad's absence that motivated Mum to leave Longframlington), I remember going down into the air-raid shelter attached to the back of the house. Having been woken from a deep sleep, I was rushed out of the back door, under the lean-to porch that protected access to the coal bunker and garage, down the steps where our shoes and wellingtons stood in line, and along the narrow passage-way between the side of the house and the tall black wooden boundary fence. Tracers lit the thin slice of sky above us before we hurried down into candlelight and darkness to sleep in wooden bunks in whatever extra security the bunker offered. After the war, its roof became a great place to put scraps for the birds and to play games although, because of its height, that was not without danger. My left leg still bears a small scar from one accident.

A few years later, when everyone thought it was safe, the shelter was demolished with pneumatic drills that smashed up the concrete and revealed the steel reinforcement that would have protected us from falling debris, but not a direct hit. The area was paved over and within a few months you would not have known it had been there, except for the pink climbing rose that had covered its south wall and now trailed unsupported over the crazy paving.

My most vivid childhood memory is of lying in bed

with Mum just before the end of the war, or immediately afterwards, and listening to her describing some of the wonderful foods that I had never seen or tasted. Foremost were fruits – pineapple, melon and peach – sweet, juicy, mouth-watering, compared to the meagre, boring rations we had to make do with. I suppose, being in the food business, we were better off than most but it took the full stretch of Mum's imagination and all her resourcefulness to maintain an interesting and satisfying menu. Tripe was reasonably available and nourishing, and appeared each week in one form or another. We all, except Gay, quite liked it, and it became a weekly challenge to provide it in a form that was unrecognizable and palatable to her. Although very young, Gay remained undefeated in this challenge, instantly recognizing it, whether it was dressed up as mince in herbs and Bisto gravy or hidden at the bottom of a shepherd's pie.

If we had something nice to eat, like meat or fish, there would only be a small helping, so we left the table wanting more. I thought this was the reason for the most regular saying in the household, 'Enough is as good as a feast.' At the time it fell on stony ground – there was nothing any of us would have liked more than a feast of meat, fish, fruit, chocolate, sweets, cakes or any of the other delicacies we tasted in tiny quantities from time to time. We dismissed the saying either as a form of madness affecting grown-ups or a deceit to make us satisfied when we were not.

As the years have passed I came to understand the great good sense it contains. At school and university I studied classics and the motto of the Greeks was 'Μηδεν αγαν' (pronounced 'maiden agan'), which, translated literally, means 'nothing too much' or 'nothing in excess'. And little by little, year by year, the truth of the saying continued to reveal itself to me. Whatever I may have thought as a young child, enough was as good as a feast. In fact, it was better. There are many all-too-familiar examples of the opposite – that unpleasant feeling after pigging out on chocolate or drinking an extra glass or two of wine. You can have too much of a good thing.

When I was interviewed on TV after Greggs went public in 1984, I was asked what changes in lifestyle my newly acquired wealth would bring. I should have been prepared for this question but I wasn't. My spontaneous response was, 'You can only eat one pie at a time.' Mum would have been proud that her lesson had been so well absorbed. It lives on in Greggs' values, which have two main pillars, both of which are based on not being greedy, on sharing and consideration of others. One pillar is our responsibility to the communities we serve and the other is our duty to the people we employ.

Our responsibility to our communities is embodied in the work of the Greggs Foundation. Although most of Greggs' charitable funds were originally distributed in the north-east of England, there are now seven regional charity committees spread around the UK. They raise increasing sums of money from collection boxes in their local Greggs shops and at fundraising events, and support an increasing number and variety of local projects. In 2012 regional grants totalled more than £600,000, but this only satisfied half of the requests received.

As well as increasing the geographical spread of the Foundation's work, we have tried to provide more continuity of funding. For example, we have now supported Sunderland Headlight's care for people with mental health problems in Sunderland city centre for eleven years. The Northern Initiative on Women and Eating, better known as NIWE Eating Distress, was funded for nine years to help women with eating disorders, after which the development officer of the project, Anne Marie Norman, became a trustee of the Greggs' Trust. More recently, a grant of £50,000 a year has been made to the local Community Foundation to establish the Local Environment Fund (LEAF). It supports and encourages local environmental initiatives that can significantly affect the quality of life of local people.

A virtuous circle can often develop between the local community, its needs and Greggs' shop employees, most of whom are part of that community. They know the problems and the requirements, can pass that information back to regional charity committees, and help to raise funds to meet local needs and solve problems. We have ambitious plans to extend the activities of the committees, including extending the hardship fund and increasing the number of Breakfast Clubs.

Many regional activities are not included in calculating the value of the contribution of the company and the Trust to the community, and some are significant, such as the People's Kitchen in Newcastle. Its continuing success is a fitting tribute to its founder Alison Kay, who received an OBE in 1992. She died in 2001, but the People's Kitchen continues to this day.

As well as the work of the Greggs' Trust, the company itself has also made increasingly significant contributions to local communities. The Breakfast

Clubs have grown from the original one in 1999 to 220 in 2012, and provide 10,000 primary school children each day with a healthy breakfast. The basis of the breakfast is toast and spreads, and this is supplemented with baked beans and also cereals, fruit drinks and occasional special treats. They result in better attendance rates and improved attention and achievement in class (benefits that have been confirmed by research by Durham Business School and Ofsted). They are run by five hundred local volunteers, including school staff, who receive some initial training from Greggs. These locally run initiatives are a positive influence in areas that often suffer from high unemployment and other related social issues. We have ambitious plans to open many more Breakfast Clubs (300 is the target), around half of which will be in partnership with other organizations. Such partnerships already exist with some twenty-five organizations, including RBS, the CBI, Etihad Airways, Typhoo Tea, Friesland Campanina, PWC, Caledonia Investments, Your Homes Newcastle and Middlesbrough Council.

Greggs' sponsorship of the North-east Children's Cancer Run has also been very important. In the twenty-nine years since it was first staged, it has raised a staggering £5.5 million, and has encouraged and inspired other fundraising initiatives throughout the north-east and helped to secure major grants from Cancer Research UK, Leukaemia and Lymphoma Research and the European Research Council. This has helped establish Newcastle as one of the leading childhood-cancer research units in the world. As a result, doctors can now cure close to 80 per cent of all children and young people diagnosed with cancer (thirty

years ago the rate was lower than 30 per cent). Despite
the progress, though, cancer remains the leading cause
of death (other than accidents) in children and young
people: about 1,700 children each year are diagnosed in
the UK with cancer – one in 600 children. The treatments sometimes come with deeply unpleasant side
effects so the money raised now will support a wider
range of research, including clinical trials offering new
drugs with the lowest levels of side effects. It will under-
pin the research that Newcastle undertakes into
childhood brain tumours, neuroblastoma and
leukaemia, which will benefit children in the north-east
and throughout the world.

Greggs' sponsorship of the Cancer Run has been
supported by many other businesses, local press, radio
and TV, educational establishments and other organizations too numerous to mention individually, but it has
been a real partnership effort. Christopher Peacock,
who inspired the run all those years ago, is now chairman of the committee. The committee manages this
huge event and co-ordinates the great network of
volunteers that has been built up, many from families
and friends of those who have received treatment but
many others simply wanting to be involved in such a
worthwhile activity.

Included in this massive volunteer effort are several
hundred Greggs' employees, who give up their weekend
to make the sandwiches, sausage rolls and cakes for the
picnic that each of the 10,000 participants receives with
their medal. They eat them in front of the racecourse
grandstand as more runners are cheered over the
finishing line amid roundabouts, bouncy castles and displays. An ex-colliery band, the Lynemouth Band, which

we sponsored after the colliery closed in 1985 and became known as the Greggs Brass Band, plays them in. Most years the runners include celebrities, like former 1,500-metre world champion Steve Cram, and Alan Shearer, who has been the starter in recent years and become a fantastic ambassador for the event. But the real heroes are all the parents and children, many of whom have never taken part in any other running event. They have the excitement and satisfaction of completing the course and of taking part in an amazing experience, which has helped so many children.

In 2001 Andrew Davison, the Greggs company secretary, took over from me as chairman of the Trust. His thoughtful and strategic approach helped to pave the way for the future and he recruited several outside trustees. At the same time he encouraged my daughters, Fiona and Felicity, to continue their support and involvement.

In 2009 Ken McMeikan led the initiative to combine the community programme of the company and the Greggs Trust, and changed the name to the Greggs Foundation. This provided a closer link between the company and all its charitable activities and enabled more ambitious fundraising and activity to take place. It also provided more co-ordinated resources to support the Greggs Foundation, which now has a dedicated professional team led by Jackie Crombie committed to using the funds available to them to reduce hardship, deprivation and unhappiness in the north-east, and increasingly provides expertise and help to the regional committees so they can achieve the same outcome elsewhere in the UK. Underlying everything they do, is their passion to get money and help to those who can make a difference in local communities, and to continue to provide support with the minimum of administration and bureaucracy.

In 2011 and 2012 donations reached £2.6 million, of which £1.5 million was donated via the Foundation (including £250,000 through the Breakfast Clubs), and £1 million was raised for the BBC's Children in Need – a huge increase from the £70,000 raised in 2006, our first year. Greggs has now raised more than £4 million for Children in Need, and is the second highest corporate fundraiser after Asda. This is all due to an amazing effort by everyone throughout Greggs, whether working in the shops, bakeries, offices or transport, often with fantastic support from customers. In 2011 the Foundation received the Corporate Foundation Award at the prestigious Business Charity Awards.

The effort and enthusiasm throughout the company for Children in Need has been remarkable, resulting in a huge variety of fundraising activities – sponsored walks, belly dancing, abseiling from the top of bakeries, raising £20,000 from dips in the cold North Sea, shop ladies dressing up as 'Pink Ladies' (Raymond Reynolds, Greggs' six-foot-seven-inch retail director, crossed London on the Underground dressed as a 'Pink Lady'), the Scotland team recording 'The Cake Song', an Airdrie shop assistant remaining handcuffed until the required amount of money was raised, and many, many more. All these activities were thought up and carried out by individuals or groups of employees at a local level in the knowledge that the funds raised would be used to make life-changing grants to children suffering from illnesses or deprivation.

Special thanks to Greggs customers who support

these and other activities so generously. They purchased 650,000 gingerbread Pudseys in 2012 for the remarkable BBC appeal, which has been held regularly since 1998 when it raised £18 million, and now raises between £40 and £50 million every year.

The original motivation for Greggs' charitable and community activities was certainly not to promote and advertise the business, and for several years we didn't publicize any of what we were doing, but many of the projects and causes that Greggs supported needed publicity for their own good reasons. Our employees were more likely to contribute to the Foundation if they knew about what it was up to, and customers liked to know what was happening in their own communities. Now there is considerable publicity surrounding Greggs' charitable activities, particularly in relation to Children in Need. This is good for the business and hopefully encourages other businesses to get involved.

The Foundation and the company work in harmony and pursue activities over and above normal grant-making and fundraising. Greggs' involvement with Business in the Community also continues to expand. In 2010, and again in 2011, Ken was appointed HRH Prince of Wales Ambassador for the north-east. During this time Greggs has become involved in helping the homeless with work placement and job opportunities; working with other companies to create apprenticeships for the long-term unemployed; refitting and opening shops in the North East for start-up businesses to share premises rent free; working with young offenders to overcome the barriers to getting a job and a home; and partnering with seven other companies to provide training in Low Newton Women's prison. In 2012, working with the Prince's Trust in Teesside and Tomorrow's People in Scotland, we agreed to put £100,000 into schemes to help 16–24 year olds into employment. We were particularly concerned that in these challenging economic times a million of them are unemployed. Richard Hutton is chairman of the regional advisory board of Business in the Community and we now have several regional Business in the Community business connectors.

Was the original motivation philanthropy? Was it to make us feel good? Was it enlightened self-interest, helping the communities that supported Greggs' business? Was it a combination of these? Or was it simply that people cared and felt that they could do something? I don't really know, but however small the beginnings, the range and extent of the activities of the Foundation now far exceed anything I could have envisaged or hoped for. These charitable and community activities comprise one of the two main pillars of the Greggs' values.

The other main pillar is our duty to our employees. We have a duty to treat them fairly. This has many facets: considering them as individuals, giving them the respect we would like to receive ourselves, paying decent wages and providing reasonable working conditions, and seeing that there is an equitable division of the wealth a business creates between shareholders and different groups of employees. These are some necessary elements of sustainable capitalism and a fair society. Yet today we seem increasingly faced with greed and selfishness, particularly in relation to senior executive pay, which in many companies now seems out of control. Change is required, not just in the form of legislation and stronger codes of conduct but also the adoption of better values and also the general public becoming more active. In the past, legislation and codes of conduct have not been enough on their own.

It had become apparent during the nineties, when corporate governance requirements increased significantly, that the UK needed better controls over the management of major public companies. The need was highlighted after Robert Maxwell drowned while cruising around the Canary Islands in 1990. He had made a number of risky acquisitions in the 1980s, resulting in high debts, which he serviced by plundering his companies' pension funds to the tune of £440 million. Following his death, it was revealed that one of his companies, the Mirror Group, had debts greatly exceeding its assets, but no action against Maxwell's estate or companies was taken by regulators in the UK or the USA. In 1992 his companies filed for bankruptcy. At around the same time, the Bank of Credit and Commerce International went bust, losing millions of dollars for its depositors, shareholders and employees. Another company, Polly Peck, reported good profits one year and filed for bankruptcy the next, owing £550 million. Its managing director, Asil Nadir, escaped justice for almost twenty years by fleeing to northern Cyprus, but was eventually convicted of embezzling £29 million from Polly Peck and sentenced to ten years in prison.

There was widespread concern among shareholders and employees that the practices leading to such events could go undetected, and in 1991 a committee, chaired by Sir Adrian Cadbury, was set up by the Financial Reporting Council, the London stock exchange and the accountancy profession to suggest improvements. Its report's main recommendations were that the role of CEO and chairman should be separated, boards should have at least three NEDs, and each board should have an audit committee composed of NEDs.

Shortly afterwards, Sir Richard Greenbury chaired another committee set up in response to public anger at spiralling executive pay, particularly in the recently privatized public utilities. He recommended further changes, including establishing remuneration committees that, apart from the chairman, would be composed solely of NEDs, and giving directors long-term, performance-related pay, which should be disclosed in the accounts.

Over the next few years, further reports added to the burgeoning well-meaning but bureaucratic burdens with which public companies had to comply. The meetings and obligations of audit sub-committees had to be increased in line with recommended practice; remuneration sub-committees were expected to carry out more surveys of executive pay, which meant using salary consultants. Nominations sub-committees were required for senior appointments. The requirements for the annual report and accounts became more complex, as did the technicalities and actuarial valuations in relation to pension schemes, which appeared to me like some dark art form! All of this distracted from the time and effort available for the business itself at main board meetings, as well as making the role of NEDs more time-consuming, technical and open to potential liability for failure to comply with the raft of legal requirements. Executive directors, particularly the chief executive, were similarly affected.

Some of the changes were necessary and effective, but the recommendations of Greenbury and others did nothing to contain senior executives' pay. On the contrary, remuneration committees achieved exactly the reverse, and none of the reports stopped the bad and risky practices that had led to the banking crisis in 2008, or the banking malpractices over the Libor rate and money laundering, which were revealed in 2012.

Selfishness, greed, excess and lack of decent values have become a global problem. Bankers, businessmen and politicians receive most criticism but all of us, the general public, share some of the responsibility. A wave of smash-and-grab consumerism has swept the world over the last twenty-five years, reaching levels that threaten life as we know it. We all seem stuck on a hedonistic treadmill of more money, more holidays, a larger home, a faster car and more designer clothes. This does not bring happiness to the developed world and drives the rest of it to aspire to similar unsustainable goals. It is fostered by capitalism and promoted by advertising. Similarly in the environment: unless we can start to reduce our carbon emissions over the next twenty-five to fifty years, the consequences will be dire. Global temperatures continue to rise, and species, habitats and ecosystems are being destroyed at an alarming and increasing rate, but we continue to want more, more, more. Planet Earth's natural resources of oil, gas, coal, rain forests and minerals are all being squandered in this global feast, and there is insufficient investment to conserve these resources and find green and sustainable alternatives.

Society seems driven by extremes: on the one hand by excessive greed and consumerism, on the other by warnings about things that have served mankind well for millennia but are suddenly seen as damaging: butter, salt, bread, meat, wine. Whatever happened to 'Everything in moderation'? Driven by these forces, the capitalist business model is out of control and has become too focused on the greed of the few at the expense of the many. Trade-union power in the 1960s and 1970s brought the country close to its knees, and double-digit inflation and excessive wage increases made it difficult to manage businesses. Margaret Thatcher fought the unions in the 1980s and checked this excess, but set the pendulum swinging, as history shows it inevitably does, too far in the opposite direction.

The bankers showed us how greedy they can be and how little they care for anyone or anything else. Having brought the country close to financial meltdown in 2008 and then been bailed out, they continued with their excessive bonuses while the rest suffered the consequences of their mismanagement. Such behaviour is offensive to common sense and decency, and it is hardly surprising that it contributed to the violence and unrest in 2011, provoking a series of protests, demonstrations and union actions. People were very angry, justifiably so.

However, it is not just the banks. The senior directors of many of the UK's major companies, who should really be setting standards and examples for others to follow, have been paid salaries, fees and bonuses that bear no relationship to increases in productivity or profitability. The trend continues, driven upwards by the very remuneration committees designed to ensure that pay in large public companies was managed in a responsible way. It is their role to ensure that the packages awarded to senior management are competitive with the market. To do this they have to review salaries, with the data collated by one of the array of consultancies that has grown up in London on the rich pickings of this activity. The data will show the market has – surprise, surprise – increased, driven further upwards by each survey containing the latest round of excessive salary awards. The position will be exacerbated by the increasing number of complex share incentive schemes, which few people can understand.

It is difficult to dispute the massive difference a good chief executive or senior director can make to the profitability of a company, to shareholder value, to job security and to future growth. Compared to those factors, the salary paid, particularly in relation to very large global businesses, can be insignificant, an argument often used to justify larger than normal remuneration increases and to encourage boards and committees to push the boat out in order to secure the very best.

Yet most people regard the pay packages of many current senior directors as unfair, exclusive and unsustainable, and have become increasingly angry about them. They accept that top achievers should be well rewarded, but believe the system has become out of control and needs a firm check. Standards of living today are higher than they have ever been but there is great dissatisfaction, which is not surprising. Poverty is relative, not absolute. Comparisons with these excessive top salaries are bound to lead to dissatisfaction and a feeling of unfairness, particularly when those making the comparison are suffering financial hardships, which should be shared more equitably.

I wrote the outline of this chapter in July 2011, in preparation for an address about sustainable capitalism to students graduating from the business school of Newcastle University. At that time I was surprised and angry that excessive top salaries were not attracting more criticism from politicians, commentators and the media. The facts since 1999 spoke for themselves:

- RPI had increased by 42 per cent
- wages had increased by 49 per cent
- the stock market had declined by 15 per cent
- top directors' packages had increased by 200–300 per cent

Of course, the stock market had suffered abnormally due to the 2008 financial crisis and subsequent recession, and running businesses during this period had been particularly difficult, but there could be no justification for pay packages that were already very high rising any more than general wages and salaries, which meant that many top salaries were double what they should have been. This situation of a small minority continuing to take excessive salaries while the vast majority suffers financial hardship is in direct contradiction of the Greggs' value of treating everyone with fairness. It is not acceptable and has to be changed.

In the face of overwhelming public indignation, the tide has now started to turn. The trickle of newspaper, radio and TV criticisms that appeared in 2010 and the first half of 2011 became an avalanche in the autumn of 2011. In September 2011, at the Labour Party Conference, Ed Miliband adopted a strong moral position on the issue. The Occupy Movement gained attention throughout the world and attracted much sympathy, despite concerns about its methods and activities. Social network organizations, such as 38 Degrees and UK Uncut, organized effective campaigns and protests. The High Pay Commission, chaired by Deborah Hargreaves, highlighted the unfairness of the position and called for major reforms.

Mike Darrington has made a significant and continuing contribution through his campaign 'Pro Business against Greed'. During 2010 and 2011 he worked hard to create a platform of support for opposing current excessive levels of directors' pay and changing the processes that drive them. It had been difficult to secure support from business leaders, institutions and 'the establishment', many of whom were reluctant to take a public stance, but by 2012 his campaign had convinced more people that senior pay was unfair, unsustainable and unrelated to performance and that shareholders should be more actively protecting their interests. More business leaders, including the Institute of Directors, the Association of British Insurers, the National Association of Pension Funds and the Local Authority Pension Fund, came to recognize that change was needed. The campaign also achieved important publicity in the newspapers, on radio and on television.

During 2012 things really started to happen. The former chief executive of RBS was stripped of his knighthood. Other senior bank and FTSE 100 senior executives were pressured into taking reduced bonuses. Protests were heard from shareholders at AGMs. The governor of the Bank of England urged the government to 'enact the reforms recommended by the independent commission on banking, chaired by John Vickers, sooner rather than later'. The government announced it would introduce binding shareholder votes on directors' pay.

Although welcome, these developments can only be regarded as token steps towards the root-and-branch change that is required to senior-executive pay structures, the composition of remuneration committees and rules governing incentive schemes. The change also needs to extend beyond pay packages to the values and ethics on which capitalism and business are based, in order to address the incidents of corruption and dishonesty that became evident later in 2012: the mis-selling of payment-protection insurance, the manipulation by leading banks of the Libor rate, laundering of drug money and funds from Iran, and the revelation that an extraordinary £13 trillion was hidden offshore by the global super-rich.

When I set out to write this book, my primary objective was to record the history of Greggs, the main events over the last eighty years and the people who have helped to make Greggs what it is today. I have done this to the best of my ability, but in the course of it I have come to realize that the book might also achieve something more important than its original intention and make a contribution to the debate on corporate greed, the need for better values and the changes that must take place.

It would be a very proud moment for everyone who has been part of the Greggs story if our example could help in some way to make capitalism and business more sustainable, to make communities stronger and society fairer and more cohesive. Such values are shared by many other companies, ranging from giants like the Co-op and John Lewis/Waitrose to medium-sized businesses like The Entertainer Ltd (which sells toys) and Cook Ltd (which sells frozen meals) to local and regional businesses like our competitors in Yorkshire, Thomas of York and Bettys & Taylors of Harrogate. These examples should send a powerful message to business leaders, decision-makers and shareholders that decent values are not incompatible with efficiently run, profitable companies. Indeed, such values can be a key factor in their success.

The time is overdue for some process that will help the public determine which companies have decent values. Companies have to report on their financial and environmental performance – why not extend this to their values and how they treat people. Perhaps a register could be compiled, ranking businesses according to these factors.

Companies that do not adopt more ethical standards and better values will increasingly lose customers to those that do. In the debate that has now started, more and more people will come to realize that they hold the power to achieve change by supporting companies with good values and voting for politicians with responsible agendas. Their support will be increasingly important. There are few indications that the current recession and economic gloom will cease in the short term. In fact, most commentators suggest they will continue for some time, perhaps a further three or four years, putting additional pressures on consumers and business. We are in uncharted territory, which will be best navigated by companies with sound ethical values that treat people fairly. Enlightened self-interest, if you like.

What is happening today in the business world, the environment and the community is not sustainable. The vast, normally silent majority is starting to recognize this and wants change. A change of mindset is needed that will stop individuals looking to others to effect change and help them understand that only they can bring about these changes by better use of their purchasing power; that any sacrifices they make will be small compared to the problems we will all face if change does not happen soon.

We cannot rely on politicians or companies to make them without pressure. Politicians cannot see beyond what will win the next election, and most companies will seek to put short-term profit before the environment and community. The general public has allowed them to do it.

People can bring about change in their own lifestyle to reduce their carbon footprint in a dozen different ways, which could save them money and increase, rather than decrease, their enjoyment of life. They can change from banking with one of the big, bad banks to a building society or co-operative, and they can support local businesses and decent companies. They can think about where they spend their money and they can bring pressure on their friends and colleagues to do likewise, all of which will make a collective difference. Most important, they can use their vote more effectively, supporting political parties with a real commitment to green agendas, community issues, and to curbing excesses in the City.

This process has started. It will be increasingly supported by social-media networks, which have demonstrated their power through the democracy movement in the Arab world. Their impact has also grown in the UK. The campaign in February 2012 on Twitter and Facebook against the government's work-experience programme showed how effective they can be in influencing both governments and companies.

The process will gather momentum. It has to, if our children and grandchildren are to enjoy the same land-scapes and communities that we have been privileged to enjoy but have seemed hell-bent on destroying in recent history. There is still time to change course. During my visit to Newcastle University in 2011, I was impressed that sustainability was at the centre of everything they do, a lesson we could all follow. We could adopt their mantra: 'Enough for all, for ever.'

Acknowledgements

I wish to thank: my first wife, Edith, for her support in the early years and for giving me two daughters who are my proudest achievement; my partner, Jane, for her encouragement in my business and charitable activities; my brother, Colin, and sister, Gay, for their continued support for almost fifty years; Mike Darrington for taking the reins from me in 1983 and steering the business so successfully for nearly twenty-five years; Ken McMeikan for encouraging me to write this book; the British Baker for supplying data about the industry; Araminta Whitley and Susanna Wadeson for their guidance and enthusiasm; Neil Hanson and Hazel Orme for their help in editing; Neil Gower for his illustrations; and last, but by no means least, Janet Arnison for typing all my illegible handwriting.

Ian Gregg, March 2013

Index